Designing Security for a Microsoft® Windows Server™ 2003 Network (70-298)

Lab Manual

Martin Grasdal

PUBLISHED BY
Microsoft Press
A Division of Microsoft Corporation
One Microsoft Way
Redmond, Washington 98052-6399

Printed and bound in the United States of America.

1 2 3 4 5 6 7 8 9 QWT 9 8 7 6 5

Distributed in Canada by H.B. Fenn and Company Ltd.

A CIP catalogue record for this book is available from the British Library.

Microsoft Press books are available through booksellers and distributors worldwide. For further information about international editions, contact your local Microsoft Corporation office or contact Microsoft Press International directly at fax (425) 936-7329. Visit our Web site at www.microsoft.com/learning/. Send comments to *moac@microsoft.com.*

Acquisitions Editor: Lori Oviatt
Project Editor: Laura Sackerman

ISBN 13: 978-0-470-76746-7

SubAssy Part No. X11-15625
Body Part No. X11-15614

CONTENTS

LAB 1

ASSESSING THE NEED FOR SECURITY

This lab contains the following exercises and activities:

- Exercise 1.1: Assessing Threat Agents and Threats
- Exercise 1.2: Developing a Threat Agent Classification
- Exercise 1.3: Organizing Threats and Threat Mechanisms According to a Threat Agent Classification
- Exercise 1.4: Assessing Threat Likelihood Arising from Intention-Based Threat Agents
- Exercise 1.5: Assessing Vulnerabilities
- Lab Review Questions
- Lab Challenge 1.1: Performing a Threat and Vulnerability Analysis

SCENARIO

Contoso Pharmaceuticals is a publicly traded company that manufactures both generic and proprietary prescription drugs for the international market. It has 18,000 employees in offices throughout the world. The company hosts its own Web servers to provide information to the public, the medical profession, and company shareholders. In addition, the Web servers host an application that allows pharmaceutical drug wholesalers to place orders for stock.

The company is considering a proposal to open an online pharmacy to sell drugs directly to consumers. Also, the company plans to manufacture a controversial generic drug that has attracted an extremely negative response from small, but vocal, interest groups opposed to its manufacture and distribution. As a consequence, there is renewed interest in developing a coherent and thorough security design.

Because of its rapid growth, Contoso Pharmaceuticals' network has been implemented in an ad hoc manner. As a result, the security design of the network is inconsistent and, in some places, nonexistent. The CIO has recently formed a security team within the company to address the lack of a security design. You have been hired as a security consultant to work with the team to provide guidance in developing a security design for the company.

In this and subsequent labs, you will help Contoso Pharmaceuticals create a security design.

After completing this lab, you will be able to:

- **Assess possible threats to an organization's assets.**
- **Distinguish threats from threat agents.**
- **Develop custom threat agent classifications.**
- **Organize and analyze threats according to threat agent classifications.**
- **Develop custom rating scales to assess and analyze threat likelihood and threat impact.**
- **Distinguish threats from vulnerabilities.**
- **Develop worksheets to assess and analyze threats and vulnerabilities.**
- **Develop strategies to mitigate vulnerabilities and threats.**
- **Use the STRIDE threat model to categorize threats.**
- **Use the CIA triad to characterize threat aspect.**
- **Apply the Principles of Information Security as general vulnerability-mitigation strategies.**

Estimated lesson time: 115 minutes

BEFORE YOU BEGIN

To successfully complete this lab, you will need to be able to do the following:

- Log on to your student computer by using the number assigned to you by your instructor.

> **NOTE** The exercises in this lab and Lab 2, "Analyzing Risk," are paper-based and discussion-oriented; a computer is not necessary to perform them. However, you will need to log on for Lab Challenge 1.1 and for the exercises in Lab 2. It is not necessary for you to complete all the steps listed in this section before proceeding with Exercise 1.1. However, you should know how to log on to your computer by the end of the lab, and you should complete all the steps in this section before you perform Lab 3, "Reducing the Risk of Software Vulnerabilities."

Understanding the Lab Environment and Logging on and Configuring Your Computer

Estimated completion time: 5 minutes

> **NOTE** In all the labs in this manual, you will see the characters *dd*, *pp*, xx, yy and zz in computer names. These directions assume that you are working on computers configured in pairs and that each computer has a number. Each pair of computers in the classroom comprises a separate Active Directory forest.
>
> When you see *dd*, substitute the number used for your domain. When you see *pp*, substitute the number of your partner's computer. When you see xx, substitute the unique number assigned to the lower-numbered computer of the pair. When you see yy, substitute the unique number assigned to the higher-numbered computer of the pair. When you see zz, substitute the number assigned to the computer which you are currently using. For example, if the partner pair of computers has been assigned the names Computer05 and Computer06, and you have been assigned Computer05, the following is true:
>
> Computer*pp* = Computer06 = your partner's computer
>
> Computerxx = Computer05 = lower-numbered computer
>
> Computeryy = Computer06 = higher-numbered computer
>
> Computerzz = Computer05 = computer you are currently using
>
> Contoso*dd*.msft = Contoso03.msft = Active Directory domain you are using
>
> Some lab exercises may require you to partner with another pair of students. In this case, you will see the characters *pd*, px, and py. The *pd* character refers to the number assigned to the domain used by the other pair of students. The px character refers to the lower computer number of the partner pair. The py character refers to the higher computer number of the partner pair. For example, imagine a lab requires you to partner with students who have been assigned Computer07 and Computer08 in the Contoso04.msft domain, and a lab step contains the instruction, "ping computerpx.contoso*pd*.msft," you would type **ping computer07.contsoso04.msft**.
>
> In general, these variables will apply throughout the labs. However, depending on the lab exercise, the meaning of these variables may change or different variables may be introduced. For example, dates are often expressed in *ddmmyy* format. In such cases, the lab instructions will be explicit as to the meaning of the variables.

When these labs ask you to log on to your domain, you can use either of two methods to log on:

- Enter your logon credentials in the User Principal Name (UPN) format, for example, ***usernamezz*@contoso*dd*.msft** (where *zz* is the unique two-digit number assigned to you by the instructor and contoso*dd* is the name of your domain).

- Enter just your username and select your domain from the Logon To drop-down list in the Logon dialog box.

The convention followed throughout these labs is to express your logon credentials as **Contoso*dd**Usernamezz*** and to express your computer name as Computer*zz* (where *zz* is the two-digit version of your student number). For example, if you are asked to log on as Contoso*dd*\Admin*zz*, and your student number is 7, you would log on to Contoso04.msft as Admin07.

The following steps provide instructions for logging on to your domain by selecting the domain name from the Log On To drop-down list:

1. Record the following information:
   - ❑ Your assigned number (*zz*)
   - ❑ Your partners's assigned number (*pp*)
   - ❑ Your domain number (*dd*)
   - ❑ Your fully qualified computer domain (FQDN) name (computer*zz*.contoso*dd*.msft)
2. Press CTRL+ALT+DEL, click Option to display the Log On To text box, and enter the following credentials:
   a. In the User Name box, type **Admin*zz*** (where *zz* is the two-digit student number that has been assigned to you by your instructor).
   b. In the Password box, type **P@ssw0rd**.
   c. In the Log On To drop-down list, select CONTOSO*DD* (where *dd* is the two-digit number representing your domain).
   d. Click OK.

   NOTE Departure from Best Practice Normally, it is a good practice to force a password change on the first logon with an account. However, to simplify the instructions for the labs, you are not required to change the password for this account.

3. In the Manage Your Server Page, click the Don't Display This Page at Logon check box.
   a. Close the Manage Your Server page.
   b. Open Internet Explorer.

c. A dialog box informs you that Internet Explorer's Enhanced Security is enabled. Select In The Future, Do Not Show This Message, and then click OK.

d. In the Address box, type **Computer*zz***, and press ENTER.

e. From the Tools menu, select Internet Options.

f. In the Internet Option dialog box, select Use Current.

g. In the Internet Explorer dialog box, click the Security tab, select Local Intranet, and then select Sites.

h. In the Local Intranet dialog box, verify that http://computer*zz* appears in the Add This Web Site To The Zone box, click Add, and then click Close.

i. Click OK.

j. Close Internet Explorer, and log off.

EXERCISE 1.1: ASSESSING THREAT AGENTS AND THREATS

Estimated completion time: 20 minutes

During an initial meeting with the security team, you discover that the company has not done any kind of assessment of the threat agents that could potentially cause harm to company assets. To start the process of developing a security design, you recommend that the security team spend some time brainstorming possible threat agents that could pose a risk to the company's assets. You remind the security team that the term "assets" includes both tangible items, such as physical hardware, and intangible items, such as employee knowledge or the company's reputation. You further remind the team that, although assessing threats and threat agents is a critical and necessary component of a formal risk analysis, it usually follows an identification of assets. However, the point is to initiate and promote an increased awareness of security issues before beginning a more formal risk analysis.

QUESTION In this exercise, you will work as a class to brainstorm and create a list of threat agents and threats that could potentially pose a risk for Contoso Pharmaceutical's assets. Your instructor will compile the results of this brainstorming exercise into a list that the class will use in Exercises 1.2 and 1.3.

QUESTION Why is it important to consider the motivation of a human threat agent when assessing possible threat agents?

QUESTION In assessing threat agents, should you restrict input exclusively to members of the IT department? Why or why not?

EXERCISE 1.2: DEVELOPING A THREAT AGENT CLASSIFICATION

Estimated completion time: 15 minutes

In your brainstorming session with members of Contoso's security team, you have come up with a substantial list of threats and threat agents. However, the list does not follow any logical order or make use of any systematic, logical categories that could be used to organize the list. You suggest that the security team devise high-level, general categories to describe threat agents. To help them get started, you suggest using categories that have the following labels: Catastrophic, Malicious Attackers, Non-Malicious Attackers, and Mechanical Failures. However, you point out that, although these categories are commonly used within the security community to classify threat agents, these categories are general recommendations only. In fact, the specific threats that an organization faces may require the use of other classifications. Other classifications of threat agents are possible as long as the classifications are informative and create a logically consistent way to organize the list of threats and threat mechanisms under the rubric of threat agents.

In this exercise, you work as a class to create alternative labels to classify threat agents into four general categories. To help you get started, consider what an error in entering sales data and an error in integrating UNIX and Microsoft Windows systems have in common, and what label you might use to classify them. Consider how these threat agents differ from a threat agent represented by a motivated attacker. Your instructor will help guide the class to a consensus of the labels for threat agents that you would like to use to classify threats and threat mechanisms. Use these labels in Exercise 1.3.

QUESTION *List four threat agent classifications.*

QUESTION *What is the difference between a threat agent and a threat or threat mechanism?*

EXERCISE 1.3: ORGANIZING THREATS AND THREAT MECHANISMS ACCORDING TO A THREAT AGENT CLASSIFICATION

Estimated completion time: 20 minutes

In this exercise, you take the information from Exercises 1.1 and 1.2 to complete each of the four tables here. For each of the tables, provide a heading that matches one of the four threat agent classifications that you determined in Exercise 1.2.

Then, below each heading, list the threats from Exercise 1.1 that belong to the particular classification. Feel free to add threats that were not uncovered in Exercise 1.1, where appropriate. When you are finished, your instructor will conduct a class discussion to review the results of your efforts.

Table 1-1 **Threat Agent 1**

Threat Agent:

Table 1-2 **Threat Agent 2**

Threat Agent:

Table 1-3 **Threat Agent 3**

Threat Agent:

Table 1-4 **Threat Agent 4**

Threat Agent:

EXERCISE 1.4: ASSESSING THREAT LIKELIHOOD ARISING FROM INTENTION-BASED THREAT AGENTS

Estimated completion time: 20 minutes

The Contoso security team has agreed to a list of threats that arise from intentional actions on the part of human agents. Now, you would like to create a rating scale that you can use to assign a probability (likelihood) to human threat agents that act intentionally. You suggest to the team that there is a direct relationship between threat agents' motivations and skill levels and their ability to cause harm. You suggest that the Contoso security team create two simple 3-point scales to rank motivation and skill level/capability. You explain to them that skill level/capability has two subcomponents: knowledge and skills to launch an attack, and access to resources (tools, techniques, and so on).

NOTE In this exercise, by devising a rating scale to take into account a threat agent's motivation and skill level, you are performing steps that are preliminary to a formal risk analysis, which involves determining risk likelihood or probability. You will learn more about risk analysis in Chapter 2 of the textbook, "Analyzing Risk," and examine the development of qualitative rating scales in more detail in Lab 2. However, for this exercise, it is important to focus on the consideration that the combination of motivation and skill determines the significance of the threat to the security of an organization. That is, not only should you develop categories to describe a threat agent's motivation, but you should also develop categories to describe the threat agent's skill level.

QUESTION For this exercise, your instructor will assign you to small groups to create descriptions for the 3-point rating systems to rank motivation and skill level. The descriptions for the first level have been completed for you. Complete the remaining descriptions and record them in the spaces below. When you are finished, your instructor will review the results with the class.

Table 1-5 **Threat Agent Motivation Ratings**

Rating	Description
1	Little or no motivation to launch an attack.
2	
3	

Table 1-6 **Threat Agent Skill-Level/Capability Ratings**

Rating	Description
1	Little or no skills or lack of access to resources to launch an attack.
2	
3	

QUESTION *If one were to combine the motivation and the skill-level capability rating tables, how many possible combinations of Motivation and Skill-Level/Capability Ratings are there?*

QUESTION *Assuming labels for the motivation ratings as M1, M2, and M3 and labels for skill level/capability ratings as C1, C2, and C3, create an ordered list in the following space, showing all the possible combinations of the two rating scales, for example, M1-C1, M1-C2, M1-C3, M2-C1, M2-C2, etc.*

QUESTION *The ordered list of possible threat combinations presents a number of equivalent probabilities. Assume the threat probability arising from the combinations of M1–C2 and M2–C1 are equivalent. Further assume that combinations of M2–C2, M1–C3, and M3–C1 represent a second set of equivalent probabilities. And, finally, assume that the combinations M2–C3 and M3–C2 represent the last set of equivalent probabilities. Given these equivalent probabilities, create an ordered, 5-point rating scale that combines the motivation and threat scales, where 1 represents the lowest threat probability and 5 represents the highest threat probability.*

QUESTION *Would the resulting 5-point rating scale be useful in assigning likelihood to threats arising from motivated threat agents? Would a rating scale that used fewer or more data points be preferable to a 5-point scale? Explain your answer.*

EXERCISE 1.5: ASSESSING VULNERABILITIES

Estimated completion time: 20 minutes

Now that the Contoso security team has done some preliminary threat analysis and determined potential ways to organize threats and rate threat likelihood, you suggest that the team look at vulnerabilities that can be potentially exploited by specific threats. You point out that normally a vulnerability assessment is a formal process that involves collecting data on system configurations, employee practices, and conformity to corporate policies. For the time being, however, you simply want to raise awareness regarding potential vulnerabilities as a way to lay the foundation for a more formal vulnerability assessment.

QUESTION *For this exercise, work with the group to which your instructor assigned you in Exercise 1.4 and complete the empty cells in the following Threat and Vulnerability Matrix table. Note that only a limited number of threats are listed for each threat agent. Depending on the threat agent, additional threats may be probable. When you have completed the task, your instructor will lead a class discussion on the results of the exercise.*

Table 1-7 Threat and Vulnerability Matrix

Threat Agent	Threat	Vulnerability
Disgruntled employee	Improper modification of data	Lack of auditing controls
Electrical storm	Denial of service, physical damage, safety	
Contractor	Theft of proprietary data	
Technical staff (system administrators, etc.)	Unauthorized access to security logs, elevation of privilege	
Technical staff (system administrators)	Error configuring services	
Nontechnical staff (managerial, administrative, clerical)	Damage, improper modification of data, denial of service, improper use of company resources	
Fire	Denial of service, physical damage, safety	
Motivated attacker (external)	Unauthorized system access	
Corporate headhunters	Loss of talent and knowledge	
Social activist (external)	Damage to reputation, unauthorized physical and systems access	

QUESTION What is the difference between a threat and a vulnerability?

LAB REVIEW QUESTIONS

Estimated completion time: 15 minutes

1. Does a threat agent or threat always imply intention? Explain your answer.
2. Recently, a number of talented individuals have left the company. During exit interviews, a number of the employees mentioned that their reason for leaving was their manager, which they all had in common. Is the manager a threat agent? If so, would you characterize the threat agent as intentional or unintentional? Explain your answer.
3. Should a threat analysis be limited to the potential impact of threats on information systems?
4. You want to assess the likelihood and potential impact of threats arising from the natural environment. Describe what you would do to gather data to assist you in making this assessment.
5. Why is it useful to rate threats according to likelihood or probability?
6. Explain why lack of employee training should be considered a vulnerability. By providing training and reducing the vulnerability, what possible threats are mitigated?
7. You want to discover the vulnerabilities that arise as a result of employee use of information systems. How would you recommend proceeding to discover this information? Explain your answer.
8. Does the existence of a threat mean that it will cause harm?
9. You are performing a threat and vulnerability analysis. You decide to use a 10-point scale to rate threat likelihood. What kind of threat and vulnerability analysis are you performing, a qualitative or quantitative threat analysis? In what circumstances would it be appropriate to use a qualitative or quantitative threat and vulnerability analysis?

LAB CHALLENGE 1.1: PERFORMING A THREAT AND VULNERABILITY ANALYSIS

Estimated completion time: 40 minutes

The Contoso Pharmaceuticals network contains a screened subnet that is used to host computers that are accessible from the Internet. The screened subnet contains a Web server and an SQL database server, along with two DNS servers. The

Web server is used to provide information about Contoso and its products, as well as to provide Web pages to process orders from business partners. The order information is stored on the SQL database server located on the screened subnet. A network diagram of the screened subnet follows.

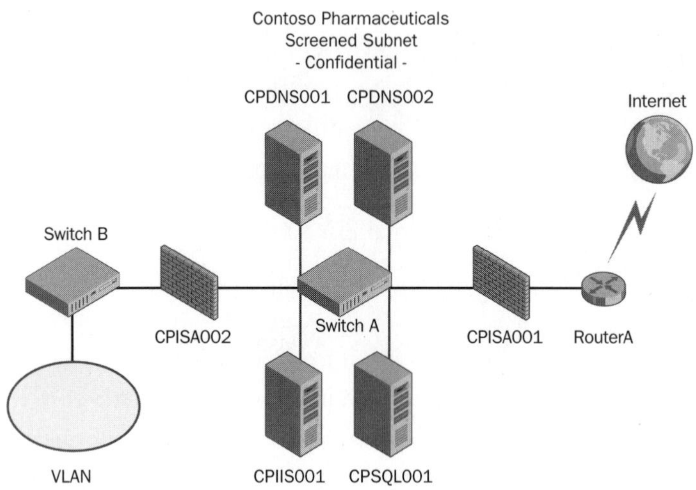

The Contoso Security Team has partially completed a threat and vulnerability analysis for the computers that reside in the screened subnet. They are requesting your help in completing a Threat and Vulnerability Matrix Worksheet they have been working on. Specifically, they would like you to assist them in designing a rating scale for threat likelihood and threat impact. They would like you to help them in using the STRIDE categories to label the threats they have identified also. Finally, they would like you to recommend strategies to reduce vulnerabilities and associate these strategies with the Principles of Information Security (from Chapter 1 of the textbook, "Assessing the Need for Security").

To complete this lab challenge, navigate to the C:\Lab 01\Labwork folder and open the Threat and Vulnerability Matrix Worksheet.doc file. Working either individually or in small groups per your instructor's directions, follow the instructions included in the worksheet to complete the matrix. When you have completed the lab worksheet, save it as C:\Lab 01\Labwork\LC1-1 [***initial of firstname_last name***].doc. If your instructor wants you to submit the lab challenge for evaluation, he or she will provide additional instructions. Be prepared to review the lab challenge as part of class discussion.

You might wish to review the STRIDE threat model and the Principles of Information Security that are discussed in Chapter 1 in the textbook.

LAB 2
ANALYZING RISK

This lab contains the following exercises and activities:

- Exercise 2.1: Determining the Steps for a Formal Risk Analysis
- Exercise 2.2: Determining the Assets to Inventory for a Risk Analysis
- Exercise 2.3: Developing Qualitative Rating Scales for Asset Valuation
- Exercise 2.4: Determining Total Impact Values for a Qualitative Risk Analysis
- Exercise 2.5: Evaluating Security Policies
- Lab Review Questions
- Lab Challenge 2.1: Comparing a Quantitative with a Qualitative Risk Analysis
- Lab Challenge 2.2: Performing a Risk Analysis

SCENARIO

You are continuing in your role as a security consultant to Contoso Pharmaceuticals. You have completed a series of initial meetings with the Contoso Pharmaceuticals security team to assess the need for a security design. As an outcome of these initial meetings, there is unanimous agreement that Contoso Pharmaceuticals needs to implement a formal, systematic, and project-based risk analysis. The purpose of the risk analysis is to help Contoso identify areas of concern and allow them to address security weaknesses in a prioritized manner.

Some members of the security team have looked at a number of standardized methodologies for performing a risk analysis. Although these methodologies have much to recommend them, the security team participants believe they might be better served by developing a custom risk analysis methodology that is specific to their organization and is tailored to the skills and knowledge of its internal staff. Furthermore, they believe that by creating their own customized risk analysis process, they will be better able to compare the strengths and weaknesses of standardized risk analysis methodologies if they decide to use a standardized methodology in the future.

After completing this lab, you will be able to:

- Construct high-level steps for a customized risk analysis project.
- Develop a customized risk analysis process.
- Organize assets into logically consistent categories for analysis.
- Determine different types of assets, such as tangible and intangible assets.
- Develop rating scales for asset valuation that take into account direct and indirect impacts associated with loss.
- Develop rating scales to help determine total risk for a qualitative analysis.
- Analyze security policies for weakness that could lead to an increased risk for an organization.
- Compare qualitative and quantitative risk analysis methodologies.
- Develop rating scales for a qualitative risk analysis that capture the relationships among risk, threat, vulnerability, and asset value.

Estimated lesson time: 115 minutes

BEFORE YOU BEGIN

To successfully complete this lab, you will need to do the following:

- Log on to your student computer as per the instructions in the Before You Begin section of Lab 1, "Assessing the Need for Security."

EXERCISE 2.1: DETERMINING THE STEPS FOR A FORMAL RISK ANALYSIS

Estimated completion time: 20 minutes

Senior management has asked the security team to present a list of the high-level tasks that need to be completed as part of a formal risk analysis and to make the appropriate recommendations.

As the security consultant hired by Contoso Pharmaceuticals to guide them through the security design process, you meet with the team to discuss the steps that are part of a formal risk analysis project.

To complete this exercise, consider the following questions. Then, either in small groups assigned by your instructor or as a general class discussion, list the high-level tasks that should comprise any formal, project-based risk analysis. Although Chapter 2 of the textbook, "Analyzing Risk," provides an ordered list of steps that can compose a risk analysis, the goal of this exercise is to arrive at a series of logical steps independently of the steps listed in the textbook. After you have made a list of tasks, place them in the order in which they should be completed. Compare your results with those listed in Chapter 2.

QUESTION Should a formal risk analysis look at the entire organization or at a portion of the organization? What should you do to limit or extend the risk analysis? What can you do to ensure that the risk analysis project meets and does not exceed its explicit goals?

QUESTION What does a risk analysis seek to protect? How do you determine what specific actions need protection from threats?

QUESTION How do you measure the value of items that require protection? Do you need to define a particular methodology as part of the risk analysis?

QUESTION Who should conduct the risk analysis? What sorts of skills, knowledge, and authority do they require? How do you ensure that the risk analysis is able to account for specific risks that individual departments face?

QUESTION What kinds of data and information do you need to collect as part of a risk analysis?

QUESTION How do you determine whether lack of compliance with existing security policies represents a vulnerability? How do you determine whether the practices and processes of technical or nontechnical staff represent a vulnerability? How do you determine the critical tasks that are performed by key personnel?

QUESTION Should a risk analysis identify threats and vulnerabilities? Does this represent a separate step in the analysis?

QUESTION Should a risk analysis identify countermeasures? Should a risk analysis identify risk management actions such as accept, transfer, mitigate, or avoid?

QUESTION Create an ordered list of the high-level tasks that should comprise a formal risk analysis. You can combine similar steps on a single line.

EXERCISE 2.2: DETERMINING THE ASSETS TO INVENTORY FOR A RISK ANALYSIS

Estimated completion time: 20 minutes

The senior management of Contoso Pharmaceuticals has decided to proceed with a comprehensive, company-wide risk analysis based on the preliminary work you and the security team have performed to date. Senior management wants the risk analysis to consider as many of the company's assets as possible and to extend beyond the IT systems. Furthermore, they like the methodologies you and the security team have been developing for your initial analysis and would like you to continue to develop custom methodologies to perform the risk analysis.

To help guide them in creating an inventory of assets, senior management has asked you to provide them with a number of high-level, general categories that each contains four or five illustrative examples.

QUESTION Should an inventory of assets include such items as employee loyalty and customer confidence? If so, how would you characterize such assets?

QUESTION Should full-time staff and other personnel be considered an asset? If so, what category would staff belong to?

QUESTION Should personal data be considered an asset? If so, what kind of personal data should be protected and under what general asset category would it belong?

QUESTION Should paper-based records, such as contracts, be considered an asset? Briefly explain your answer.

QUESTION Would a server room be considered an asset, separate from the computer systems that reside in it? If so, what general category would you use to characterize it?

QUESTION Either in small groups assigned by your instructor or as a general class discussion, list from three to five high-level asset categories. For each high-level asset category, provide four or five examples to illustrate the asset category.

EXERCISE 2.3: DEVELOPING QUALITATIVE RATING SCALES FOR ASSET VALUATION

Estimated completion time: 20 minutes

As a pilot project, the Contoso security team decides to conduct a risk analysis that uses a qualitative rating scale to indicate the value of assets. You point out that the asset value rating scale should have the following characteristics:

- Be simple and easy to use.
- Take into account the value of the information, not just the value of the physical device or media on which that information is stored.
- Take into account the importance of the business process facilitated by the hardware and software to the overall health of the business, for example, an online ordering process that is implemented on a Web server and database server.
- Take into account the level of impact on the business if the confidentiality, integrity, or availability of the asset were compromised.
- Take into account not only direct consequences, but also indirect consequences. For example, if information subject to regulatory statutes, such as personally identifiable medical information, is compromised, the company might face substantial fines and possibly loss of public confidence.

To help the security team get started, you suggest that it is useful to consider the value of the information that is stored on various devices and media as a guide to determining the value of a particular physical asset. Following are examples of the kinds of information assets they might consider grouping into easy-to-use categories for asset valuation:

- Proprietary data, trade secrets
- Authentication credentials
- Information subject to regulatory statutes, such as the Health Insurance Portability and Accountability Act (HIPAA) or the European Union (EU) Data Protection Directive
- Detailed information on personnel
- Company directory
- Network diagrams and other information that relates to internal IT systems

- Detailed organization chart
- High-level organization chart
- Credit card data
- Financial Profit and Loss statements of a publicly traded company
- Detailed financial records
- White papers
- Outdated financial information
- Public Web pages
- Information about the IT platforms used internally
- Public Domain Name System (DNS) records
- DNS records used for name resolution on the internal network

To complete this exercise, work in small groups assigned by your instructor. Within your group, define three to five asset-value rating scale categories that reflect the importance of the asset to the business or the impact on the business if the confidentiality, integrity, and availability of the asset were compromised. Include a brief definition of each rating scale category. Then group the items from the previous bulleted list to provide representative examples of the asset rating categories. When you have completed the exercise, your instructor will take up the results as a class discussion.

QUESTION Consider the effect on an organization if the confidentiality of its public DNS records were compromised (for example, an attacker performed an unauthorized zone transfer from the publicly available DNS server) against the effect on an organization if the integrity or availability of the public DNS records were compromised. Would there be a sufficient difference in the impact to justify including the public DNS records into more than one asset rating category? Explain your answer.

EXERCISE 2.4: DETERMINING TOTAL IMPACT VALUES FOR A QUALITATIVE RISK ANALYSIS

Estimated completion time: 10 minutes

The Contoso security team is now ready to move on to deciding on a methodology for determining the qualitative values for total summary risk that will compose a well-formed definition of risk. You inform the security team members that total risk can be defined as the combination of the threat, the vulnerability, and the total impact. The total impact itself can be defined as the combination of the asset value and the exposure factor (the extent of potential damage). You recommend that the team use two five-point scales to describe qualitative asset value and the exposure factor, respectively. Then, the team should combine the scales to create a meaningful range of values to describe the total impact. The two rating scales are as follows:

Table 2-1 **Asset Value Classification**

1.	Negligible asset value. Negligible or no impact on business if confidentiality or integrity of asset is compromised. Compromise of availability results in negligible or no increase of support costs or loss of productivity.
2.	Low asset value. Impact on business so low that it cannot be measured if confidentiality or integrity of asset is compromised. Compromise of availability results in distractions that are easily absorbed by internal business process; possible slight increase in support costs.
3.	Medium asset value. Medium impact on business (internal processes, etc.) if confidentiality or integrity is compromised, resulting in revenue loss and increase in support costs. Compromise of availability results in work delays with noticeable increase in support costs and loss of productivity.
4.	Substantial asset value. Serious impact on business if confidentiality or integrity of asset is compromised, resulting in loss of profitability or success. Compromise of availability results in work interruptions, causing quantifiable increase in support costs or delay in business commitments (for instance, clients and customers not able to connect to Web sites, unable to make commitments for contract deliverables on time, etc.).
5.	High asset value. Severe or catastrophic impact on business if confidentiality of asset is compromised, resulting in high losses to business profitability or success. Compromise of availability results in significant work stoppages, causing substantial increase in support costs or cancellation of business commitments.

Table 2-2 **Exposure Classification**

1.	Negligible or no loss of asset confidentiality, integrity, or availability. Effects of compromise to asset effectively contained with no subsequent threat of compromise to other assets.
2.	Low loss of asset confidentiality, integrity, or availability. Effects of compromise to asset tightly contained with negligible or low subsequent threat to other assets.

Table 2-2 **Exposure Classification**

3.	Moderate or limited loss of asset confidentiality, integrity, or availability. Effects of compromise to asset can involve more than one system or service and cause an increased threat to other assets. Compromise or exploit may be externally visible.
4.	Serious loss of asset confidentiality, integrity, or availability. Effects of compromise are likely to have negative effects on other assets and cause a noticeable increase in threats to other assets. Compromise or exploit may be externally visible.
5.	Severe or complete loss of asset confidentiality, integrity, or availability. Results in significant increase in threats to other assets. High probability that compromise or exploit may be externally visible.

To complete this exercise, combine the two scales into a matrix to create a 10-point total impact rating scale. A number of entries have already been completed to help you infer a pattern. When you have completed the matrix, work with your lab partner to determine three summary ranges that represent a low, medium, and high impact.

Table 2-3 **Total Impact Matrix**

	Exposure Factor: 1 = Negligible, 2 = Low, 3 = Medium, 4 = Serious, 5 = Severe					
Asset Value Classification	0	1	2	3	4	5
1 = Very low or negligible	1	2				
2 = Low	2					
3 = Medium	3					
4 = Substantial	4					9
5 = High	5				9	10

Table 2-4 **Summary Total Impact**

Total Impact Range	**Summary Level**
	High
	Medium
	Low

QUESTION What advantages are there, if any, of combining two simple scales with relatively few data points into a scale that has more data points?

EXERCISE 2.5: EVALUATING SECURITY POLICIES

Estimated completion time: 30 minutes

You have begun the initial phase of the threat and risk analysis for Contoso Pharmaceuticals and are in the process of collating and analyzing existing security policies. You explain to the risk assessment team that, at this point in the process, you want to make note of where the security policies are lacking and make recommendations for changes that you will implement at a later phase in the process.

To complete this exercise, navigate to the \Lab Manual\Lab 02 folder and open the file rfc2196.txt (the Site Security Handbook). In the Site Security Handbook, read section 2, Security Policies (pages 6 through 11). Then, in the Lab Manual\Lab 02 folder, open the Contoso Pharmaceuticals Security Policies.doc and read the security policies. Working individually or in small groups assigned by your instructor, answer the following questions with regard to the existing Contoso security policies. When you are finished, your instructor will take up your responses as part of a class discussion.

QUESTION Should the onus for understanding legislation, such as the Health Insurance Portability and Accountability Act (HIPAA), be compelled through a security policy? Does this represent a misuse of a security policy?

QUESTION Are employees likely to understand what is meant by the phrase "objectionable subject matter" in the Internet Use policy? If not, what would you put in place of this phrase?

QUESTION The E-mail Usage policy places the onus on the user for placing a corporate disclaimer at the end of all email messages sent outside the company. What is wrong with this approach from the point of view of security policy enforcement?

QUESTION Consider the password policy. Does this policy clearly discriminate between administrator and user responsibility? If not, what would you do to differentiate user and administrator responsibility?

QUESTION Consider the password policy again. Is a user likely to understand what is meant by the phrase "strong passwords that meet industry standard complexity requirements"? If not, what would you put in place of this phrase?

QUESTION Why might it be important for security policies to provide reasons for compliance and implementation?

QUESTION *Do the policies provide any information on users' expectations of privacy? If not, why would it be a good idea to include such information?*

QUESTION *Are these security policies likely to fail? Explain your answer in general terms.*

LAB REVIEW QUESTIONS

Estimated completion time: 15 minutes

1. You want to perform a risk and threat analysis on a Web server that resides in a screened subnet. What information should you collect as a preliminary step of your analysis? Make your answer as detailed as possible.
2. What factors can constrain (limit) a risk analysis? Where would you express these constraints in a formal risk analysis?
3. Your organization implements a number of software-based processes to ensure the integrity of data entered into a database. Would you consider a process to be an asset?
4. Your organization has a security policy that states users may not install unauthorized software on the company's computers. Would you consider relying exclusively on user understanding of the security policy, user behavior, and penalties for noncompliance as an effective way to enforce this policy? If not, how should you enforce the policy?
5. Your organization's Acceptable Use policy states that users may not use e-mail for personal correspondence. However, as a result of a survey of user behavior, you discover that use of e-mail for personal correspondence is widespread throughout all levels of the company. Furthermore, you discover that management has been aware of the lack of compliance to the policy for a considerable period and has done nothing to address the situation. A supervisor wants to fire an employee whom he finds difficult to manage, but cannot find any substantial grounds to do so, except for the employee's use of e-mail for personal correspondence. Why would the supervisor firing the employee increase the risk of harm to the company? Explain your answer in terms of threats and vulnerabilities that compose the risk.
6. What are the relationships among risk, threat, vulnerability, and asset value?

7. When attempting to assess the risk to an asset, why is it important to take into account the probability of threats and the exposure factor of the assets?

8. You are working with a risk analysis team and trying to determine a rating scale to use for assigning qualitative values to assets. One team member recommends using a 10-point scale. Another team member recommends using a 3-point scale. Briefly describe the pros and cons of both approaches.

LAB CHALLENGE 2.1 COMPARING A QUANTITATIVE WITH A QUALITATIVE RISK ANALYSIS

Estimated completion time: 20 minutes

The Contoso security team has reached an impasse with regard to the methodology for performing a risk analysis. A group of team members wants to use empirical and quantifiable financial, accounting, and statistical data to perform a thorough cost–benefit analysis for implementing risk management strategies. Another group of team members wants to use qualitative data to rank asset values, threat probabilities, and exposure factors to determine risk management strategies. To help the team reach a consensus regarding the methodology to use for the risk analysis, you suggest that the team list the pros and cons of both a quantitative and a qualitative risk analysis.

For this exercise, work individually or in small groups assigned by your instructor to devise a list of pros and cons for quantitative and qualitative risk analysis. To complete this exercise, open the Microsoft Word file named Risk Analysis Comparison.doc in the Lab Manual\Lab 02\Labwork folder. In the file, list the pros and cons for each method. When you have finished, save the file as Lab Manual\Lab 02\Labwork\ LC2-1_[***initial of firstname_last name***].doc. If your instructor wants you to submit the lab challenge for evaluation, he or she will provide additional instructions. Be prepared to take up the lab challenge as part of a class discussion.

QUESTION Is it necessary to use one method of risk analysis (quantitative or qualitative) to the complete exclusion of another method? Briefly explain your answer.

LAB CHALLENGE 2.2 PERFORMING A RISK ANALYSIS

Estimated completion time: 30 minutes

The Contoso security team has decided to continue its development of a risk analysis methodology based on the previous work it has performed. To evaluate the utility and effectiveness of the custom risk analysis methodology, it wants to perform an ad hoc risk analysis of the screened subnet that exists between the Internet and the corporate intranet.

The screened subnet contains a number of computers that are important to the operations and profitability of Contoso Pharmaceuticals. In particular, the screened subnet contains a Web and a SQL server that are responsible for processing orders from customers and business partners. The SQL server contains personally identifiable medical data that is covered under the Health Insurance Portability and Accountability Act (HIPAA).

All the computers in the screened subnet are members of a Microsoft Windows Server 2003 Active Directory directory service domain. A forest trust is configured between the Active Directory domain in the screened subnet and the Contoso.com domain on the corporate intranet. The Contoso.com DNS zone files on the DNS servers in the screened subnet contain Address (A) records that point to domain controllers on the corporate intranet to support the trust relationship. Furthermore, the domain controller in the screened subnet communicates with the Contoso.com domain controllers on the corporate intranet through a virtual private network (VPN).

A network diagram of the screened subnet follows.

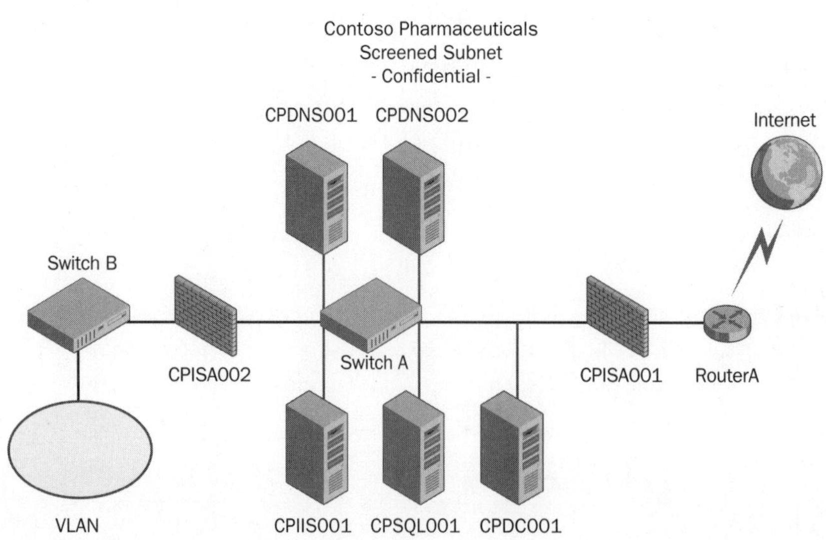

Additional details of the configuration of the computers in the screened subnet can be found in the Lab Manual\Lab 02\CP Screened Subnet Computer Details.doc file.

Instructions

To complete this exercise, navigate to the Lab Manual\Lab 02 folder and open the Risk Analysis Worksheet.doc using WordPad or Word (if it is available). Further instructions for completing the lab challenge are included in the Risk Analysis Worksheet.doc file.

LAB 3

REDUCING THE RISK OF SOFTWARE VULNERABILITIES

This lab contains the following exercises and activities:

- Exercise 3.1: Using MBSA to Check Computers for Missing Security Updates
- Exercise 3.2: Extending Reporting Functionality of MBSA by Using Custom Scripts
- Exercise 3.3: Installing and Configuring Software Update Services
- Exercise 3.4: Using Group Policy to Configure Automatic Update Clients
- Exercise 3.5: Using MBSA to Check for Missing Security Updates Against a List of SUS-Approved Items
- Lab Review Questions
- Lab Challenge 3.1: Automating Scans for Missing Security Updates
- Lab Challenge 3.2: Designing an SUS Infrastructure

SCENARIO

You work as a network support specialist for Contoso, Ltd. Currently, the company has a small peer network. Your job is to install servers and manage users and access to network shares. Your responsibilities require you to do the following:

- Install Windows Server 2003
- Be familiar with Windows Server 2003
- Manage local users and groups
- Create, share, and view shared folders and their permissions
- Verify, test, and configure network settings

After completing this lab, you will be able to:

- Install Microsoft Baseline Security Analyzer (MBSA) and Software Update Services (SUS).
- Configure MBSA to scan computers for vulnerabilities and missing security updates.
- Use the command-line version of MBSA to automate scans of computers.
- Extend the reporting capabilities of MBSA through the use of scripts.
- Configure MBSA to scan computers against a list of SUS-approved updates.
- Configure SUS in a parent/child hierarchy.
- Configure SUS options for approving updates.
- Create Group Policy to apply Microsoft Windows Update settings to member computers in an Active Directory domain.
- Analyze Software Update Service log files.
- Design an SUS infrastructure and hierarchy.

Estimated lesson time: 115 minutes

BEFORE YOU BEGIN

Before you begin these labs, you need to be familiar with the classroom lab environment and know how to log on to your computers. If you haven't done so already, perform the "Before You Begin" section of Lab 1, "Assessing the Need for Security."

> **NOTE** In this lab, you will see the characters *dd*, *pp*, *xx*, *yy*, and *zz*. These directions assume that you are working on computers configured in pairs and that each computer has a number.
>
> When you see *dd*, substitute the number used for your domain. When you see *pp*, substitute the number of your partner's computer. When you see *xx*, substitute the unique number assigned to the lower-numbered (odd-numbered) computer of the pair. When you see *yy*, substitute the unique number assigned to the higher-numbered (even-numbered) computer of the pair. When you see *zz*, substitute the number assigned to the computer you are currently using. The following example assumes that the partner pair of computers has been assigned the names Computer05 and Computer06, and that you have been assigned Computer05.
>
> Computer*pp* = Computer06 = your partner's computer
>
> Computer*xx* = Computer05 = lower-numbered computer
>
> Computer*yy* = Computer06 = higher-numbered computer
>
> Computer*zz* = Computer05 = computer you are currently using
>
> Contoso*dd*.msft = Contoso03.msft = Active Directory domain you are using

SCENARIO

You are a network security administrator for a branch office of Contoso Pharmaceuticals. There are over 150 client computers at the branch office. Keeping the client computers and servers up to date with current security updates and hotfixes is challenging. Aside from the time you spend installing security updates and otherwise keeping computer software up to date, you spend a significant amount of time documenting the status of security updates on computers you administer.

Your manager has approved your recommendation to investigate the effectiveness of Microsoft Baseline Security Analyzer (MBSA) and Software Update Services (SUS) as a means to reduce administrative overhead and mitigate risk resulting from unpatched computers. If your testing of MBSA and SUS is successful, she would like you to design and implement an automated security update infrastructure based on these products.

EXERCISE 3.1: USING MBSA TO CHECK COMPUTERS FOR MISSING SECURITY UPDATES

Estimated completion time: 20 minutes
In this exercise, you use MBSA to determine the identity of computers that are missing security updates and are subsequently at risk. You then investigate using the command-line version of MBSA to automate the creation of reports that identify the patch status of individual computers.

Installing Microsoft Baseline Security Analyzer

1. Log on as Contoso*dd*\Admin*zz* (where *dd* is the two-digit number assigned to your domain and *zz* is the two-digit number assigned to your computer), using P@ssw0rd as the password.
2. Click Start, select Run, type **C:\Lab Manual\Lab 03\MBSASetup-en.msi** in the Open box, and click OK. The Windows Installer dialog box appears.
3. On the Welcome To The Microsoft Baseline Security Analyzer page, click Next.
4. On the License Agreement page, select I Accept the License Agreement, and click Next.
5. Accept the default location on the Destination Folder page and click Next.

6. On the Start Installation page, click Install, and then click OK when the installation completes.
7. On the desktop, double-click the Microsoft Baseline Security Analyzer 1.2.1 shortcut. The Microsoft Baseline Security application opens.
8. In the left pane, click Microsoft Baseline Security Analyzer Help.
9. If a message appears indicating that Microsoft Internet Explorer Enhanced Security Configuration is enabled, select the In The Future, Do Not Show This Message check box, and click OK.
10. In the Microsoft Security Baseline Analyzer help, click the System Requirements link and review the contents of the section.

> **QUESTION** What services must be running on a system that you want to scan remotely?

11. Close the Microsoft Baseline Security Analyzer Version 1.2 Help window and leave MBSA open for the next section.

Scanning for Missing Security Updates

> **NOTE** To scan for missing security updates, MBSA needs to have access to a file named Mssecure.xml. When you launch an MBSA scan for security updates, MBSA attempts to download the most recent version of this file from the Microsoft Web site. If MBSA cannot download this file, it will check for the presence of a local copy of the file and use that version of the file for the scan. If this file is not present locally, MBSA cannot scan for missing security updates. Note that MBSA cannot download this file if a proxy server or firewall requires authentication for outbound HTTP traffic. In such an event, you can download the file from the Microsoft Web site before running a scan for missing security updates.

> **IMPORTANT** Perform steps 1 through 3 only if you do not have a connection to the Internet. If you have a connection to the Internet, start the exercise at step 4.

1. Click Start, select Windows Explorer, and then browse to C:\Lab Manual\Lab 03.
2. In the Lab 03 folder, right-click Mssecure.xml and select Copy.

3. Browse to C:\Program Files, select the Microsoft Baseline Security Analyzer folder, and press CTRL+V to copy the Mssecure.xml file to this folder.
4. Switch to the instance of Microsoft Baseline Security Analyzer that you left open from the previous section.
5. In the left pane, click Pick Multiple Computers To Scan.
6. In the Domain Name box, type **Contoso*dd*** (where *dd* is the two-digit number assigned to your domain).
7. In the Options section, clear all the selected options except Check For Security Updates.

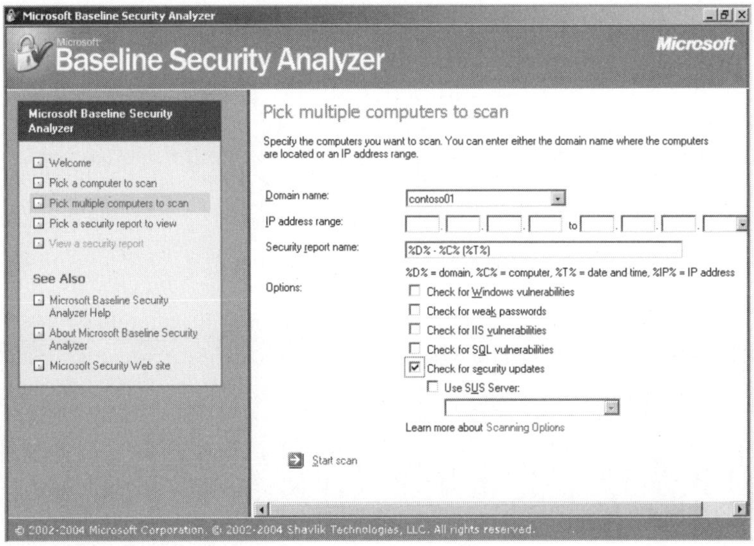

NOTE In this lab, you are focusing on only one of the capabilities of MBSA—the ability to scan computers for missing security updates.

8. Click Start Scan. The Scanning progress bar appears with a message informing you that it is downloading security update information from Microsoft. If you do not have a connection to the Internet, MBSA will use the Mssecure.xml file you copied to its program folder. It will take a few minutes to complete the scan.
9. Wait for the scan to complete, and then, below Pick A Security Report To View, click the link for the topmost item to view the report details.

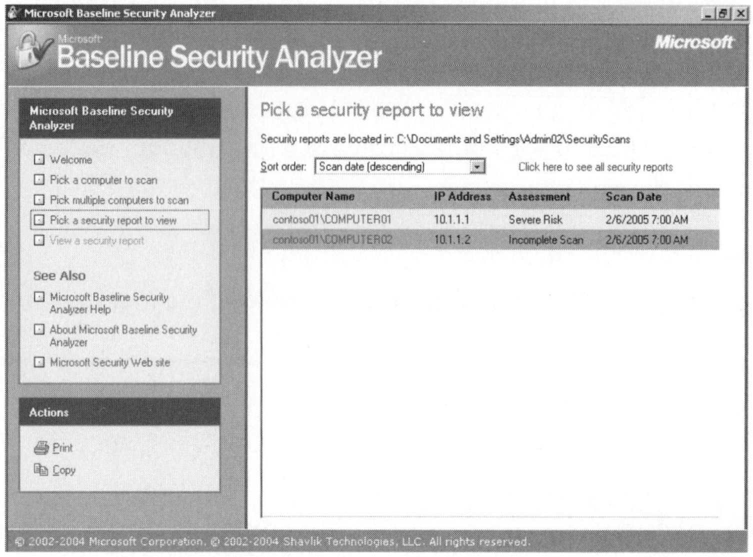

QUESTION *How many Windows security updates are missing or could not be confirmed?*

10. Click Next Security Report and view the report details.

QUESTION *Can you perform remote scans for Office Security Updates by MBSA?*

Using the MBSA Command Line Utility to Check for Missing Security Updates

1. Close the Microsoft Baseline Security Analyzer.
2. Click Start, select Run, type **cmd** in the Open box, and then click OK.
3. At the command prompt, type **cd\Program Files\Microsoft Security Baseline Analyzer**, and press ENTER.
4. At the command prompt, type **ping Computer*pp*** (where *pp* is the two-digit version of your partner's student number), press ENTER, and note the Internet Protocol (IP) address.
5. At the command prompt, type **Ipconfig**, press ENTER, and note your IP address.

6. At the command prompt, type **notepad fips.txt**, press ENTER, and click Yes when prompted if you want to create this file.

   You are creating this file to provide a list of IP addresses that the command-line version of MBSA (Mbsacli.exe) will use to perform an MBSA scan.

7. In Notepad, type your lab partner's IP address on one line, and then type your IP address on another line.
8. From the File menu, select Save, and then close Notepad.
9. At the command prompt, type **mbsacli –hf -?**, press ENTER, and review the options that can be specified with the HFNetChk-style command.

   QUESTION *In what circumstance is verbose output the default when you run the mbsacli command with the –hf flag?*

10. At the command prompt, type **mbsacli –hf –b –fip fips.txt –x mssecure.xml –f hotfix-summary.txt** and press ENTER. Note the information concerning the use of the –v flag that is displayed on the screen.
11. When the scan completes, type **notepad hotfix-summary.txt**, press ENTER, review the contents of the file, and leave Notepad open.

    NOTE *The output of the command lists security bulletin and Microsoft Knowledge Base identifiers to provide a means of locating information easily on the missing updates.*

12. At the command prompt, type **mbsacli –hf –b –v –fip fips.txt –x mssecure.xml –f hotfix-detail.txt** and press ENTER.
13. When the scan completes, type **notepad hotfix-detail.txt**, press ENTER, and review the contents of the file.

    QUESTION *What is the effect of using the –v flag?*

14. Close both instances of Notepad, and all open windows.

EXERCISE 3.2: EXTENDING REPORTING FUNCTIONALITY OF MBSA BY USING CUSTOM SCRIPTS

Estimated completion time: 20 minutes

Your manager likes the reports that MBSA generates. However, she would like the data to be available in different formats. In particular, she wants to be able to view all the computers that are vulnerable to specific threats as a result of missing security updates. For example, she would like a report that shows computer vulnerabilities grouped by missing security updates. In this exercise, you explore the use of custom scripts that you can use to display MBSA data in different formats.

1. Open Windows Explorer, browse to C:\Documents and Settings\Admin*zz* (where *zz* is your student number), and select the Security Scans folder. The reports from the MBSA scan you ran previously are stored here. Unless you ran extra scans, you will see two XML report documents.
2. Select the first XML report, press and hold the SHIFT key, select the last XML report, release the SHIFT key, press DELETE, and then click Yes when prompted to delete the files and send them to the Recycle Bin.

> **IMPORTANT** Be careful not to delete the \Config folder in step 2.

3. On the taskbar, click the Desktop icon, and then double-click on the Microsoft Baseline Analyzer 1.2.1 shortcut. MBSA opens. Notice that the options to view reports are dimmed because you deleted the two XML report documents.
4. In the left pane, click Pick Multiple Computers to Scan.
5. In the Domain Name box, verify that your domain name is entered.
6. In the Options section, verify that only the Check For Security Updates check box is selected.
7. Click Start Scan.
8. Wait for the scans to complete, and then switch to Windows Explorer.
9. In Windows Explorer, browse to C:\Lab Manual\Lab 03 and select the MBSA_SampleScripts folder.

> **NOTE** This folder contains sample scripts and supporting files that were downloaded from *http://www.microsoft.com/technet/security/tools/mbsascript.mspx*.

10. Right-click Rollup.js, select Edit, and briefly review the script.

> **QUESTION** *What is the purpose of the g_SecurityScans variable?*

11. Close Notepad.
12. In the MBSA_SampleScripts folder, right-click the MultiPatchRollup-Demo.bat file and select Edit from the menu. Note the list of Microsoft Security Update identifiers to the right of the –b switch. This list determines the updates that will appear in the output of the script. You can customize this list to show fewer or more updates in the output of the script.
13. Close Notepad.
14. Double-click MultiPatchRollupDemo.bat to run this file. A command prompt window opens showing the report is being processed. When the script has completed, it creates a file named MultiPatchRollup-Demo.xml in the folder.
15. Double-click the MultiPatchRollupDemo.xml file. Internet Explorer opens showing the report.

> **NOTE** *The output display in Internet Explorer is managed by the rollup.xslt file in the same folder as the XML report file output. Unless you have the Wingdings 2 fonts installed on your computer, a number of the icons in the first row of the table will display incorrectly. A copy of the Wingdng2.ttf file has been provided in the Lab 03 folder if you want to install these fonts through Control Panel\Fonts and correct the problems with the display output. To install the Wingdings fonts, copy the Wingdng2.ttf file to the clipboard, open the Fonts folder through Control Panel, and paste the file to the Fonts folder.*

16. In the MultiPatchRollupDemo.xml file, review the output by clicking the >> elements on the left-hand side for various items in the report.

> **QUESTION** *What is an advantage of using these reports over the standard reports available in the MBSA GUI?*

17. Switch to the Microsoft Baseline Security Analyzer, and then, below Pick A Security Report To View, select the topmost item to view the report details.
18. In the row that lists Windows Security Updates in the Issue column, click Result Details.

19. Briefly compare the items that are listed in the Result Details page with the items listed in the MultiPatchRollupDemo.xml file.

> **QUESTION** Why are fewer items listed in the MultiPatchRollupDemo.xml file?

20. Close all open windows.

EXERCISE 3.3: INSTALLING AND CONFIGURING SOFTWARE UPDATE SERVICES

Estimated completion time: 25 minutes

After extensive testing with Software Update Services (SUS), your manager has approved your recommended design for an SUS deployment. Your design calls for staging an SUS server that will download updates from the Microsoft Web site at 3:00 A.M. daily. You will review and test the updates in the lab. If an update passes your review, you will manually approve it on the staging SUS server. A production child SUS server will copy updates from the staging parent SUS server. Any updates that you approve on the staging SUS server are automatically approved on the production SUS server.

In this exercise, you and your lab partner install and configure Software Update Services to receive updates from another SUS server on the intranet.

Installing Software Update Services

1. On both computers, click Start, select Run, type **C:\Lab Manual\Lab 03\sus10sp1.exe**, and click OK. A dialog box showing the progress of the installation file extraction appears, followed by a command prompt window in which the setup command is executed, and then you see the Windows Installer dialog box.
2. On the Welcome To The Microsoft Software Update Services Setup Wizard page, click Next.
3. On the End-User License Agreement page, select I Accept The Terms In The License Agreement, and then click Next.
4. On the Choose Setup Type page, click Custom.
5. On the Choose File Locations page, verify that the locations for the SUS Web site files and update storage are C:\SUS\ and C:\SUS\content\, and click Next.

6. On the Language Settings page, select the English Only option, and then click Next.
7. On the Handling New Versions Of Previously Approved Updates page, ensure that the option I Will Manually Approve New Versions Of Approved Updates is selected, and then click Next.
8. Review the information on the Ready To Install page, and then click Install. The wizard installs SUS with the settings you specified. It will take a few minutes to install SUS. To save time in the lab, try to answer some of the Lab Review questions while you are waiting for the installation to complete.
9. On the Completing The Microsoft Software Update Services Setup Wizard page, note the URL for the SUS administration Web site, and then click Finish. The Microsoft Software Update Services Web administration page appears in Internet Explorer.
10. Leave the SUS administration Web page open for the next section.

Configuring Software Update Services

1. On the Microsoft Software Update Services page, in the left pane, click Set Options.
2. On the Set Options page, select the Do Not Use A Proxy Server To Access The Internet option.

> **NOTE** Note that the proxy server configuration settings include the ability to specify an account credential that the SUS server can use for authentication with the proxy server for outbound HTTP access. You can use credentials for proxy server access only if the SUS server is configured to download updates from the Microsoft Web site. You cannot use proxy server authentication credentials if you are configuring SUS to download updates from an upstream parent SUS server, other than the servers at the Microsoft Web site, or the downloading of SUS updates will fail.

3. Scroll down and below Select Which Server To Synchronize Content From, select Synchronize From A Local Software Update Services Server.
4. In the Synchronize From A Local Software Update Services Server text box, enter the following information, according to your computer number.

a. On the odd-numbered computer (the domain controller) for your student domain, type **Instructor01**, and verify that the check box option to Synchronize List Of Approved Items Updated From This Location (Replace Mode) is *not* selected.

> **NOTE** For the lab scenario, the role of the odd-numbered computer is that of a staging SUS server to provide updates for a second SUS server, pending approval of the updates. This SUS server is the parent server in a parent/child SUS hierarchy. The even-numbered computer is the child SUS Server in a parent/child SUS hierarchy. On the odd-numbered computer, make sure that the check box option to Synchronize List of Approved Items Updated From This Location (Replace Mode) has been cleared; otherwise, you will receive an error.

b. On the even-numbered computer (the member server in the domain), type **Computer*pp*** (where *pp* is the two-digit version of your lab partner's student number), and verify that the check box option to Synchronize List of Approved Items Updated From This Location (Replace Mode) *is* selected.

5. Review all other options without changing them, and then click Apply.
6. In the VBScript message box, click OK.

> **IMPORTANT** Perform steps 7 through 14 on only the odd-numbered computer (the domain controller for the domain). The student sitting at the even-numbered computer should wait until his or her lab partner has finished step 14 before proceeding to step 15.

7. Click Synchronize Server.
8. On the Synchronize Server page, click Synchronize Now. It will take a few minutes to synchronize the server. To save time in the lab, try to answer some of the lab review questions while you are waiting for synchronization to complete.
9. When synchronization has finished, in the VBScript message box, click OK.
10. If necessary, on the Microsoft Software Update Services page, in the left pane, click Approve Updates.

> **NOTE** You should see a sample list of updates. To save time in the lab, a number of sample update files have been installed on Instructor01 to simulate a real Software Update Services environment. Normally, you would see a much larger list of updates.

11. On the Approve Updates page, select the check boxes for each of the six available updates and click Approve.
12. In the Vbscript: Software Update Services message box, click Yes to continue.
13. In the Software Update Services–Web Page Dialog dialog box, click Accept.
14. In the Vbscript: Software Update Services message box, click OK.

> **IMPORTANT** You should perform steps 15 through 17 on only the even-numbered computer (the member server for the domain). Before proceeding, make sure that you have selected the Synchronize List of Approved Items Updated From This Location (Replace Mode) option for this server.

15. On the even-numbered computer, in the left pane, click Synchronize Server.
16. On the Synchronize Server page, click Synchronize Now. It will take a few minutes to synchronize the server. To save time in the lab, try to complete some of the Lab Review questions while you are waiting for synchronization to complete.
17. When synchronization has finished, in the VBScript message box, click OK. Note that the check box options for the approved items are grayed out, indicating that the items were approved on an upstream SUS server.

> **IMPORTANT** Both students perform the following steps.

18. On both computers, in the left pane, click View Synchronization Log and briefly review the items that SUS downloaded.
19. Click View Approval Log and briefly review the items in the approval log.

> **QUESTION** What computer is listed as having approved the updates on both the odd-numbered and even-numbered computers?

20. Click Monitor Server and review the statistics on available updates.
21. Close all open windows.

EXERCISE 3.4: USING GROUP POLICY TO CONFIGURE AUTOMATIC UPDATE CLIENTS

After installing SUS, your next step is to configure the automatic update clients to receive updates from the production SUS server. The most effective way to configure update clients is to use Group Policy. However, you do not want to use a single Group Policy for both your domain controllers and your member computers in a number of scenarios. For example, you might want to have a Group Policy setting for the domain controllers that downloads the updates, but does not install them automatically, whereas for your member computers, you might want to download and install updates automatically.

Estimated completion time: 25 minutes

In this exercise, you and your lab partner create a Group Policy to configure SUS settings on computers in your domains. You create two Group Policies: one for the domain controller (the odd-numbered computer) and another for the member server (the even-numbered computer). Because you will not be modifying the default domain Group Policy to configure SUS settings on member computers, you first create an organizational unit (OU) for member servers and then move the member server object from the Computers container in Active Directory.

> **NOTE** In Active Directory, you can link Group Policy to an organizational unit, domain, or site object, but not to a container object, such as Computers or Users.

1. Click Start, point to Administrative Tools, and select Active Directory Users And Computers.
2. From the View drop-down menu, select Advanced Features. Additional container objects appear in the tree view.

> **IMPORTANT** Perform steps 3 through 7 on only the even-numbered computer (the member server). If you are sitting at the odd-numbered computer (the domain controller), watch your lab partner perform these steps before proceeding with step 8.

3. In the Active Directory Users And Computers console, expand Contoso*dd*.msft (where *dd* is your domain number), right-click the Contoso*dd*.msft node, point to New, and select Organizational Unit.
4. In the New Object–Organizational Unit dialog box, in the Name text box, type **Member Servers**, and click OK.

5. In the tree view, in the left pane, select the Computers container. You see the computer object for the member server in the details pane.
6. Right-click on Computer*yy* (where *yy* is the two-digit version of the even-numbered student computer), and select Move.
7. In the Move dialog box, select the Member Servers OU, and click OK.

> **IMPORTANT** Both students perform the following steps.

8. Access the property pages of the Domain Controllers and Member Servers OUs by performing the following steps:
    a. If you are sitting at the odd-numbered computer, expand Contosodd.msft, right-click on the Domain Controllers OU and select Properties.
    b. If you are sitting at the even-numbered computer, right-click the Member Servers OU and select Properties.
9. In the *Name-Of-OU* Properties dialog box, click the Group Policy tab. The tab informs you that the Group Policy Management snap-in has been installed.
10. Click Open. The Group Policy Management Console (GPMC) opens with the appropriate object, either the Domain Controllers or the Member Servers OU highlighted, depending on at which computer you are sitting.
11. In the GPMC, right-click your OU, either the Domain Controllers or the Member Servers OU, and select Create And Link A GPO Here.

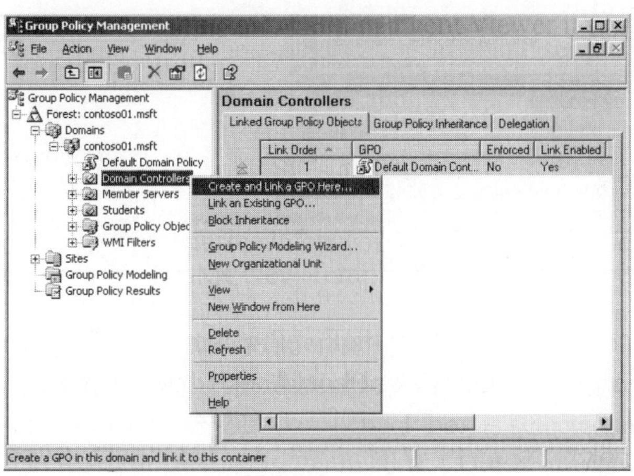

12. In the New GPO dialog box, in the Name text box, type either **SUS Domain Controllers Policy** or **SUS Member Servers Policy**, depending on your computer role, for the name of the Group Policy, and click OK.

13. Right-click the Group Policy object you just created under the OU and click Edit.

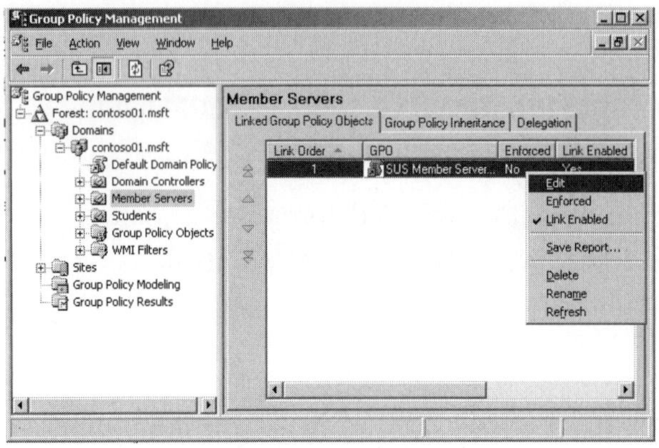

14. In the Group Policy Object Editor, in the tree pane, browse to Computer Configuration\Administrative Templates\Windows Components and select Windows Update.

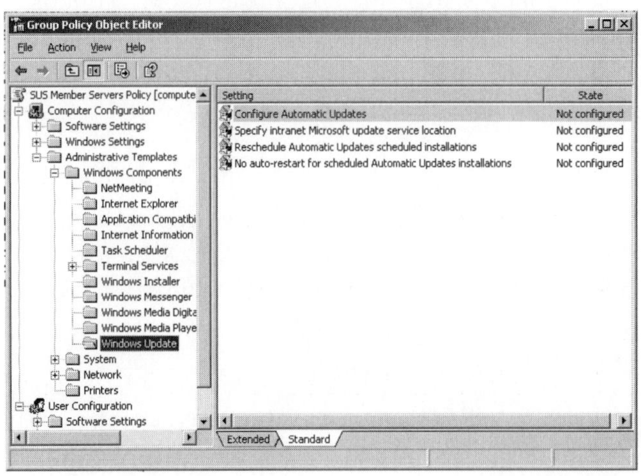

NOTE *On a Windows 2000 domain controller, you would have to add the administrative template that provides the client SUS Group Policy settings.*

15. In the details pane, double-click the Configure Automatic Updates policy setting.

16. In the Configure Automatic Updates Properties dialog box, select Enabled. From the Configure Automatic Updating drop-down list, select 2–Notify for Download And Notify For Install. Click Next Setting.
17. In the Specify Intranet Microsoft Update Service Location Properties dialog box, select Enabled.
18. In both the Set The Intranet Update Service For Detecting Updates and the Set The Intranet Statistics Server text boxes, type **http://computer*yy*** (where *yy* is the even number of the member server in the domain), and click OK.
19. In the details pane, double-click on the two remaining SUS settings, click the Explain tab, and read the description of these settings.

    QUESTION *In what circumstance would you configure either or both of these settings?*

20. Close the Group Policy Object Editor and the Group Policy Management Console.
21. Click Start, choose Run, type **cmd** in the Open text box, and then click OK.

    NOTE *The next step is necessary to ensure that the Group Policy you just created is applied immediately on both computers.*

22. At the command prompt, type **gpupdate /target:computer /force**, press ENTER and, when the command finishes executing, close the command prompt window. After a few minutes, the Windows Update icon will appear in the System Tray.

    IMPORTANT *Do not download or install the updates that you see in the Windows Update box.*

Examining Changes to Computer After Application of Automatic Update Client Group Policy

In this section, you examine changes to your computer as a result of the application of Group Policy.

1. Click Start, right-click My Computer, and select Properties.

2. On the System Properties page, click the Automatic Updates tab. The configuration options should be dimmed. If they are not dimmed, you might have to wait a few more minutes or restart your computer.

> **QUESTION** Why are the Automatic Update options dimmed?

3. Close the System Properties page.
4. Click Start, select Run, type **regedt32** in the Open text box, and click OK.

> **IMPORTANT** In the next steps, you examine changes to values in the registry. Be very careful that you do not change any values in the registry.

5. In the Registry Editor, browse to HKEY_LOCAL_MACHINE\Software\Policies\Microsoft\Windows and select WindowsUpdate.

> **QUESTION** What data do you see for the WUServer and the WUStatusServer values?

6. Expand the WindowsUpdate key and select the AU key.

> **QUESTION** What data do you see for the AUOptions and the UseWUServer values, and what do they mean?

7. Close Registry Editor.

Examining Windows Update Log Files

In this section, you examine the client Windows Update log files and the Internet Information Services (IIS) log files on the Windows Update server.

> **NOTE** Wait for the Windows Update icon to appear in the system tray before proceeding with the following steps. The files you examine may not show complete entries unless this icon is present.

1. Click Start, select Run, type **%windir%\Windows Update.log**, and click OK.

> **QUESTION** What file is being requested from the Windows Update server that contains the software update catalog?

2. Look for an entry that indicates an error.

> **QUESTION** What file is being requested?

3. Close Notepad.
4. Click Start, select Run, type **\\computerxx\admin$\system32\LogFiles\W3SVC1** (where *xx* is the odd number of the domain controller), and click OK.
5. In Windows Explorer, double-click ex*yymmdd*.log (where *yy* is the year, *mm* is the month, and *dd* is the current numeric date).
6. In Notepad, select Edit, and then select Find.
7. In the Find dialog box, type **<10.1.1.*yy*>** (where *yy* is the last octect of the member server's IP address), and click Find Next.

> **QUESTION** Aside from the sampleExe-exclAnexcl.cab file, which is part of the SUS sample files used for this lab and you would not normally see them on a production SUS server, what three files does the member server (the child SUS server) request?

8. Close Notepad.
9. Click Start, select Run, type **\\computeryy\admin$\system32\LogFiles\W3SVC1** (where *yy* is the even number of the member server), and click OK.
10. In Windows Explorer, double-click ex*yymmdd*.log (where *yy* is the year, *mm* is the month, and *dd* is the current numeric date).
11. Review the log file and note that both computers in the domain request the */autoupdate/getmanifest.asp* file.
12. Close all open windows.

EXERCISE 3.5: USING MBSA TO CHECK FOR MISSING SECURITY UPDATES AGAINST A LIST OF SUS-APPROVED ITEMS

Estimated completion time: 15 minutes

You have completed your testing of SUS and MBSA. One of your concerns about MBSA reports is that they report security updates that haven't been approved by your organization as missing. You want to ensure that MBSA will report on the patch status of only the security updates that have been approved by your organization. Before deploying both MBSA and SUS, test the ability of MBSA to perform scans of computers using a list of SUS-approved updates. Explore, also, the ability of MBSA to perform scans against a list of SUS-approved updates in the event that the SUS server is unavailable or can't be contacted.

1. Click Start, select Run, type **cmd** in the Open text box, and press ENTER.
2. At the command prompt, type **cd\Program Files\Microsoft Baseline Security Analyzer** and press ENTER.
3. Type **mbsacli –hf –v –b –x mssecure.xml** and press ENTER. The output of the command shows a number of missing security updates. Review the output of the command and leave the command prompt window open.
4. Click Start, select Run, type **cmd** in the Open text box and press ENTER.
5. At the command prompt, type **cd\Program Files\Microsoft Baseline Security Analyzer**, and press ENTER.
6. Type **mbsacli –hf –v –b –x mssecure.xml –sus http://computer*zz*** (where *zz* is the two-digit version of your student number), and press ENTER. The output of the command shows a number of missing security updates.
7. Review the output of the command. In particular, note the hotfix information under the first heading, Windows Server 2003, Enterprise Edition Gold. Leave the command prompt window open.
8. Switch to the first command prompt window and compare the output of both commands.
9. Open Windows Explorer, and navigate to C:\Inetput\Wwwroot.
10. In the C:\Inetput\Wwwroot folder, double-click the file named ApprovedItems.txt, and review the contents of the file.
11. Close Notepad.
12. In Windows Explorer, right-click ApprovedItems.txt, select Rename, and rename the file to **ApprovedItems.txt.bak**. Press ENTER and click Yes when prompted to confirm the change.
13. In Windows Explorer, navigate to C:\Lab Files\Lab 03, right-click the file named ApprovedItems.txt, and select Copy.

14. In Windows Explorer, navigate to C:\Inetpub\Wwwroot, right-click in the folder and select Paste.
15. In the C:\Inetpub\Wwwroot folder, double-click the ApprovedItems.txt file and briefly review its contents.
16. Close Notepad.
17. Switch to the second command prompt window, type **mbsacli -hf -v -b -x mssecure.xml -sus http://computer*zz***, and press ENTER.
18. Review the output of the command. In particular, note the hotfix information under the first heading, Windows Server 2003, Enterprise Edition Gold.

> **QUESTION** What accounts for the difference in the output of these commands?

19. In Windows Explorer, delete the ApprovedItems.txt file and rename the ApprovedItems.txt.bak file back to ApprovedItems.txt.
20. Close all open windows.

LAB REVIEW QUESTIONS

Estimated completion time: 10 minutes

1. You want to use MBSA to check for missing security updates against a list of SUS-approved updates. Do the MBSA components need to be able to contact an actual SUS server?
2. List some of the advantages that the command-line version of the MBSA has over the GUI version.
3. You have configured a client update Group Policy to apply to computers within a particular OU. What happens to the update configuration on a computer when you move it from one OU to another?
4. You manage a group of computers that are used by temporary employees. You want to apply updates to these computers with a minimum of interaction on the part of the end user. How would you configure the Windows Update policy settings?

5. You are responsible for managing updates on both Windows servers and client computers. For the Windows servers, you want to be notified when new updates are ready to be downloaded and installed. For the client computers, you want the updates to automatically install and restart the computer if a particular update requires it. Both groups of computers belong to the same OU. Describe two solutions that would allow you to apply different Windows Update configurations to these two groups of computers.

6. You are a security consultant working on contract for Contoso Pharmaceuticals. An administrator asks you for help in performing MBSA scans of a Web server in a screened subnet. She says that she is unable to scan the computer remotely. Depending on whether she is trying to scan the Web server according to its host name or IP address, she receives an error message indicating that the server is not found or that she lacks administrative rights. You and she confirm that the account has sufficient administrative rights. However, you also confirm that a number of services on the Web server have been disabled to mitigate potential vulnerabilities. What services have to be running to perform remote MBSA scans, and what do you recommend the administrator do to scan the computers for missing security updates using MBSA?

LAB CHALLENGE 3.1: AUTOMATING SCANS FOR MISSING SECURITY UPDATES

Estimated completion time: 20 minutes

Your manager is happy with the progress you have made in creating an effective security update infrastructure. The current update infrastructure you have implemented for your office is as follows:

- Updates are downloaded at 3:00 A.M. each day from the Microsoft Web site to an SUS server used to stage updates. These updates are subsequently tested in a lab prior to deployment from a production SUS server.
- On Friday of each week, updates that have passed testing are approved on the staging SUS server by the close of business at 5:00 P.M.
- The synchronization schedule of the production SUS server is set to download approved updates automatically from the staging SUS server at 10:00 P.M. on Friday of each week.

- Approved security updates downloaded from the staging SUS server are automatically approved on the production SUS server.
- A Group Policy object that applies to client-enabled computers schedules Automatic Updates to occur at 3:00 A.M. every Saturday.
- All client computers on the same subnet receive IP address configurations from a Dynamic Host Configuration Protocol (DHCP) server.
- An MBSA-style scan runs from a command line every Sunday at 3:00 A.M. The report is copied to a central location.

One of the problems with your design is that employees must leave their computers on over the weekend for the security updates to be applied. Although employees have been instructed to do this, occasionally they will turn computers off when they leave the office for the weekend nevertheless. Because you do not want to interfere with employee productivity during the week, you do not want to configure the SUS Group Policy to apply the security updates automatically when the computers are restarted. Rather, you would like to know which computers did not receive the security updates over the weekend and contact the employees directly to schedule a convenient time to perform the update.

Your manager is pleased with the MBSA report formats you have produced using modified demo scripts from the Microsoft Web site. However, she would like to see the scan data in a format that can be imported to a database for easier and more flexible analysis.

For this lab challenge, create a batch file that will run at 3:00 A.M. every Tuesday and scan all the client computers for a detailed list of missing security updates that have been approved on the SUS server. The report format needs to be such that it can be easily imported into a database for analysis.

To complete this lab challenge, create a batch file that performs the required task. Save the batch file as C:\Lab Manual\Lab 03\Labwork\<*LastNamezz*>_MissingUpdate.bat (where *LastName* is your last name and *zz* is your student number). In the batch file, point to any file(s) that you might need to create for the command to meet the requirements of the lab challenge, but do not create the actual file(s) unless you want to test the command. Then, using the Scheduled Tasks application, configure the file to run at 3:00 A.M. every Tuesday. Take a screen shot of the Schedule Tasks folder to show the schedule for the file and save the screen shot as C:\Lab Manual\Lab 03\Labwork\ <*LastNamezz*>_schedule.bmp. If your instructor requires you to copy the file to another location for evaluation, he or she will provide specific instructions for doing so.

TIP *To create a screen shot, with the window of interest in the foreground, press ALT+PRT SCR. Open Paint, press CTRL+V to paste the screen shot into the Paint application, and then save the file.*

LAB CHALLENGE 3.2: DESIGNING AN SUS INFRASTRUCTURE

Estimated completion time: 20 minutes

You are a security consultant working for Contoso Pharmaceuticals. The company is currently applying security updates manually to computers on its network. However, this is a labor-intensive activity that has significant costs associated with it. Contoso Pharmaceuticals would like to deploy Software Update Services to reduce these costs and minimize the risk associated with applying unapproved security updates or not applying security updates that have been approved.

The network administrator has tentatively suggested that an SUS infrastructure start with the placement of an SUS server in the screened subnet located at the Contoso Pharmaceuticals headquarters. However, the network administrator is unclear how best to leverage an SUS server installed in the screened subnet to deliver updates to client computers in the corporate network and Contoso's geographically distributed branch offices.

Figure 3-1 below shows a high-level diagram of the Contoso network infrastructure. One representative branch office in Toronto, Ontario, is shown to represent a typical branch office configuration.

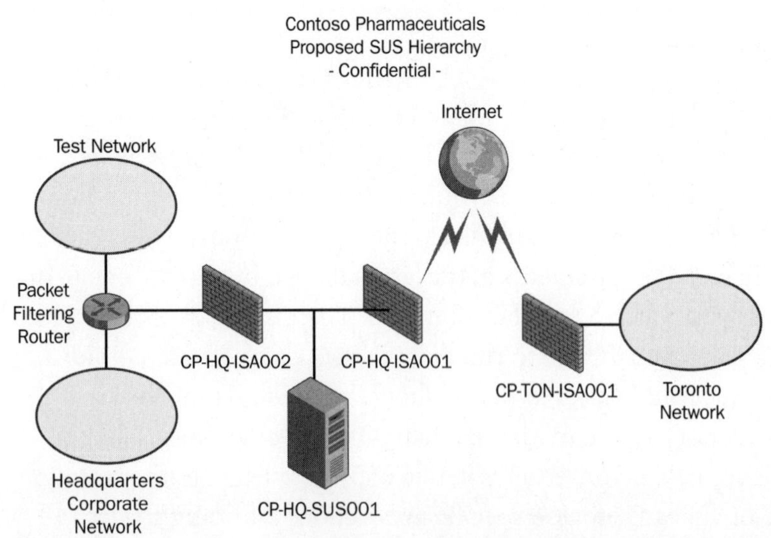

Figure 27-1 Contoso network diagram for proposed SUS infrastructure

To assist with the design of the SUS infrastructure, you learn the following information:

- All updates must be tested before they can be deployed through SUS.
- Local administrators in branch offices must apply only approved updates and should have no control over what updates to apply.
- All approved updates to client computers must be installed and users should not have the option to delay the installation of the updates.
- All approved updates to servers must be available as soon as possible on server computers, but the installation of any updates that require a restart must be scheduled through a change management process.
- A log of all updates that has occurred on client and server computers should, if possible, be recorded in a single location.
- All outbound HTTP access to the Internet through Internet Security And Acceleration (ISA) Server at the branch offices requires authentication.
- A sufficient budget has been approved to deploy as many SUS servers as are needed to fulfill these requirements.

Instructions

Working with your lab partner, spend a few minutes considering how you would deploy and configure an SUS infrastructure for the stated scenario. Consider, for example, how many SUS servers you need to deploy and how they should be configured. Consider, also, circumstances that might warrant changes to current security policies, or that might require a change to the network infrastructure or your OU design, and so on. When you are finished, your instructor will lead a class discussion to examine the merits and demerits of the various solutions that the class proposes.

POSTLAB CLEANUP

Estimated completion time: 5 minutes

Perform the following steps before proceeding to the next lab:

1. Click Start, point to Administrative Tools, and select Group Policy Management.
2. In the tree view pane, expand the Forest node, the Domains node, the contosodd.msft node and, finally, the Group Policy Objects node.

3. Select the Group Policy Object you created earlier in the lab, either the SUS Domain Controllers Policy or the SUS Member Servers Policy.

> **IMPORTANT** Ensure that you right-click the Group Policy object you created, either the SUS Domain Controllers Policy or the SUS Member Servers Policy, and *not* the Default Domain Controllers Policy or the Default Domain Policy. Deleting the wrong GroupPolicy Object could have serious consequences for subsequent labs.

4. Right-click the Group Policy Object you created earlier in the lab, either the SUS Domain Controllers Policy or the SUS Member Servers Policy, and select Delete.
5. In the Group Policy Management dialog box, select OK to delete the SUS Group Policy object.
6. Click Start, type **cmd**, and press ENTER.
7. In the command prompt window, type **gpupdate /target:computer /force** and press ENTER.
8. Close all open windows and log off.

LAB 4
DESIGNING A MANAGEMENT INFRASTRUCTURE

This lab contains the following exercises and activities:

- Exercise 4.1: Understanding the Need for a Secure Management Infrastructure Design
- Exercise 4.2: Designing a Secure Emergency Management Services Infrastructure
- Exercise 4.3: Restricting Customized MMCs for Delegated Tasks
- Exercise 4.4: Securing Remote Desktop Protocol
- Lab Review Questions
- Lab Challenge 4.1: Designing a Secure Management Infrastructure

SCENARIO

You are a security consultant currently working on contract for Contoso Pharmaceuticals. You have been working for some time with Contoso's security team to help them mitigate threats, vulnerabilities, and risks to their IT infrastructure. During this phase of your work with Contoso, you are analyzing issues related to the network management infrastructure. In general, the security team recognizes that the current network management security model is weak and exposes the company to a number of significant vulnerabilities and threats.

After completing this lab, you will be able to:

- **Determine the vulnerabilities associated with network administration.**
- **Determine strategies for mitigating vulnerabilities associated with network administration.**

- **Design a secure Emergency Management Services Infrastructure.**
- **Restrict the use of Microsoft Management Consoles.**
- **Use the Runas command to observe the principle of least privilege.**
- **Design a secure Remote Desktop Protocol strategy for managing servers.**
- **Configure Terminal Services to use an alternate port.**
- **Configure Terminal Services for greater security.**
- **Design a secure management infrastructure.**

Estimated lesson time: 120 minutes

BEFORE YOU BEGIN

This lab assumes that you have previously performed the "Before You Begin" section of Lab 1, "Assessing the Need for Security," and steps 3 through 7 of "Lab Exercise 3.4: Using Group Policy to Configure Automatic Update Clients" in Lab 3, "Reducing the Risk of Software Vulnerabilities."

Exercises 4.3 and 4.4 in this lab depend on the presence of organizational units (OUs) and user accounts that are not created as part of the lab setup. In addition, the default security policy for the domain controller in the Contoso*dd*.msft domain will have to be weakened to allow users to log on locally. To complete this lab successfully, the student sitting at the odd-numbered computer (the domain controller for the Contoso*dd*.msft domain) must perform the following steps:

1. Log on to Contoso*dd*\Admin*zz* (where *dd* is the number assigned to your domain and *zz* is your student number) using **P@ssw0rd** as the password.
2. Click Start, point to Administrative Tools, and then select Domain Controller Security Policy. Be careful not to confuse this item with the Domain Security Policy.
3. In the Default Domain Security Settings console, in the tree pane, expand the Local Policies node, and then select User Rights Assignment.
4. In the details pane of the User Rights Assignment node, double-click Allow Logon Locally.
5. In the Allow Logon Locally Properties dialog box, click Add User Or Group.

6. In the Add User Or Group dialog box, type **Domain Users**, and then click OK.
7. Click OK to close the Allow Log On Locally Properties dialog box.
8. Close the Default Domain Security Settings console.

> **NOTE** In a production environment, configuring a domain controller to allow users the right to log on to it locally represents significant security vulnerability. On domain controllers and other servers on your network, log on with administrative credentials, perform your tasks, and log off after you have finished.
>
> Security on the domain controller is relaxed only to allow the student sitting at the odd-numbered computer the ability to perform lab exercises while logged on with an account that does not have administrative privileges. This represents a weakening of security in a typical production environment and is not a recommended best practice.

9. Click Start, select Run, type **c:\lab manual\lab 04\Lab04Setup.cmd** in the Open box, and press ENTER. A batch file executes that creates a number of OUs and user accounts used in the lab.
10. When the batch file completes, click Start, select Run, type **cmd** in the Open box, and press ENTER.
11. In the command prompt, type **gpupdate /target:computer /force**.
12. Log off.
13. To verify that the new rights assignment for the Domain Users group has been successfully configured, log on as Contoso*dd*\Student*zz* using P@ssw0rd as the password.
14. Log off.

> **NOTE** In this lab, you will see the characters dd, pp, xx, yy, and zz. These directions assume that you are working on computers configured in pairs and that each computer has a number.
>
> When you see dd, substitute the number used for your domain. When you see pp, substitute the number of your partner's computer. When you see xx, substitute the unique number assigned to the lower-numbered computer of the pair. When you see yy, substitute the unique number assigned to the higher-numbered computer of the pair. When you see zz, substitute the number assigned to the computer you are currently using. The following example assumes that the partner pair of computers has been assigned the names Computer05 and Computer06 and that you have been assigned Computer05:
>
> Computerpp = Computer06 = your partner's computer

Computerxx = Computer05 = lower-numbered computer

Computeryy = Computer06 = higher-numbered computer

Computerzz = Computer05 = computer you are currently using

Contosodd.msft = Contoso03.msft = Active Directory domain you are using

EXERCISE 4.1: UNDERSTANDING THE NEED FOR A SECURE MANAGEMENT INFRASTRUCTURE DESIGN

Estimated completion time: 20 minutes

The Contoso security team recognizes the problem and has asked your help in developing strategies that will help them mitigate some of the vulnerabilities and threats that are a consequence of the weak network management security model. They have identified a preliminary list of some of the threats posed by administrators and have asked your help in expanding the list and providing some guidance for developing strategies for mitigating the risk arising from these threats and vulnerabilities.

To complete this lab exercise, spend a few minutes working with your assigned lab partner or in a small group assigned by your instructor to complete the Vulnerability and Mitigation Strategy columns in the Administrator Threat Table that follows. Note that there may be more than one vulnerability and mitigation strategy for each threat. After you have finished adding items to the columns, answer the following questions. When you have completed the exercise, your instructor will take up the results with the classroom as a whole.

Table 4-1 **Administrator Threat Table**

Threat	Vulnerability	Mitigation Strategy
Administrator accidentally deletes important system or corporate data.		
Administrator accidentally compromises data confidentiality by making it available to unapproved users.		
Administrator is tricked into granting unapproved elevated privileges to a user.		

Table 4-1 **Administrator Threat Table**

Threat	Vulnerability	Mitigation Strategy
Intruder gains access to unlocked workstation used by administrator and creates account credentials with elevated privileges.		
Account administrator intentionally elevates unapproved privileges for his or her user account.		
Administrator makes error in configuration of services and causes disruption of availability.		
Administrator disables security measures to allow for easier performance of duties.		
Administrator uses penetration tools, such as Nmap, on the network without prior approval.		
Administrator inadvertently introduces Trojan horse while logged on to network.		
Administrator learns personal details of an employee through unauthorized monitoring of communications.		

QUESTION Many security policies within an organization can be enforced through software. For example, software restriction policies can be implemented to prevent the use of particular software on the network. Are administrators generally subject to the same degree of control in an organization as users are? That is, are administrator actions more or less likely to be circumscribed by enforcement of security policies through software? Briefly explain your answer.

QUESTION Given your answer to the question above, what implications does this have for the design of secure network management infrastructure? For example, should an organization design security policies that are specific to administrative behavior?

QUESTION Administrators often need access to specialized tools, such as protocol analyzers, to perform their tasks. Should an organization's security policies determine where these tools can be installed?

QUESTION Many organizations employ the principle of separation of duties to reduce the risk created by administrators. Give an example of an activity that administrators should not be able to perform in an organization that employs the principle of separation of duties.

EXERCISE 4.2: DESIGNING A SECURE EMERGENCY MANAGEMENT SERVICES INFRASTRUCTURE

Estimated completion time: 20 minutes

The Contoso security team has been meeting to discuss the implementation of Emergency Management Services (EMS) on the computers running Microsoft Windows Server 2003 that are physically located in a server room at Contoso's headquarters. One of their concerns is that an incorrect implementation of EMS will create significant security vulnerabilities to the servers. Consequently, one of their requirements for the EMS design is that only one or two administrators have access to the EMS components. Another requirement is that the EMS administrators should be able to access the EMS components from the workstations they use on the corporate local area network (LAN). However, this requirement notwithstanding, the EMS components should have a maximum degree of isolation from the corporate LAN. Although cost is not a primary factor for this project, the security team would like to implement EMS as a lower-cost solution that uses a terminal concentrator, rather than a more expensive solution that relies on application-specific integrated circuit (ASIC)–based service processors.

The security team has asked you to recommend a security design for EMS based on these requirements.

To complete this lab exercise, work with your lab partner or in small groups assigned by your instructor to answer the following questions. When you are finished, the instructor will discuss the results with the class.

QUESTION What precautions should you take to prevent unauthorized individuals from connecting to the management ports on the EMS-enabled servers?

QUESTION What precautions should you take to ensure the physical security of the terminal concentrator?

QUESTION One of the design requirements is that the EMS components be isolated as much as possible from the corporate LAN. How would you accomplish this isolation? What EMS component(s) would you isolate?

QUESTION What security features should the terminal concentrator possess? For example, how would you protect user names and passwords that cross the wire between the management server and the terminal concentrator?

QUESTION One of the security team members has recommended using a remote access server (RAS) to provide dial-in access to the terminal concentrator and enhance fault tolerance and availability. What security feature should you implement on the RAS to mitigate the discovery of the phone number used to provide dial-in access to the terminal concentrator?

QUESTION Would you consider using either a firewall or a secure packet-filtering router to protect the EMS components? If so, where would you place the firewall or the packet-filtering router?

QUESTION Aside from the EMS administrators, would you inform IT staff in general about the presence of EMS management components?

EXERCISE 4.3: RESTRICTING CUSTOMIZED MMCS FOR DELEGATED TASKS

Estimated completion time: 30 minutes

Contoso Pharmaceuticals uses a distributed administration model based on geographic location to structure its OUs. You are responsible for administering the OUs for your particular location.

Recently, Contoso Pharmaceuticals issued a new security policy stipulating that specific departmental managers should have the ability to reset passwords on user accounts for employees that they manage. However, in granting this ability, the security policy stipulates that the principle of least privilege should extend to the use of Microsoft Management Consoles (MMCs) that managers will need to reset passwords. Finally, the security policy stipulates that, whenever possible, administrators should log on with nonadministrative user accounts and use the Runas command to perform administrative tasks.

An Enterprise Administrator has already delegated permissions on specific OUs to allow managers to reset passwords for employees they manage. You have been asked to create MMCs that the managers will use.

In this exercise, you log on with your Student*zz* account, configure your user profile to perform administrative tasks, and use the Runas command to perform the administrative tasks. You create a custom MMC that can be used by the sales manager, Carol Philips, to reset the sales employee passwords. Finally, you use the authoring features of the MMC to create a Group Policy to restrict the MMC use.

Configuring the Studentzz Profile to Perform Administrative Tasks Using the Runas Command

1. Log on as Contoso*dd*\Student*zz* using **P@ssw0rd** as the password.
2. Right-click the Start menu and select Properties.
3. In the Taskbar And Start Menu Properties dialog box, click Customize.
4. In the Customize Start Menu dialog box, select the Advanced tab.
5. In the Start menu items box, scroll down to the bottom of the list, locate the System Administrative Tools heading, select Display On The All Programs And The Start Menu, and click OK.
6. In the Taskbar And Start Menu Properties dialog box, click OK.
7. Click Start, point to All Programs, point to Accessories, right-Windows Explorer, and select Pin To Start Menu.
8. On the Start menu, select Windows Explorer.
9. From the Tools menu, select Folder Options.
10. In the Folder Options dialog box, click the View tab, and configure the folder options as follows:
    a. Select the Show Hidden Files And Folders option.
    b. Clear the Hide Extensions For Known File Types check box.
    c. Clear the Hide Protected Operating System Files (Recommended) check box. In the Warning dialog box, click Yes to confirm you want to be able to view these files.
11. In the Folder Options dialog box, click OK.
12. Close all open windows. Right-click the desktop, point to New, and then select Text Document.
13. Rename the text document ADUC.cmd. In the Rename dialog box, click Yes to confirm the change of extension.
14. Right-click ADUC.cmd, and select Edit.

15. In Notepad, type **runas /user:Contoso*dd*\Admin*zz* "mmc c:\windows\system32\dsa.msc"** (including the quotes), and then save and close the file.

Creating a Custom MMC

In this section of the exercise, you use the Runas command from the Run dialog box to launch an empty MMC in author mode to customize it.

1. Click Start, select Run, type **runas /user:Contoso*dd*\Admin*zz* "mmc /a"** in the Open box, and press ENTER.
2. In the command prompt window, type the password for your Admin*zz* account, and press ENTER.
3. In the Console1 console, click the File menu, and select Add/Remove Snap-in.
4. In the Add/Remove Snap-in dialog box, click Add.
5. In the Add Standalone Snap-In dialog box, select Active Directory Users And Computers, click Add, and then click Close.

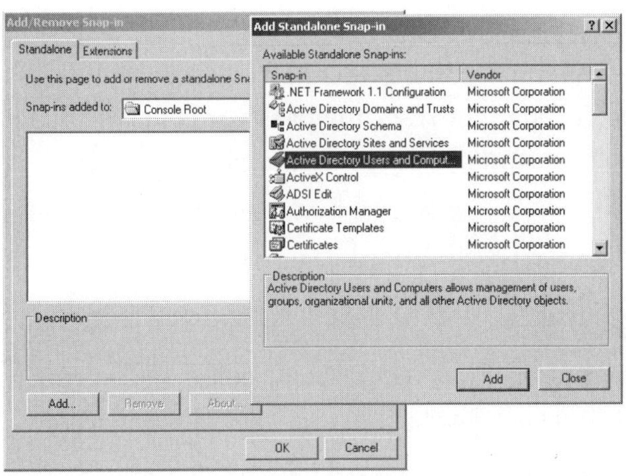

6. In the Add/Remove Snap-In dialog box, click OK.
7. In the Console1 console, in the tree pane, expand Active Directory Users And Computers, expand Contoso*dd*.msft, and expand the Location*zz* OU.
8. Right-click the Sales OU and select New Window From Here.
9. From the Window menu, select 1 Console Root.

10. Being careful *not* to close the entire MMC 1 console, close the Console Root window so that the Console1–[Sales] window is displayed.

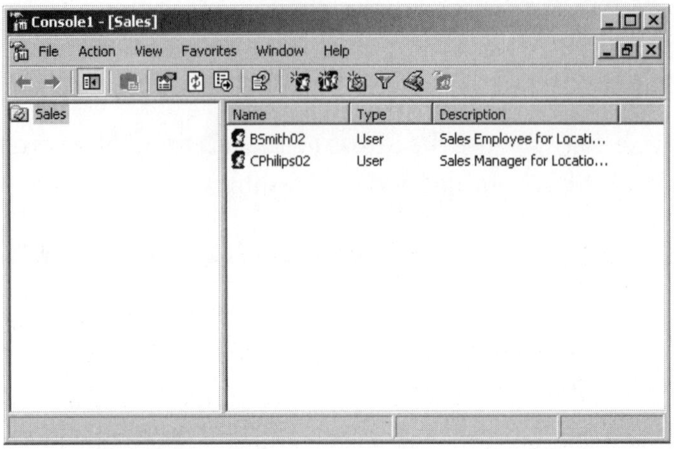

11. In the Console1–[Sales] console, right-click the Sales OU and select New Taskpad View. The New Taskpad View Wizard appears.
12. On the Welcome To The New Taskpad View Wizard page, click Next.
13. On the Taskpad Display page, accept the default selections and click Next.
14. On the Taskpad Target page, accept the default selections and click Next.
15. On the Name And Description page, type **Taskpad for Sales Managers** in the Name box, type **Taskpad for resetting passwords** in the Description box, click Next, and then click Finish. The New Task Wizard appears.
16. On the Welcome To The New Task Wizard page, click Next.
17. On the Command Type page, accept the default setting, and then click Next.
18. On the Shortcut Menu command, in the Available commands area, select Reset Password, and click Next.

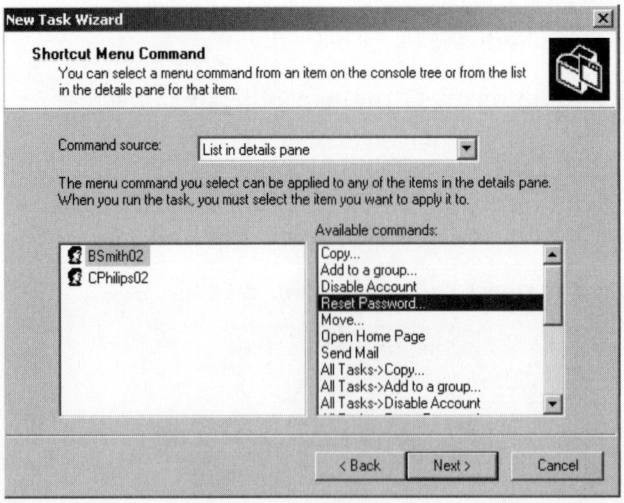

19. On the Name And Description page, click Next to accept the default values.

20. On the Task Icon page, find and select an appropriate icon for the reset password task, such as the icon that displays a key alongside a monitor, click Next, and then click Finish.

21. In the Console1–[Sales] console, from the File menu, select Options.

22. In the Options dialog box, perform the following actions:

    a. Type **Sales OU Console** to replace Console1–[Sales] as the name of the console.

    b. From the Console Mode drop-down list, select User Mode–Limited Access, Single Window.

    c. Select the Do Not Save Changes To This Console check box.

    d. Clear the Allow The User To Customize Views check box.

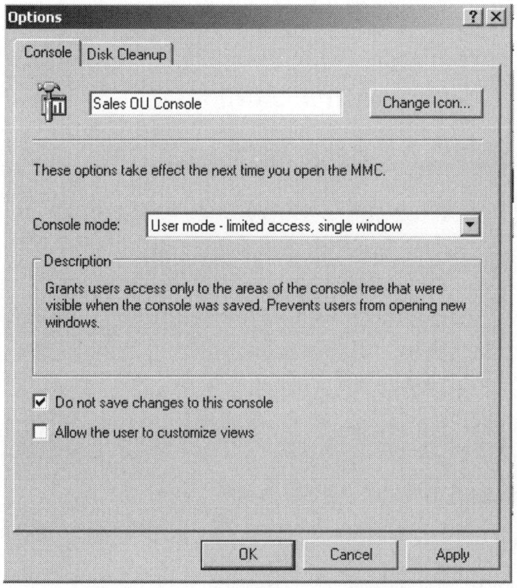

23. In the Options dialog box, click OK.

24. In the Sales OU Console, from the View menu, select Customize.

25. In the Customize View dialog box, clear the Console Tree, Standard Menus (Action And View), and Standard Toolbar check boxes, and click OK.

26. In the Sales OU Console, from the File menu, select Save As.

27. In the Save As dialog box, select the Save In drop-down list, and navigate to C:\Lab Manual\Lab 04\Labwork.

28. In the File Name text box, type Sales Console, and click Save.
29. Close the Sales OU Console.
30. Close all open windows, but do not log off.

Creating a Group Policy to Restrict the Use of MMCs

In this section, you create a Group Policy that restricts the use of MMCs and links the Group Policy to the Sales OU.

1. On the desktop, double-click the ADUC.cmd batch file that you created earlier in this exercise.
2. When prompted, type the password for your Contoso*dd*\Admin*zz* account and press ENTER. The Active Directory Users And Computers console opens.
3. In the Active Directory Users And Computers console, click the View menu and verify that the Advanced Features menu option is checked.
4. In the tree pane of Active Directory Users And Computers, expand Contoso*dd*.msft if necessary, and then expand Location*zz*.
5. Right-click on the Sales OU and select Properties.
6. In the Sales Properties dialog box, click the Group Policy tab, and then click Open. The Group Policy Management Console opens.
7. In the tree pane of the Group Policy Management Console, expand Forest:Contos*dd*.msft if necessary, expand Domains, expand Contoso*dd*.msft, expand Location*zz*, right-click Sales, and select Create And Link A GPO Here.

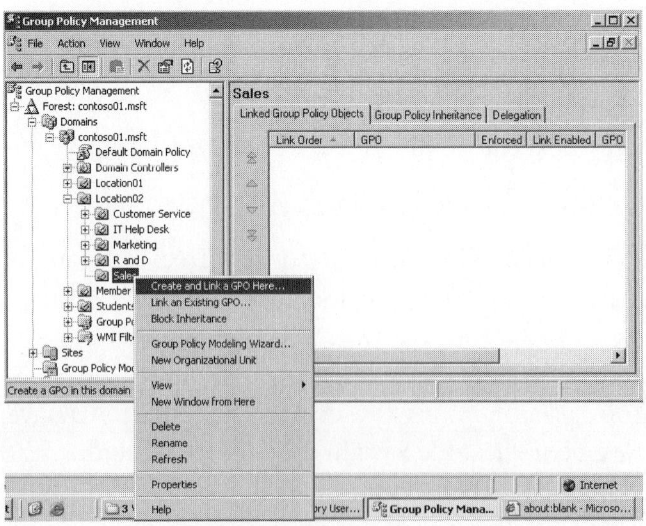

8. In the New GPO dialog box, type **Sales*zz* MMC Restrictions** and click OK.

9. In the details pane, right-click the Sales*zz* MMC Restrictions object and select Edit. The Group Policy Object Editor appears.

10. In the tree pane of the Group Policy Object Editor, under the User Configuration node, expand Administrative Templates, expand Windows Components, and select Microsoft Management Console.

11. In the details pane, double-click the Restrict The User From Entering Author Mode setting.

12. In the Restrict The User From Entering Author Mode Properties dialog box, select Enabled, and then click OK.

13. Double-click the Restrict Users To The Explicitly Permitted List Of Snap-Ins setting, select Enabled, and then click OK.

14. Double-click the Restricted/Permitted Snap-Ins folder. You now see a list of the available snap-ins to which you can restrict or permit access in the Group Policy.

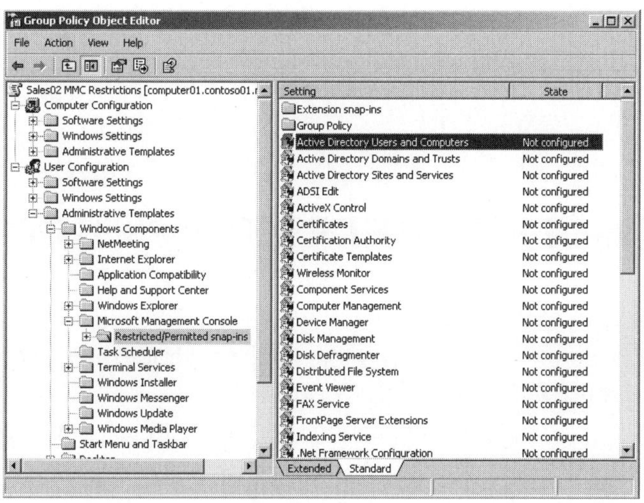

15. Double-click the Active Directory Users And Computers setting, select Enabled, and click OK.

16. Close all open windows and log off.

Verifying MMC Restrictions and Delegated Authority

In this section, you log on as Carol Philips to verify the restrictions you have created for the use of the custom MMC.

1. Log on as Contoso*dd*\Cphilips*zz* using **P@ssw0rd** as the password.

2. Right-click the desktop, point to New, and select Shortcut.
3. In the Create Shortcut dialog box, type **c:\lab manual\lab 04\labwork\Sales Console.msc**, click Next, and then click Finish.
4. On the desktop, double-click the Sales Console shortcut.
5. In the MMC dialog box, read the warning concerning the policy restriction and then click OK.
6. In the SalesOU console, select the Bsmith*zz* object, and then select the Reset Password task.
7. In the Reset Password dialog box, type **P@ssw0rd** in the New Password and Confirm Password text boxes, select the User Must Change Password At Next Logon check box, and click OK twice.
8. Right-click the Bsmith*zz* object and select Properties.

   Note that you can change the telephone number, but cannot alter any other properties of the user account. The ability to change the telephone numbers of user objects in the Sales OU, along with the ability to reset passwords, were delegated to the Cphilips*zz* account.
9. In the Bsmith*zz* Properties dialog box, type **555-1212** in the Telephone Number text box and click OK.
10. Close all open windows and log off.

EXERCISE 4.4: SECURING REMOTE DESKTOP PROTOCOL

Estimated completion time: 30 minutes

Your manager has informed you that there is some concern about the use of Remote Desktop For Administration in the organization and that a new security policy states that the default port used for Remote Desktop Protocol (RDP) needs to be changed to TCP Port 3390. In addition to changing the port used for RDP, she wants to provide remote access to a newly created global group. Finally, she would like you to provide secure RDP settings through a Group Policy object.

Enabling Remote Desktop and Adding Remote Desktop Users

In this section, you enable Remote Desktop For Administration and grant access to the remote desktop to a global group in Active Directory directory service.

1. Log on as Contoso*dd*\Admin*zz* using **P@ssw0rd** as the password.
2. Click Start, right-click My Computer, and select Properties.

3. In the System Properties dialog box, click the Remote tab.
4. In the Remote Desktop area, select the Allow Users To Connect Remotely To This Computer check box.
5. In the Remote Sessions message box, read the message and click OK.
6. In the System Properties dialog box, in the Remote tab, click Select Remote Users.
7. In the Remote Desktop Users dialog box, click Add.

> **NOTE** *Complete steps 8 and 9 on only the even-numbered member server in the domain (Computeryy).*

8. In the Select Users or Groups dialog box, click Locations.
9. In the Locations dialog box, select Entire Directory and click OK.
10. In the Select Users Or Groups dialog box, click Object Types.
11. In the Object Types dialog box, clear the Users check box, select the Groups check box, and click OK.
12. In the Select Users Or Groups dialog box, in the Enter The Object Names To Select box, type **GG-RemoteAdmins**, and click OK.
13. In the Multiple Names Found dialog box, press CTRL and, while holding the key down, select both groups, and then click OK.
14. In the Remote Desktop Users dialog box, click OK.
15. In the System Properties dialog box, click OK.

Configuring the Network Interface and Changing the Port Number Used for RDP

You now open a command prompt window and use the Netstat utility to examine the configuration of the listening port for RDP.

1. Click Start, select Run, type **cmd** in the Open box, and press ENTER.
2. At the command prompt, type **netstat –na**, press ENTER, and examine the output of the command.

> **QUESTION** *Note that the local address for TCP Port 3389 is listed as 0.0.0.0. (Use the vertical scroll bar to scroll up so that you can review the output of the command.) What does it mean when the 0.0.0.0 address is listed as the address for a listening port?*

3. Leave the command prompt window open and click Start, point to Administrative Tools, and then select Terminal Services Configuration.

4. In the tscc–[Terminal Services Configuration\Connection] console, in the tree pane, select the Connections node. In the details pane, right-click the RDP-TCP object and select Properties.
5. In the RDP-TCP Properties dialog box, click the Network Adapter tab. The Network adapter drop-down list displays All Network Adapters Configured With This Protocol.
6. From the Network Adapter drop-down list, select the network adapter that is installed on your computer. Ensure that the entry All Network Adapters Configured With This Protocol is *not* displayed.
7. Click OK, leave the tscc–[Terminal Services Configuration\Connection] console open and switch to the command prompt window.
8. At the command prompt, type **netstat –na** again, and press ENTER.

> **QUESTION** What local address is listed for TCP Port 3389?

9. Click Start, select Run, type **regedt32** in the Open text box, and press ENTER. The Registry Editor appears.

> **IMPORTANT** In the following steps, you make changes to the registry to change the TCP port used for RDP. Incorrect modifications to the registry can lead to system instability and failure. Be very careful when performing steps 16–19 below.

10. In the Registry Editor console, expand HKEY_LOCAL_MACHINE\SYSTEM\CurrentControlSet\Control\Terminal Server\WinStations, and select the RDP-TCP key.
11. In the details pane, locate and double-click the PortNumber REG_DWORD object.
12. In the Edit DWORD dialog box, in the Base area, select the Decimal option.
13. In the Value data box, replace 3389 with **3390** and click OK.

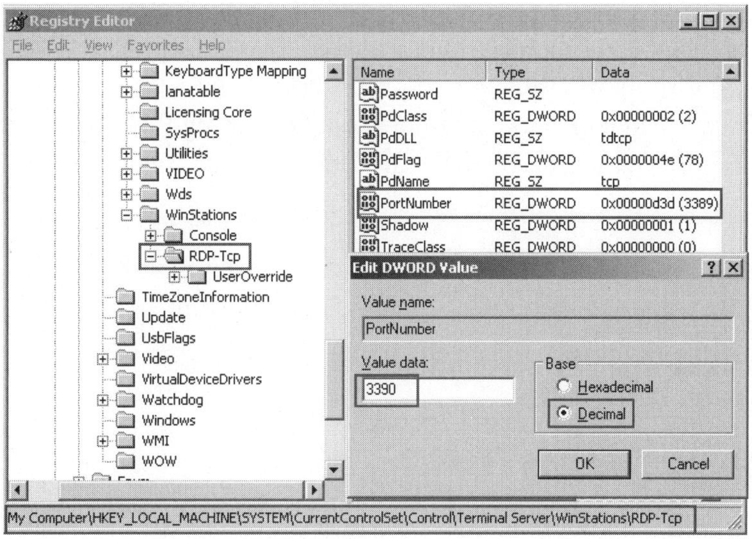

14. Close the Registry Editor console and all other open windows.

    For this change to take effect, it is necessary to restart your computer.

15. Click Start, and then select Shut Down.

16. In the Shut Down Windows dialog box, select Restart from the What Do You Want The Computer To Do? drop-down list, enter **Restart to change the port number for Terminal Services connections** in the Comment area, and click OK. The computer restarts.

17. Log on as Contoso*dd*\Admin*zz*.

18. Click Start, select Run, type **cmd** in the Open box, and press ENTER.

19. At the command prompt, type **netstat –na**, and press ENTER.

> **QUESTION** *Does either TCP Port 3389 or TCP Port 3390 appear in the output of the command?*

In the next step, you verify that the TCP Port used for RDP has been changed on your lab partner's computer by using the PortQry (version 1.22) Support Tools utility. This step requires that the Microsoft Windows 2003 Support Tools are installed on your computer according to the lab setup instructions.

20. At the command prompt, type **portqry computer*pp* –n –r 3380:3391** (where *pp* is the two-digit number of your partner's computer), and press ENTER. The PortQry utility scans a range of ports between 3380 and 3391 on your partner's computer.

> **QUESTION** *What port is shown in a listening state in the output of the portqry command?*

Verifying Remote Desktop Connectivity

In this section, you verify whether a remote desktop user named Contoso*dd*\Kberg*zz* can connect to a remote computer using RDP. In cases in which the RDP connection fails, you make the appropriate configuration changes to ensure that the account can connect to a remote computer.

1. Click Start, point to All Programs, point to Accessories, point to Communications, and then select Remote Desktop Connection.
2. In the Computer box, type **computer*pp*** and click Connect.

   QUESTION *Why does the connection attempt fail?*

3. In the Remote Desktop Disconnected dialog box, click OK.
4. In the Remote Desktop Connections dialog box, click Options.

   In step 5, you configure a client RDP connection object to connect to your partner's computer using the authentication credentials Contoso*dd*\Kberg*zz*. The Kberg*zz* account is a member of one of the groups you earlier authorized to use Remote Desktop. However, aside from this, the account has no additional permissions and is used for demonstration purposes.

5. In the Logon settings area on the General tab of the Remote Desktop Connection dialog box, configure the following:
   a. In the Computer box, type **computer*pp*:3390**.
   b. In the User Name box, type **Kberg*zz***.
   c. In the Password box, type **P@ssw0rd**.
   d. In the Domain Name box, verify that Contoso*dd* is listed as the domain name.
   e. Select the Save My Password check box.
6. Click Save As.
7. In the Save As dialog box, select Desktop from the Save In drop-down list, type **Lab04.rdp** in the File Name text box, and click Save.
8. In the Remote Desktop Connection dialog box, click Connect. The connection attempt from the odd-numbered computer to the even-numbered computer should be successful.

NOTE Even if the account credentials are configured correctly, the RDP connection attempt from the even-numbered computer (Computeryy) to the odd-numbered (Computerxx) will fail with a message stating that the "local policy of this system does not allow you to log on interactively." In steps 9a through 9k, the student sitting at Computerxx resolves the problem.

9. On Computer*yy*, click OK to acknowledge the Logon Message dialog box, and observe your lab partner as he or she performs the following steps:

   a. On Computer*xx*, minimize the Terminal Services window by clicking the minimize icon in the tab at the top of the screen.

   b. Click Start, point to Administrative Tools, and select Domain Controller Security Policy, being careful not to confuse this item with the Default Domain Policy.

   c. In the Default Domain Controller Security Settings console, in the tree pane, expand the Local Policies node, select User Rights Assignment and, in the details pane, double-click Allow Logon Through Terminal Services.

   d. In the Allow Logon Through Terminal Services Properties dialog box, select the Define These Policy Settings check box, and click Add User Or Group.

   e. In the Add User Or Group dialog box, click Browse.

   f. In the Select Users Or Groups dialog box, in the Enter The Object Names To Select box, type **GG-RemoteAdmins** and click OK.

   g. In the Multiple Names Found dialog box, press CTRL and, while pressing the key down, select both groups, and then click OK.

   h. In the Add User Or Group dialog box, click OK.

   i. In the Allow Logon Through Terminal Services Properties dialog box, click OK, and then close the Default Domain Security Settings console.

   j. Click Start, select Run, type **cmd** in the Open text box, and press ENTER.

   k. At the command prompt, type **gpupdate /target:computer /force**, and press ENTER to update the new security settings on the domain controller.

   l. On Computer*yy* (the even-numbered computer), on the desktop, double-click the Lab04.rdp object to connect to Computer*xx*. The connection should be successful.

10. On Computer*yy*, when the remote logon has completed, minimize the Terminal Services window. Both students should perform the following steps:

    a. Click Start, point to Administrative tools, and select Terminal Services Manager.

    b. In the Terminal Services Manager dialog box, click OK to acknowledge the informational message.

    QUESTION *How many sessions are listed in the Terminal Service Manager console?*

11. Switch to the Terminal Services window showing your session on your partner's computer, click Start, click Run, type **notepad** in the Open text box, and press ENTER.

12. Close the Terminal Services window by clicking the close icon (X) in the tab at the top of the screen.

13. In the Disconnect Windows Session dialog box, click OK.

14. On the desktop, double-click the Lab04.rdp object to connect to your partner's computers using the same authentication credentials.

    QUESTION *Was the remote desktop preserved as you had left it when you disconnected from the session? What would cause a session to end, rather than remain active?*

15. In the Terminal Services window, log off from your partner's computer.

16. When your partner has logged off, switch to the Terminal Services Manager window, and note that only the console session is active.

17. Close the Terminal Services Manager console.

Configuring Remote Desktop Security Settings

In this section, you configure Group Policy settings to provide additional security for Remote Desktop connections.

1. Click Start, point to Administrative Tools, and select Active Directory Users And Computers.

2. Depending on whether you are sitting at the odd-numbered computer (Computer*xx*) or the even-numbered computer (Computer*yy*), perform either of the following steps:

   a. On Computer*xx*, in the tree pane of Active Directory Users And Computers, right-click the Domain Controllers OU and select Properties.

   b. On Computer*yy*, in the tree pane of Active Directory Users And Computers, right-click the Member Servers OU, and select Properties. (This OU was created in steps 3 through 7 of "Lab Exercise 3.4: Using Group Policy to Configure Automatic Update Clients" in Lab 3.)

3. In the Name of OU Properties dialog box, click the Group Policy tab and click Open.

4. In the Group Policy Management console, in the tree pane, right-click the Domain Controllers or the Member Servers OU (depending on whether you are sitting at Computer*xx* or Computer*yy*, respectively) and select Create And Link A GPO Here.

5. In the New GPO dialog box, in the Name box, type **TS Policies Settings** ***zz*** and click OK.

6. In the details pane, right-click the TS Policy Settings *zz* GPO, and select Edit.

7. In the Group Policy Object Editor console, in the tree pane, navigate to the Computer Configuration\Administrative Templates\Windows Components node and select Terminal Services.

8. In the tree pane, underneath the Terminal Services node, select the Encryption And Security node.

9. In the details pane, double-click the Always Prompt Client For Password Upon Connection setting, select the Enabled option, and then click Next Setting.

10. In the Select Client Encryption Level Properties dialog box, select the Enabled option. From the Encryption Level drop-down list, select High Level, and click OK.

11. Double-click the RPC Security Policy folder and then double-click the Secure Server (Require Security) setting. Select the Enabled option and then click OK.

12. In the tree pane of the Group Policy Object Editor console, underneath the Terminal Services node, select the Sessions node.

13. Use the following information to enable and configure the settings in the details pane of the Session node:

    - Set Time Limit For Disconnected Sessions: 3 hours
    - Sets A Time Limit For Active Terminal Services Sessions: 1 day
    - Sets A Time Limit For Active But Idle Terminal Services Sessions: 15 minutes
    - Terminate Session When Time Limits Are Reached: Disabled

    QUESTION Why is it a good idea to use a very short interval for the setting Time Limit For Active, But Idle Terminal Server Sessions?

    QUESTION What is the effect of disabling the setting Terminate Session When Time Limits Are Reached? When would a session be terminated, rather than disconnected?

    QUESTION A number of the Sessions settings appear in both the Computer and the User Group Policy nodes. Which Terminal Server Session settings take precedence, the Computer settings or the User settings?

14. Close the Group Policy Object Editor, close the Group Policy Management console, close the Name of OU Properties dialog box, and then close Active Directory Users And Computers.

15. Click Start, type **cmd** in the Open box, and press ENTER.

16. At the command prompt, type **gpupdate /target:computer /force**, and press ENTER.

17. Close the command prompt window.

18. Click Start, click Run, type **tscc.msc** in the Open box, and press ENTER. The tscc–[Terminal Services Configuration\Connections] console appears.

19. In the details pane of the console, right-click the RDP-TCP connection object, and select Properties.

20. In the RDP-TCP Properties dialog box, click the General, Logon Settings, and Sessions tabs, and note the settings that are dimmed as a result of the Group Policy object you configured.

21. Close the RDP-TCP Properties dialog box and, in the tscc–[Terminal Services Configuration\Connections] console, select the Server Settings node. Note that the Active Desktop setting is set to Enable.

> **QUESTION** *Why would it be a good idea to disable Active Desktop for remote desktop connections?*

22. In the details pane, right-click Active Desktop, and select Disable.
23. Close the tscc–[Terminal Services Configuration\Connections] console.
24. On the desktop, double-click the Lab04.rdp object you created earlier. The remote desktop window appears, prompting you to enter a password in the Log On To Windows dialog box.

> **QUESTION** *Why are you prompted for a password in this instance, when previously you were not prompted for a password?*

25. In the Password box, type **P@ssw0rd** and click OK.
26. Log off the Terminal Services session, close all open windows, and log off.

LAB REVIEW QUESTIONS

Estimated completion time: 20 minutes

1. You have enabled Remote Desktop For Administration on a computer that has two network adapters. From a command prompt, you execute the command Netstat –na. The output of the command shows the local address for TCP Port 3389 to be 0.0.0.0. What are the implications of this configuration for connecting to the computer using RDP?
2. Why should you prevent Remote Desktop users from logging on with saved passwords?
3. Consider the phrase "Trust but audit." Briefly explain the relevance of this phrase as it applies to managing the risks created by systems and network administrators.
4. As part of a threat and vulnerability analysis, you have conducted a survey of the work behaviors and practices of the network administrators in your organization. You have discovered that the network administrators will typically install management tools on any server or workstation that it is convenient for them to do so. The organization's

security policy is silent on the issue of the installation of management tools. Does the ad hoc installation of management tools represent an increased vulnerability and should the organization's security policy restrict the installation of management tools?

5. The help desk of a large organization is overwhelmed with requests to change passwords of employees who have forgotten them. You have recommended that local managers or administrative support personnel be delegated the ability to change passwords for the employees in their business units. Does this delegation increase or decrease the security risk to the organization? Briefly explain you answer.

6. You want to implement EMS. To complement EMS, you are considering a vendor-specific Service Processor solution that would allow the out-of-band management of servers through an onboard 100 megabit-per-second (Mbps) Ethernet card. These cards provide access to a virtual desktop for the server from a dedicated management server, regardless of the state of the server and even before the operating system is installed or starts. For example, the service processor firmware can turn on the computer, restart it, and so on. This solution would allow both normal administration of the servers and administration of the server when EMS is required. Briefly explain the vulnerabilities inherent in this solution and what countermeasures you would implement to mitigate these vulnerabilities.

7. You have created a restrictive MMC for use by junior administration staff. You need to modify the console to provide additional functionality. How would you open the console so that you could modify it?

LAB CHALLENGE 4.1: DESIGNING A SECURE MANAGEMENT INFRASTRUCTURE

Estimated completion time: 30 minutes

You are a security consultant assisting Contoso Pharmaceuticals in developing a secure network infrastructure design. The CIO has asked you to a meeting to express concerns regarding the security of the management infrastructure of the screened subnet where Contoso hosts its Web, SMTP, and other servers that require communication with the Internet. At the meeting, the CIO tells you the following:

"The overall security of the screened subnet is a matter of some concern. When we implemented the screened subnet, we did take potential risks into account. For example, we implemented a separate Active Directory forest in the screened subnet and have not permitted any trusts to be established across the internal firewall with the Active Directory forest in the corporate network. We also implemented a dedicated management server that was supposed to have been used exclusively for management tasks. We also purchased some expensive multilayer (routing) switches to provide an additional layer of security for the network traffic.

"However, we don't seem to have created an effective design to safeguard the servers. We don't seem to be leveraging the capabilities that could be provided by the layer 3 switches to secure the management infrastructure. Furthermore, our enforcement of security policies with regard to the use of management tools has been lax. The Web Application developers have installed a number of tools on the Web servers, and all the servers in the screened subnet have, over time, acquired both the Windows Server 2003 Support Tools and the Windows Server 2003 Resource Kit tools. Also, the Administration Pack has been installed on the member servers. I am very concerned that if one of these servers were compromised, our exposure to additional vulnerabilities would be unnecessarily high.

"Both developers and administrators require access to servers in the screened subnet. We provide this access through Remote Desktop for Administration. Although this solution has worked for the most part, on some occasions administrators and developers are prevented from doing their work because the maximum number of allowed RDP connections has been exceeded on particular servers.

"I would like you to provide your thoughts on what measures we might consider implementing in the short term to improve the security of the management infrastructure in particular. I am willing to authorize a budget to purchase any additional hardware, software, or licenses to secure the management infrastructure if the expenditure can be justified. If you have any thoughts about the overall security of the screened subnet outside this topic, I would be pleased to hear those as well."

Instructions

To complete this lab exercise, examine the network diagram of the screened subnet in Figure 4-1. Then, working individually or in small groups assigned by your instructor, discuss the scenario and possible solutions to improve the security of the management infrastructure for the screened subnet. When you are finished, your instructor will conduct a classroom-wide discussion on the scenario.

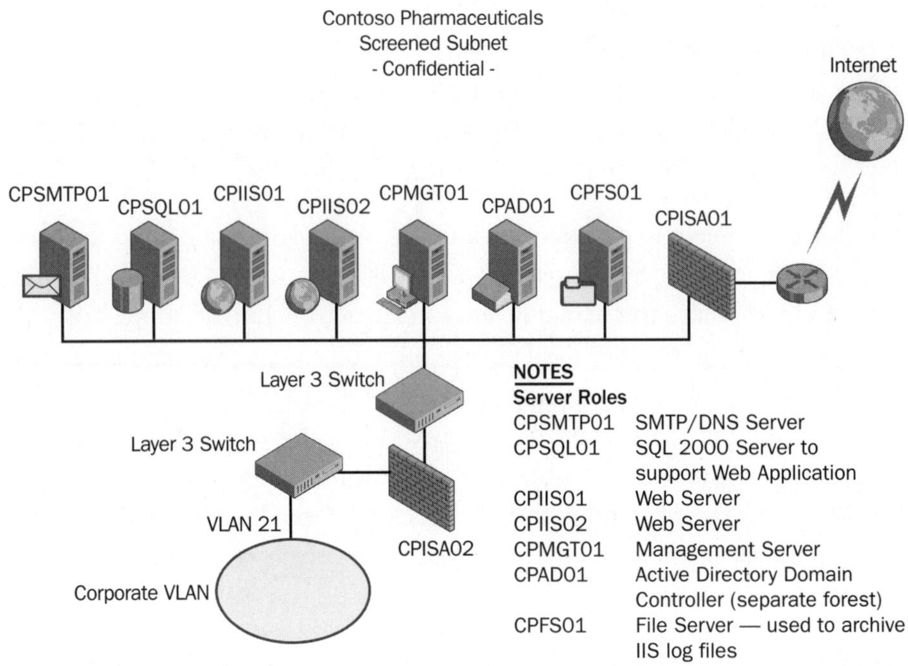

Figure 4-1 Partial diagram of Contoso Pharmaceutical's screened subnet

As an alternative to these instructions, your instructor may ask you to write up your recommendations and submit them for evaluation. If this is the case, your instructor will provide further instructions.

The following questions are provided to assist you in designing the management infrastructure. Note that the answers to these questions provide only a partially complete list of actions to consider taking to implement a more secure management infrastructure. Consider issues that go beyond the limited set of questions in this scenario.

QUESTION What capabilities of multilayer (routing) switches could you leverage to enhance security of the management infrastructure?

QUESTION Would you recommend implementing an additional subnet in the screened subnet? If so, what would it be used for? What servers would belong to which network?

QUESTION The CIO has expressed a concern about the availability of remote desktops when multiple administrators and developers are connecting. How would you mitigate this vulnerability?

QUESTION Where would you allow the Resource Kit and Support Kit tools to be installed?

QUESTION What levels of access should you give to management tools? For example, should you make a distinction, reflected in the ACLs on the tools folders, between senior and junior administrators?

QUESTION Would you create a separate subnet in the corporate network to manage the computers in the screened subnet? If so, what could you do to provide additional security?

QUESTION What is the minimum protocol to allow between the corporate network and the screened subnet to manage the servers in the screened subnet?

LAB 5

DESIGNING ACTIVE DIRECTORY SECURITY

This lab contains the following exercises and activities:

- Exercise 5.1: Assessing the Risks to Authentication
- Exercise 5.2: Implementing Password and Authentication Security
- Exercise 5.3: Establishing a Forest Trust with Selective Authentication
- Exercise 5.4: Granting Access to Objects from a Trusted Forest with Selective Authentication Enabled
- Lab Review Questions
- Lab Challenge 5.1: Designing Security for Interforest Trusts

SCENARIO

You are working as a security consultant to Contoso Pharmaceuticals. The company has become concerned about risks to authentication in its environment. You are assisting Contoso in evaluating the specific risks and implementing solutions to mitigate those risks. Also, the company has entered into a partnership with another firm, for which Contoso must establish a forest trust. You will assist Contoso in implementing the forest trust.

After completing this lab, you will be able to:

- **Analyze and assess various risks to authentication.**
- **Configure Group Policy settings to mitigate authentication vulnerabilities.**
- **Verify Group Policy settings by using the Group Policy Results Wizard.**
- **Establish a forest trust with selective authentication enabled.**
- **Enable access to resources in a trusting forest across an interforest trust that has selective authentication enabled.**

- **Understand the impact of the default permissions granted to users who authenticate across an interforest trust.**
- **Limit the permissions of objects that authenticate across an interforest trust.**

Estimated lesson time: 115 minutes

BEFORE YOU BEGIN

To complete this lab, you will need to have done the following:

- Performed the "Before You Begin" section of Lab 1, "Assessing the Need for Security."
- Created a Member Servers organizational unit (OU) and moved the Computer*yy* member server object to this OU, as instructed in steps 3 through 7 of Lab Exercise 3.4, "Using Group Policy to Configure Automatic Update Clients" in Lab 3, "Reducing the Risk of Software Vulnerabilities."

> **NOTE** In this lab, you will see the characters *dd*, *pp*, *xx*, *yy*, and *zz*. These directions assume that you are working on computers configured in pairs and that each computer has a number.
>
> When you see *dd*, substitute the number used for your domain. When you see *pp*, substitute the number of your partner's computer. When you see *xx*, substitute the unique number assigned to the lower-numbered (odd-numbered) computer of the pair. When you see *yy*, substitute the unique number assigned to the higher-numbered (even-numbered) computer of the pair. When you see *zz*, substitute the number assigned to the computer you are currently using. The following example assumes that the partner pair of computers has been assigned the names Computer05 and Computer06, and that you have been assigned Computer05.
>
> Computer*pp* = Computer06 = your partner's computer
>
> Computer*xx* = Computer05 = lower-numbered computer
>
> Computer*yy* = Computer06 = higher-numbered computer
>
> Computer*zz* = Computer05 = computer you are currently using
>
> Contoso*dd*.msft = Contoso03.msft = Active Directory domain you are using

EXERCISE 5.1: ASSESSING THE RISKS TO AUTHENTICATION

Estimated completion time: 25 minutes

You are a working with Contoso Pharmaceutical's security team to assist them in assessing the level of risk to authentication in the company's environment. The security team has compiled the results of questionnaires that employees have completed regarding their actual work practices. The results of the survey show that some employee practices do not conform to recognized best practices as regards password security. For example, some employees indicated that they regularly write down passwords and then leave the written passwords in obvious places. Other employees indicated that they use common words and phrases in their passwords.

The security team has integrated these questionnaire results into a preliminary risk analysis that helps qualify current risks to authentication. The results from the questionnaires have helped the security team identify specific vulnerabilities and threats related to authentication. The team has asked for your participation in a meeting that will provide a qualitative risk analysis of these and other vulnerabilities related to authentication.

Qualitative Analysis of Risks to Authentication

In this exercise, you will work with your lab partner or in a group assigned by your instructor to perform a qualitative analysis of risks to authentication, based on a preliminary threat and vulnerability analysis. To complete this exercise, log on to your computer, navigate to the C:\Lab Manual\Lab 05 folder, and, using WordPad or Microsoft Word, open the Authentication Risk Analysis Worksheet.doc file. The file contains a Risk Analysis Matrix and instructions for completing the matrix. When you have finished your analysis and provided values for the various aspects of the risk assessment, transfer the Total Risk value from the worksheet matrix to Table 5-1. When you are finished, your instructor will take up the risk analysis as a classroom discussion.

Table 5-1 **Total Risk to Authentication**

Asset	Threat	Vulnerability	Total Risk
1. Personally identifiable medical information stored on a SQL Server computer	Account credentials of data entry clerk stolen	Overly complex password requirements cause users to write down passwords and leave them in obvious places.	
2. Personally identifiable medical information stored on a SQL Server computer	Help desk resets password for an account used by data entry clerk based on request from unauthorized individual (social engineering attack)	Lack of policies and procedures in place to verify identity of individual requesting password reset.	
3. Nonproprietary and nonconfidential company data	Summer intern's password guessed by attacker	Use of familiar names and words in passwords.	
4. Exchange Server	Attacker runs online brute-force attack to determine password of account used for Exchange Services and causes account lockout on service account	Account lockout thresholds set to 5 bad attempts on domain.	
5. Network infrastructure	Account credentials of administrator stolen by individual "shoulder surfing" administrator performing daily tasks	Lack of multifactor authentication. Lack of secure work area for administrators.	
6. Company data residing on individual workstations of Human Resources department employees	Attacker runs brute-force attack against local SAM of workstation in attempt to acquire account credentials of local administrator account	Account lockout thresholds not set on member workstations.	

Table 5-1 **Total Risk to Authentication**

Asset	Threat	Vulnerability	Total Risk
7. Random company data throughout organization	Attacker exploits older authentication mechanisms	Windows 95 and 98 clients are using LM authentication.	
8. Random company data throughout organization	Attacker intercepts network packets and attempts to replay them	Kerberos authentication not used throughout the network.	
9. Random company data throughout the network	Attacker attempts to replay Kerberos authentication packets	Kerberos setting for maximum tolerance for clock synchronization set to 3 times default (3 x 5 minutes) to accommodate poor time synchronization on network.	
10. Random company data throughout the network	Attacker intercepts network authentication packets that contain password hashes attempts to break them offline	NT LAN Manager (NTLM) and LAN Manager (LM) authentication used on the network.	

QUESTION What are the two highest and the two lowest threats?

EXERCISE 5.2: IMPLEMENTING PASSWORD AND AUTHENTICATION SECURITY

Estimated completion time: 30 minutes

After reviewing the risk analysis performed by the Contoso security team, management would like to implement some recommended changes to reduce risks to authentication and password security. One concern management wants to address is the security of local accounts on critical member servers that are located in the Member Servers OU. Another concern is that there are legacy computers in the environment. All Windows 95 and Windows 98 computers will have Microsoft Internet Explorer 6.0 and the Active Directory Client Extensions installed. All Windows NT 4.0 computers will be upgraded to Service Pack 6A, unless the service pack causes problems with a mandatory application. A final concern is that some of these settings may be overly aggressive for some legacy clients in the environment and entail a number of compatibility risks; however, *not* enabling some of these settings also entails security risks. There are only a few legacy client operating systems in the environment, so one of the recommendations is to proceed with the more aggressive settings and relax them to a lower level if it is impossible to upgrade client computers or computers that host mission-critical applications.

In this exercise, you will implement Group Policy settings on your computer. Table 5-2, Account and Security Options Settings, indicates the changes that management want to make to the Group Policy settings linked to the domain, the Domain Controllers OU, and the Member Servers OU. You will need to refer to this table when you configure the Group Policy settings for your computer.

Table 5-2 **Account and Security Options Settings**

GPO Location	Group Policy Setting Change
Domain Controllers	Account Policy\Password Policy: ■ Minimum password age: 2 days ■ Minimum password length: 8 characters
Domain Controllers	Account Policy\Account Lockout Policy: ■ Account lockout duration: 30 minutes ■ Account lockout threshold: 50 invalid logon attempts ■ Reset account lockout after: 30 minutes
Member Servers OU	Account Policy\Password Policy: ■ Minimum password length: 12 characters
Member Servers OU	Account Policy\Account Lockout Policy: ■ Account lockout duration: 15 minutes ■ Account lockout threshold: 5 invalid logon attempts ■ Reset account lockout after: 15 minutes
Domain Controllers/ Member Servers OUs	Security Options\Accounts: ■ Limit local use of blank passwords to console logon only: Enabled

Table 5-2 **Account and Security Options Settings**

GPO Location	Group Policy Setting Change
Domain Controllers/ Member Servers OUs	Security Options\Domain Member: ■ Digitally encrypt secure channel data (when possible): Enabled (Configure Setting only on Member Servers OU) ■ Digitally sign secure channel data (when possible): Enabled (Configure setting only on Member Servers OU) ■ Maximum machine account password age: 30 days ■ Require strong (Windows 2000 or later) session key: Enabled
Domain Controllers/ Member Servers OUs	Security Options\Microsoft Network Client: ■ Digitally sign communications (if server agrees): Enabled
Domain Controllers/ Member Servers OUs	Security Options\Microsoft Network Server: ■ Digitally sign communications (if client agrees): Enabled (Configure setting on Member Servers OU only) ■ Amount of idle time required before suspending session: 15 minutes
Domain Controllers/ Member Servers OUs	Security Options\Network Access: ■ Do not allow anonymous enumeration of SAM accounts: Enabled ■ Do not allow anonymous enumeration of SAM accounts and shares: Enabled ■ Let Everyone permissions apply to anonymous users: Disabled

Table 5-2 **Account and Security Options Settings**

GPO Location	Group Policy Setting Change
Domain Controllers/ Member Servers OUs	Security Options\Network Security: ■ Do not store LAN Manager hash value on next password change: Enabled ■ LAN Manager authentication level: Send NTLM v2 Response only, refuse LM ■ LDAP client signing requirements: Negotiate signing ■ Minimum session security for NTLM SSP based (including secure RPC) clients: Require message integrity Require message confidentiality Require NTLMv2 session security Require 128-bit encryption ■ Minimum session security for NTLM SSP based (including secure RPC) servers: Require message integrity Require message confidentiality Require NTLMv2 session security Require 128-bit encryption

NOTE You and your lab partner will perform different steps, depending on what computer has been assigned to you. Pay close attention to the instructions in each section to ensure that you perform the steps that are specific to the computer you have been assigned.

1. Log on as Contoso*dd*\Admin*zz* using **P@ssw0rd** as the password.
2. On the desktop, select the Aduc.cmd batch file you created in Exercise 4.3 and, when prompted to enter your password in the command prompt window, type **P@ssw0rd**, and press ENTER.

   If you did not create the Aduc.cmd file in Exercise 4.3, you can launch Active Directory Users and Computers by using the following procedure:

   a. Click Start, point to Administrative Tools, right-click Active Directory Users And Computers, and select Run As.
   b. In the Run As dialog box, click The Following User, type **Contoso*dd*\Admin*zz*** in the User Name box, type **P@ssw0rd** in the Password box, and then click OK.

3. In the tree pane, right-click the Contoso*dd*.msft node and select Properties.

4. In the Contoso*dd*.msft Properties dialog box, select the Group Policy tab, and click Open. The Group Policy Management Console opens.

5. In the tree pane of the Group Policy Management Console, expand the Contoso*dd*.msft node beneath the Domains node.

> **NOTE** *Perform the following section only if you are sitting at the odd-numbered computer (Computerxx). If you are sitting at the even-numbered computer (Computeryy), proceed to the section titled "Configuring Account Policy Settings on a Member Server," later in this lab.*

Configuring the Default Domain Account Policy Settings

1. In the tree pane, select the Contoso*dd*.msft node, right-click Default Domain Policy and select Edit.

2. In the tree pane of the Group Policy Object Editor, under the Computer Configuration node, expand the Windows Settings\Security Settings\Account Policies node, and select the Password Policy node.

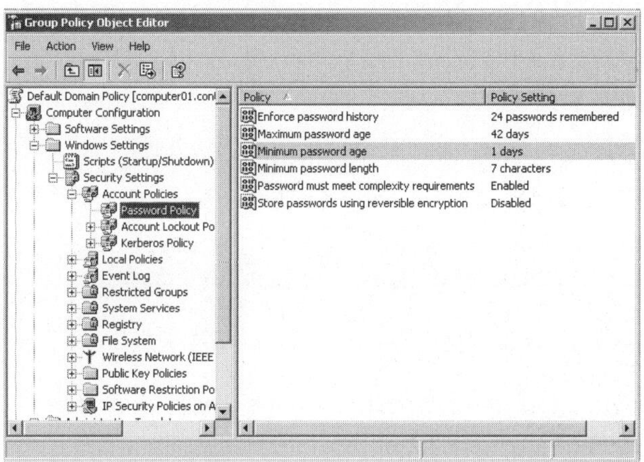

3. In the details pane, double-click Minimum Password Age, enter **2** in the Password Can Be Changed After: Days scroll box, and click OK.

4. In the details pane, double-click Minimum Password Length, enter **8** in the Password Must Be At Least: Characters scroll box, and click OK.

5. In the tree pane, select the Account Lockout Policy node.

6. In the details pane, double-click Account Lockout Threshold.
7. In the Account Lockout Threshold Properties dialog box, if necessary, select the Define This Policy Setting check box. Enter **50** in the Invalid Logon Attempts scroll box, click OK, and then, in the Suggested Value Changes dialog box, click OK to accept the recommended changes to the Account Lockout Duration and Reset Account Lockout Counter After policy settings.
8. Close the Group Policy Object Editor, and leave the Group Policy Management Console open.

> **NOTE** Perform the following section only if you are sitting at the even-numbered computer (Computeryy). If you are sitting at the odd-numbered computer (Computerxx), proceed to the section titled "Configuring Security Option Settings," later in this lab.

Configuring Account Policy Settings on a Member Server

1. In the tree pane of the Group Policy Management Console, right-click the Member Servers OU, and select Create And Link A GPO Here.
2. In the New GPO dialog box, type **Member Servers Account Policies** in the Name text box, and then click OK.
3. In the details pane, right-click the Member Servers Account Policies Group Policy object, and select Edit.
4. In the tree pane of the Group Policy Object Editor, under the Computer Configuration node, expand the Windows Settings\Security Settings\Account Policies node, and select the Password Policy node.
5. In the details pane, double-click Minimum Password Length.
6. In the Minimum Password Length Properties dialog box, select the Define This Setting checkbox. Enter **12** in the Password Must Be At Least: Characters scroll box, and click OK.
7. In the tree pane, select the Account Lockout Policy node.
8. In the details pane, double-click Account Lockout Duration.

9. In the Account Lockout Duration Properties dialog box, select the Define This Policy Setting check box. Enter **15** in the Account Is Locked Out For: Minutes scroll box and then click OK. In the Suggested Value Changes dialog box, click OK to accept the recommended changes to the Account Lockout Threshold and Reset Account Lockout Counter After policy settings.

10. Close the Group Policy Object Editor, and leave the Group Policy Management Console open.

> **NOTE** *Perform the following section on both the odd-numbered (Computerxx) and even-numbered (Computeryy) computers.*

Configuring Security Option Settings

1. In the Group Policy Management Console, in the tree pane, perform one of the following steps, depending on the computer assigned to you:

   a. On the odd-numbered computer (Computer*xx*), right-click the Domain Controllers node, and select Create And Link A GPO Here.

   b. On the even-numbered computer (Computeryy), right-click the Member Servers node, and select Create And Link A GPO Here.

2. In the New GPO dialog box, type **Security Option Settings** *zz* (where *zz* is your assigned number) and then click OK.

> **NOTE** *Normally, to increase the efficiency of Group Policy processing, we would group similar GPO settings into a single Group Policy object. In this lab exercise, we are creating multiple Group Policy objects for demonstration purposes. In a production environment, we want to limit the number of Group Policy objects that need to be processed.*

3. In the details pane, right-click the Security Option Settings *zz* Group Policy object, and select Edit. The Group Policy Object Editor appears.

4. In the tree pane of the Group Policy Object Editor, under the Computer Configuration node, expand the Windows Settings\Security Settings\Local Policies node, and select the Security Options node.

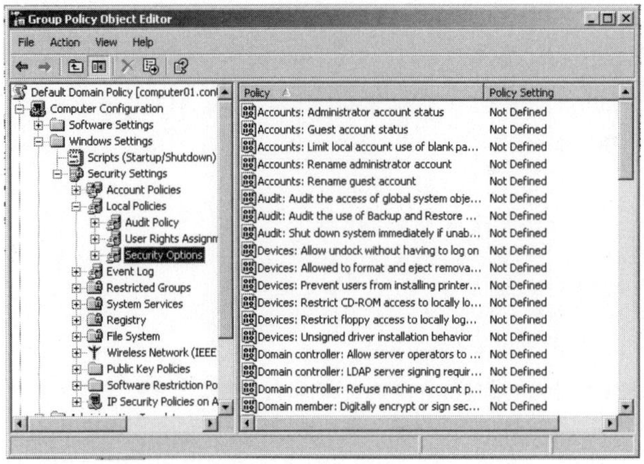

5. In the details pane, double-click Accounts: Limit Local Account Use Of Blank Passwords To Console Logon Only.

6. In the Accounts: Limit Local Account Use Of Blank Passwords To Console Logon Only Properties dialog box, select the Define This Policy Setting check box, and click OK.

> **NOTE** *Perform steps 7 through 9 on the even-numbered computer (Computeryy) only. The default domain controllers policy already defines settings for Digitally Encrypt Secure Channel Data for the domain controller.*

7. In the details pane of the Group Policy Object Editor, double-click Domain Member: Digitally Encrypt Secure Channel Data (When Possible).

8. In the Domain Member: Digitally Encrypt Secure Channel Data (When Possible) Properties dialog box, select the Define This Policy Setting check box, and then click OK.

9. In the details pane, double-click Domain Member: Digitally Sign Secure Channel Data (When Possible), and enable the policy setting.

10. On both computers, complete the remaining Group Policy settings in the Security Option Settings *zz* GPO as specified in Table 5-2: Account and Security Options Settings. You have already configured some of these settings in the previous steps.

    Pay attention to whether the policy should be applied to both the Domain Controllers and the Member Servers OU. Also, read the explanations for each setting by right-clicking the setting and selecting Help.

11. When you have finished making the changes, close the Group Policy Object Editor, but leave the Group Policy Management Console open.
12. On both computers, click Start, select Run and type **cmd** in the Open box. Click OK.
13. At the command prompt, type **gpupdate /target:computer /force**, and press ENTER to cause an immediate refresh of Group Policy. Close the command prompt window.

Verifying Group Policy Settings by Using the Group Policy Results Wizard

In this section, you will use the Group Policy Results Wizard in the Group Policy Management Console on both computers to verify the Group Policy settings you configured previously.

1. In the tree pane of the Group Policy Management Console, right-click Group Policy Results, and select the Group Policy Results Wizard.

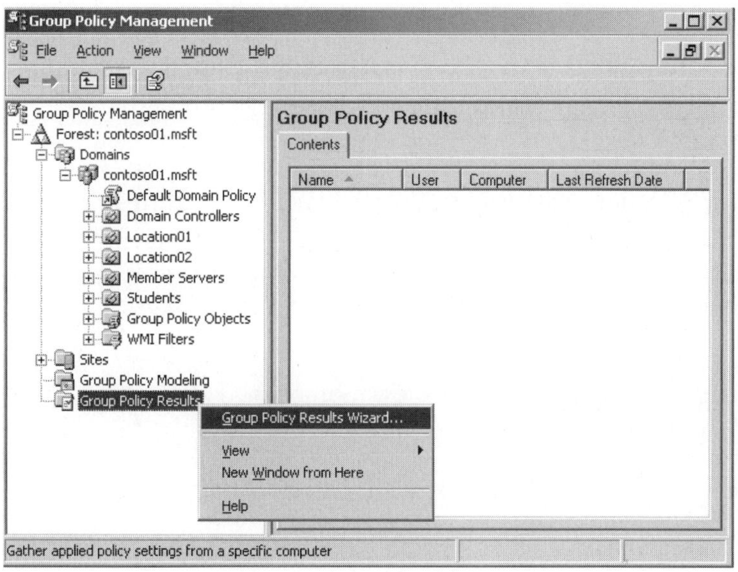

2. On the Welcome To The Group Policy Results Wizard page, click Next.
3. On the Computer Selection page, ensure that This Computer is selected, and click Next.

4. On the User Selection page, select Do Not Display User Policy Settings In The Results (Display Computer Policy Settings Only), and then click Next.
5. On the Summary of Selections page, click Next.
6. On the Completing The Group Policy Results Wizard page, click Finish. An HTML report is generated. After a few moments a warning message appears in an Internet Explorer dialog box. You see this dialog box because the Internet Explorer Enhanced Security Configuration is enabled by default.
7. In the Internet Explorer dialog box, read the information and then click Close.

   You will now generate Group Policy results for your partner's computer (Computer*pp*).

8. In the tree pane of the Group Policy Management Console, right-click Group Policy Results, and select the Group Policy Results Wizard.
9. On the Welcome To The Group Policy Results Wizard page, click Next.
10. On the Computer Selection page, select Another Computer, type your partner's computer name (**Computer*pp***) in the text box, and click Next.
11. On the User Selection page, select Do Not Use Policy Settings In The Results (Display Computer Policy Settings Only), and then click Next.
12. On the Summary of Selections page, click Next.
13. On the Completing the Group Policy Results Wizard page, click Finish. An HTML report is generated. After a few moments, a warning message appears in an Internet Explorer dialog box.
14. In the Internet Explorer dialog box, read the information and then click Close.
15. In the tree pane of the Group Policy Management Console, under the Group Policy Results node, select one of the reports you created, and, in the details pane, select the Settings tab.

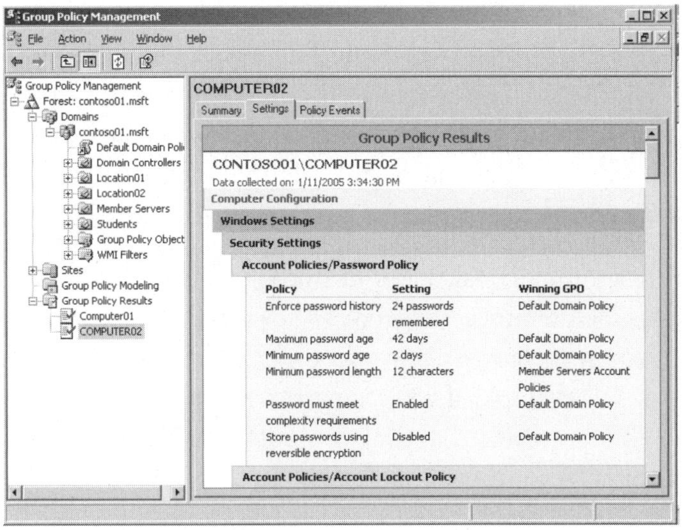

16. Scroll through the settings and note where the Group Policy settings come from in the Winning GPO column.

17. Select the other report you created and note where the various Group Policy settings come from in the Winning GPO column.

> **QUESTION** If you were to create a local account on Computeryy, what is the minimum password length you would have to provide the account? What is the Winning GPO for this setting?

> **QUESTION** List at least two Security Options settings from Table 5-2 that mitigate man-in-the-middle vulnerabilities. (A man-in-the-middle attack occurs when a third party intercepts communications between a sender and a recipient and modifies the communications between the sender and recipient. Any client-server network request is vulnerable to a man-in-the middle attack.)

18. Close all open windows and log off.

EXERCISE 5.3: ESTABLISHING A FOREST TRUST WITH SELECTIVE AUTHENTICATION

Estimated completion time: 20 minutes

In this exercise, you will establish a forest trust with another student domain in the classroom. To complete this exercise, you will first need to verify that DNS name resolution is working in your environment and then raise the forest functional level to Windows Server 2003.

Your instructor will assign you another partner to work with in the lab. This lab works best if there is an even number of student domains in the classroom. If there are an odd number of student domains in the classroom, your instructor might assign one student domain to partner with two other domains. If you are partnering with two other student domains, you will find relevant notes in the steps that have been included to assist you in that case.

Alternatively, your instructor might ask a pair of students to double up with another pair of students. Before proceeding, enter the partner domain information in the table. Refer to the table when you encounter instructions that use the *pd*, *px*, and *py* variables. For example, if you are partnered with the Contoso05.msft domain and you are asked to ping computer*py*.contoso*pd*.msft, you would type **ping computer10.contoso05.msft**.

> **NOTE** If you are partnered with two other student domains, you will need to create entries for two domain controllers and two member servers in the following table.

Partner Name Variables	Fully Qualified Domain Name (FQDN)
Partner domain: Contoso*pd*.msft	Example: Contoso16.msft
Domain controller in partner domain: Computer*px*.contoso*pd*.msft	Example: Computer31.contoso16.msft
Member server in partner domain: Computer*py*.contoso*pd*.msft	Example: Computer32.contoso16.msft

Raising Domain and Forest Functional Level

In this section, you will verify that DNS name resolution works for your partner domain, then raise the domain and forest functional levels to Windows Server 2003. The student sitting at the even-numbered computer will raise the domain functional level. The student sitting at the odd-numbered computer will raise the forest functional level.

> **NOTE** The forest functional level must be Windows Server 2003 before you can create a forest trust.

1. On both computers, log on as Contoso*dd*\Admin*zz* using **P@ssw0rd** as the password.

   You will verify that DNS name resolution is working properly in the classroom by pinging the FQDN of the member computer in the partner domain.

2. Click Start, select Run, type **cmd** in the Open box, and then click OK.

> **NOTE** If you are partnered with two other student domains, you will need to perform step 3 twice: once for each of your two partner domains.

3. At the command prompt, type **ping computer*py*.contoso*pd*.msft**, and then press ENTER.

> **NOTE** If the Ping command fails, inform your instructor. DNS name resolution must be working to complete this lab exercise.

You will now raise the domain functional level to Windows Server 2003. Perform steps 4 through 6 on only the even-numbered computer (Computer*yy*).

4. Click Start, point to Administrative Tools, and select Active Directory Users And Computers.

> **TIP** You can also raise the domain functional level by using Active Directory Domains And Trusts.

5. In the tree pane of Active Directory Users And Computers, right-click the contoso*dd*.msft node, and select Raise Domain Functional Level.

6. In the Raise Domain Functional Level dialog box, select Windows Server 2003 from the Select An Available Domain Functional Level drop-down box.

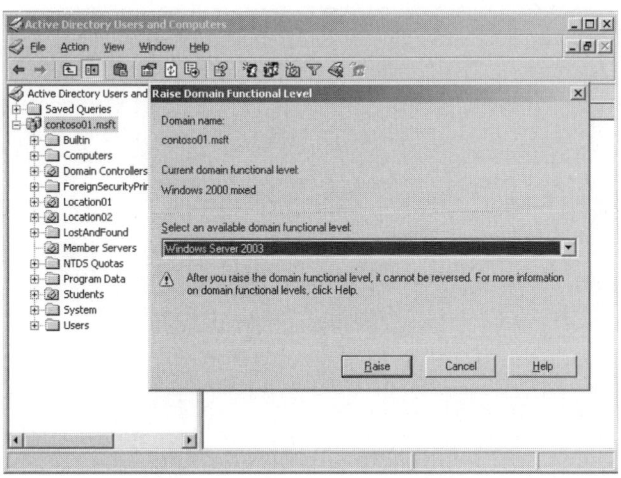

Click Raise, and then click OK twice to acknowledge that the operation cannot be reversed and that it may take awhile for the changes to replicate, depending on the replication topology.

> **QUESTION** *What are the mandatory prerequisites that must be satisfied before you can raise the domain functional level to Windows Server 2003?*

7. Minimize Active Directory Users And Computers. Your partner will now raise the forest functional level.

   Perform steps 8 through 10 on only the odd-numbered computer (Computer*xx*).

8. Click Start, point to Administrative Tools, and select Active Directory Domains And Trusts.
9. In the tree pane of Active Directory Domains And Trusts, right-click the Active Directory Domains And Trusts node, and select Raise Forest Functional Level.
10. In the Raise Forest Functional Level, click Raise, and then click OK twice to acknowledge that the operation cannot be reversed and that it may take awhile for the changes to replicate depending on the replication topology.

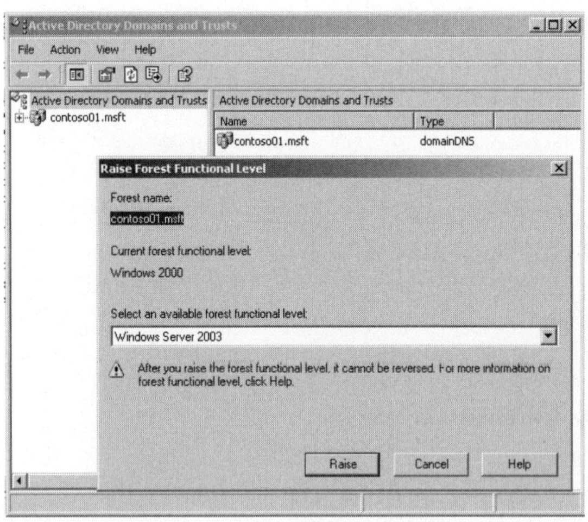

QUESTION What are the mandatory prerequisites that must be satisfied before you can raise the forest functional level to Windows Server 2003?

11. Leave Active Directory Domains And Trusts open for the next section.

Creating Forest Trust with Selective Authentication

NOTE If you are partnered with two other student domains, you will need to perform steps 1 through 14 twice: once for each of your two partner domains.

1. On the odd-numbered computer (Computer*xx*), in the tree pane of Active Directory Domains And Trusts, right-click the Contoso*dd*.msft node, and select Properties.
2. In the Contosodd.msft Properties dialog box, click the Trusts tab, and click New Trust. The Welcome To The New Trust Wizard page appears.

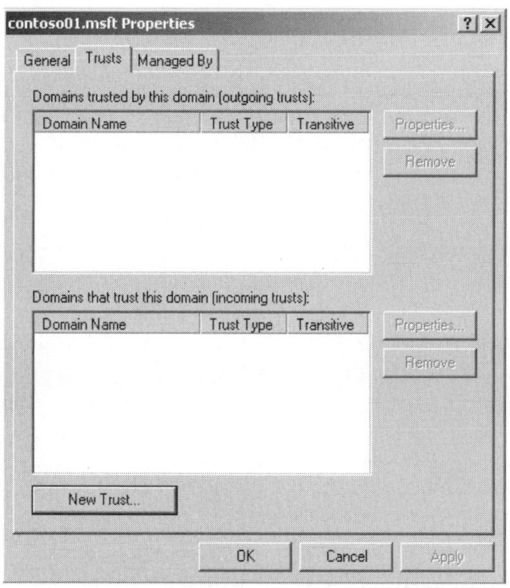

3. On the Welcome To The New Trust Wizard page, click Next.
4. On the Trust Name page, in the Name text box, type **contoso*pd*.msft** (where *pd* is the number assigned to your partner's domain), and then click Next.
5. On the Trust Type page, select Forest Trust, and click Next.

6. On the Direction Of Trust page, verify that the Two-Way option is selected, and click Next.
7. On the Sides Of Trust page, verify that This Domain Only is selected and then click Next.
8. On the Outgoing Trust Authentication Level page, select Selective Authentication, and click Next.

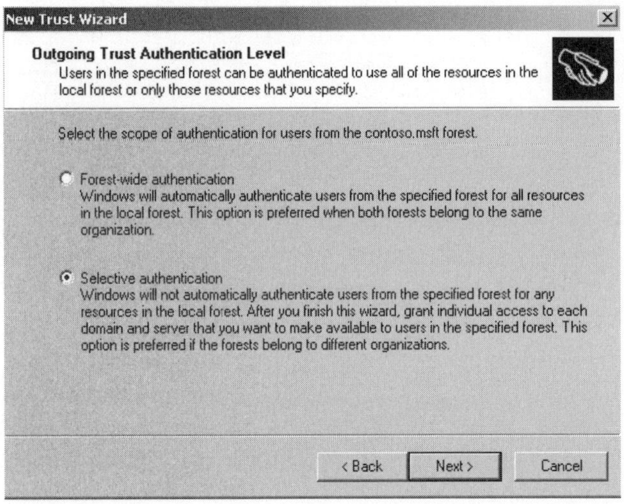

9. On the Trust Password page, in the Trust Password and Confirm Trust Password text boxes, type **P@ssw0rd**, and then click Next.
10. On the Trust Selections Complete page, click Next.
11. On the Trust Creation Complete page, click Next.

> **NOTE** Wait until the student sitting at the odd-numbered computer in your partner domain has finished the previous steps before proceeding to step 12.

12. On the Confirm Outgoing Trust page, select Yes, Confirm The Outgoing Trust, and then click Next.
13. On the Confirm Incoming Trust page, select Yes, Confirm The Incoming Trust, type **administrator** in the User Name text box, type **P@ssw0rd** in the Password text box, and click Next. The Completing The New Trust Wizard page appears, showing the status of your changes.

14. On the Completing The New Trust Wizard page, click Finish, and then click OK to close the Contoso*dd*.msft Properties dialog box.

EXERCISE 5.4: GRANTING ACCESS TO OBJECTS FROM A TRUSTED FOREST WITH SELECTIVE AUTHENTICATION ENABLED

Estimated completion time: 25 minutes

In this exercise, you will examine the impact of the Allowed to Authenticate permission on the Active Directory server object and the impact of default folder permissions for interforest access.

You will create and then share a folder named C:\Docs\MergerDocs with the default permissions. Then, the student at the even-numbered computer will grant the Allowed To Authenticate permission on the Computer*yy* server object to the Domain Admins group from the trusted (partner) domain.

The instructions in this exercise prompt you to perform steps on specific computers and to wait for your lab partners to complete steps on their computers. If you ignore these prompts, the steps will not work.

1. Click Start, select Run, and, in the Open text box, type **c:\lab manual\lab 05\lab5share.cmd** and press ENTER. This batch files creates and shares a folder named C:\Docs\MergerDocs as MergerDocs with the default share permissions.

Perform steps 2 through 10 on only the even-numbered computer (Computer*yy*).

2. Maximize Active Directory Users And Computers and, from the View menu, verify that Advanced Features is selected.
3. In the tree pane of Active Directory Users And Computers, select the Member Servers OU, right-click the COMPUTER*YY* object, and select Properties.

> **NOTE** If you are partnered with two other student domains, you will need to perform steps 4 through 10 twice: once for each of your two partner domains.

4. In the COMPUTER*YY* Properties dialog box, click the Security tab, and then click Add.
5. In the Select Users, Computers, Or Groups dialog box, click Locations.
6. In the Locations dialog box, select your partner's domain, Contoso*pd*.msft, and then click OK.
7. In the Select Users, Computers Or Groups dialog box, verify that Contoso*pd*.msft appears in the From This Location text box. In the Enter The Object Names To Select text box, type domain admins and then click OK. The Enter Network Password dialog box appears.
8. In the Enter Network Password dialog box, type **Administrator** in the User Name text box, type **P@ssw0rd** in the Password text box, and then click OK.
9. On the Security tab, verify that the Contoso*pd*\Domain Admins object is selected in the Group Or User Names box and then, in the Permission For Domain Admins box, select the Allow column check box for the Allowed To Authenticate permission.

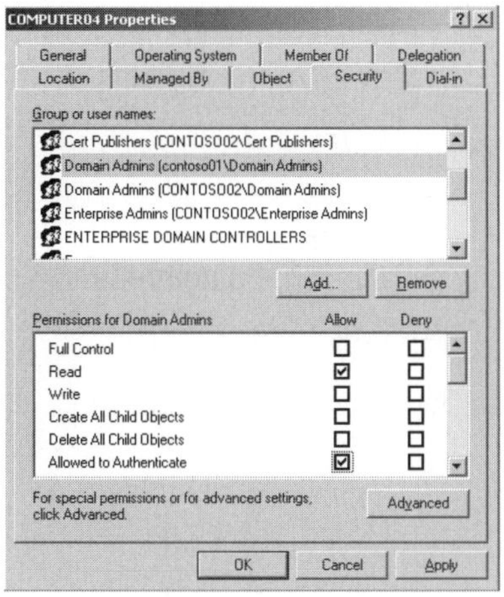

10. In the COMPUTER*YY* Properties dialog box, click OK.

> **NOTE** Wait until the student sitting at Computer*py*.contoso*pd*.msft in the partner domain has completed step 10 before proceeding.

In steps 11 through 22, you will first try to connect to the odd-numbered computer (Computer*px*) in the partner domain. You will then connect to the even-numbered computer (Computer*py*) in the partner domain. Both students should perform these steps.

> **NOTE** If you are partnered with two other student domains, you need only perform steps 11 through 22 once. You can choose one of your partner domains to use for these steps.

11. Click Start and select Run. Type **\\computer*px*\MergerDocs** in the Open text box to attempt to connect to the shared folder on the odd-numbered computer in your partner's domain, and then click OK. The connection attempt fails.

> **QUESTION** What is the error message that appears when you attempt to connect to \\computer*px*\MergerDocs?

12. Click OK to acknowledge the message.

13. Click Start and select Run. Type **\\computer*py*\MergerDocs** in the Open text box to attempt to connect to the shared folder on the even-numbered computer in your partner's domain, and then click OK. The connection attempt is successful.

14. Close the \\Computer*py*\MergerDocs shared folder.

    You will now examine the impact of changing the default NTFS permissions on the C:\Docs\MergerDocs folder. Perform the following steps on both computers.

15. Open Windows Explorer, navigate to the C:\Docs folder, right-click the MergerDocs folder, and then select Properties.
16. In the MergerDocs Properties dialog box, click the Security tab.

    QUESTION *Do you see any objects from the Contoso*pd *domain in the Group or User Names box?*

17. On the Security tab, click Advanced.
18. In the Advanced Security Settings for MergerDocs dialog box, clear the Allow Inheritable Permissions From The Parent To Propagate To This Object And All Child Objects check box. The Security dialog box appears.
19. In the Security dialog box, click Copy.
20. In the Advanced Security Settings For MergerDocs dialog box, click OK.
21. In the MergerDocs Properties dialog box, in the User Or Group Names box, do either of the following, depending on the computer to which you have been assigned:
    a. On the even-numbered computer, select the Users (COMPUTER*YY*\Users) object, and click Remove, and then click OK.
    b. On the odd-numbered computer, select the Users (CONTOSO*DD*\Users) object, and click Remove, and then click OK.

    NOTE *Wait until the student sitting at Computer*py*.contoso*pd*.msft in the partner domain has completed step 21 before proceeding.*

22. Click Start and select Run. Type **\\computer*py*\MergerDocs** in the Open text box to attempt to connect to the shared folder on the even-numbered computer in your partner's domain, and then click OK. The connection attempt fails.

> **NOTE** *Wait until your domain partner has completed step 22 before proceeding with step 23.*

23. Open Windows Explorer, navigate to the C:\Docs folder, right-click the MergerDocs folder, and select Properties.

> **NOTE** *If you are partnered with two other student domains, you will need to perform steps 24 through 29 twice: once for each of your two partner domains.*

24. In the MergerDocs Properties dialog box, click the Security tab, and then click Add.
25. In the Select Users, Computers Or Groups dialog box, click Locations.
26. In the Locations dialog box, select Contoso*pd*.msft, and click OK.
27. In the Select Users, Computers Or Groups dialog box, verify that Contoso*pd*.msft appears in the From This Location box. In the Enter The Object Names To Select box, type **domain admins** and then click OK.
28. If the Enter Network Password dialog box appears, type **Administrator** in the User Name box, type **P@ssw0rd** in the Password box and then click OK.
29. In the MergerDocs Properties dialog box, click OK.

> **NOTE** *Wait until the student sitting at the even-numbered computer (Computerpy.contosopd.msft) in your partner domain has completed step 29 before proceeding.*

> **NOTE** *If you are partnered with two other student domains, you need only perform steps 30 through 33 once. You can choose one of your partner domains to use for these steps.*

30. Click Start, select Run, type **\\computer*py*\MergerDocs** in the Open box, and then click OK. The connection attempt is successful.
31. Switch to Active Directory Users And Computers, select the Builtin node in the tree pane, and then, in the detail pane, double-click the Users object.
32. In the Users Properties dialog box, click the Members tab. You should see the Authenticated Users special group listed as a member of the Users group.

The Authenticated Users group is a system group whose membership is automatically determined by Windows Server 2003. You cannot manually modify its membership. Windows Server 2003 automatically adds the Authenticated Users security identifier (SID) to the authorization data for users who authenticate across an interforest trust.

33. Close all open windows and log off.

> **QUESTION** *What conclusion, or conclusions, can you draw about the default permissions that apply to users who authenticate across an interforest trust?*

LAB REVIEW QUESTIONS

Estimated completion time: 15 minutes

1. It is possible to implement technical controls to enforce password-related security policies. For example, a requirement for a minimum password length can be defined in a Group Policy linked to the domain OU. However, technical controls for password policies have limitations and the intent of those controls can be circumvented. Briefly describe the limitations of technical password controls and propose a general solution to address those limitations.
2. You have enabled a Group Policy setting to Send NTLM v 2 only and refuse LM. What risks does this setting create for environments with Windows 95 and Windows 98 clients? What is the best way to address those risks?
3. You have enabled a number of Group Policy settings to mitigate authentication vulnerabilities. Now, however, the Windows 95, Windows 98, and Windows NT clients are experiencing problems related to authentication. One problem is that Windows 95 and Windows 98 users are unable to change their passwords. You have installed the latest version of Internet Explorer and installed the Active Directory Client Extensions on these clients. What Security Option setting is likely responsible for the problem?
    a. Microsoft Network Client: Digitally Sign Communications (Always): Enabled
    b. Microsoft Network Server: Digitally Sign Communications (Always): Enabled

   c. Network Access: Do Not Allow Anonymous Enumeration Of SAM Accounts: Enabled

   d. Network Security: LAN Manager Authentication Level: Send NTLM v 2 Only And Refuse LM

4. You have enabled a number of Group Policy settings to mitigate authentication vulnerabilities. Now, however, your Windows Server 2003 RAS servers are not functioning properly. What Group Policy setting is most likely responsible for the problem?

   a. Network Security: Minimum Session Security For NTLM SSP (Including Secure RPC) Servers: Enabled All Settings

   b. Network Access: Restrict Anonymous Access To Named Pipes And Shares: Enabled.

   c. Network Access: Let Everyone Permissions Apply To Anonymous Users: Disabled.

   d. Network Security: LAN Manager Authentication Level: Send NTLM V 2 Only\ Refuse LM & NTLM

5. You have established an interforest trust with another organization. You have enabled selective authentication on the trust. You are concerned that accounts from the trusted forest have many of the same default permission as accounts in your forest. What other step should you take to ensure only authorized users from the trusted forest can access only the appropriate resources in your forest?

LAB CHALLENGE 5.1: DESIGNING SECURITY FOR INTERFOREST TRUSTS

Estimated completion time: 40 minutes

Contoso Pharmaceuticals has submitted an offer to purchase Fabrikam, Inc., a company that provides complementary expertise in pharmaceutical research and development. The purchase is pending regulatory approval, but both parties are confident that the approval will be granted. Contoso has entered a planning stage to decide how best to merge the companies.

The CIO invites you to a meeting to discuss establishing communications between the Contoso and the Fabrikam forests. At the meeting, the CIO tells you the following:

"As you know, we are waiting for regulatory approval to confirm the purchase of Fabrikam, Inc. We want to be ready to implement a strategy to enable communications between our two forests when the approval comes through. As a result of the due diligence process, we have learned that Fabrikam is partway through a migration process to Windows Server 2003 from Windows NT 4.0. I suspect that the where they are in the process will drive some of the decisions with regard to how we want to proceed.

"Contoso and Fabrikam management have decided that, for the short term at least, Fabrikam will maintain a separate identity. However, we are considering migrating the Fabrikam users into the Contoso forest. Fabrikam has more than 5,000 employees, so we will probably have to do the migration in stages when the time comes.

"Initially, however, we want to make sure that we can access resources in the Fabrikam forest and that Fabrikam users can access resources in our forest. We do have some special security requirements. For example, during the initial stages of the merger, only a limited number of individuals from the Fabrikam forest should have access to resources in the Contoso forest. We are going to set up a special folder on CPFS001 that will contain confidential documents to which only the Fabrikam management and some departments, such as human resources and IT, will have access. After the initial phase of the merger, however, users in both forests will need widespread access.

"This said, we have just been through a rigorous process to mitigate authentication risks, and I am reluctant to make too many changes to the Contoso forest. In fact, the bulk of the changes probably should occur in Fabrikam's forest. And I really want to keep the management of the communications with the Fabrikam forest as simple as possible without compromising security. For me, that is the primary goal. I don't really want to have to create too many configurations that we are going to have to change. I would like to hear your thoughts on how best to proceed to enable communications between the two forests."

To complete this exercise, assume that Contoso has implemented the policy settings that are listed in Table 5-2 in Exercise 5.2. The Contoso and the Fabrikam forests are shown in Figure 5-1. Consider both the Group Policy settings and the forest architecture, and then answer the questions that follow. When you are finished, your instructor will take up the questions as part of a class discussion.

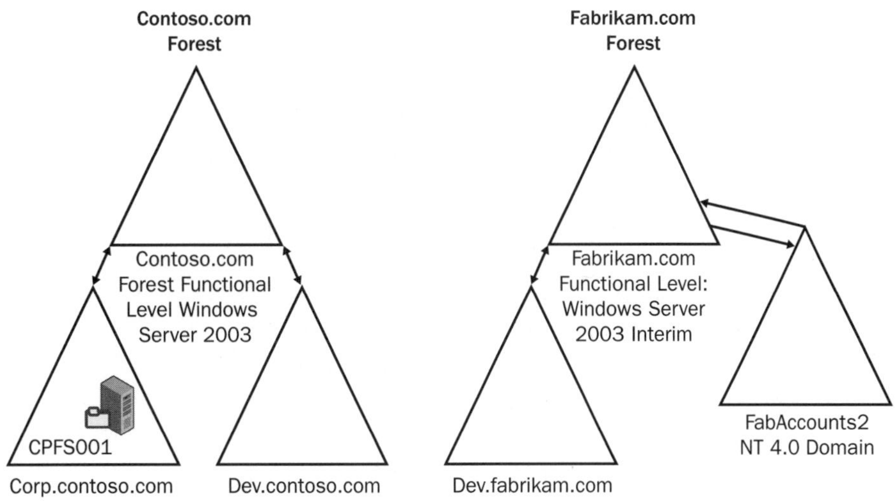

Figure 5-1 Contoso and Fabrikam forests

QUESTION What kind of trust relationship exists between the Windows NT 4.0 accounts domain and the Fabrikam forest root domain?

QUESTION Are the trusts that exist between the Windows NT 4.0 accounts domain and the Fabrikam forest root domain transitive or nontransitive?

QUESTION What kind of trust relationship exists between the *Fabrikam.com* and the *Dev.fabrikam.com* domains? Is this a transitive or nontransitive trust relationship?

QUESTION Given the current functional levels of both forests, what kind of trust relationship can be established between Contoso and Fabrikam?

QUESTION Some users in the Windows NT 4.0 accounts domain require access *Corp.contoso.com* domain. Given the current Security Options settings that Contoso has implemented, would it be possible to grant this access? If not, why not?

QUESTION Assume that you could establish a trust relationship between the *Corp.contoso.com* domain and the *FabAccounts2* Windows NT 4.0 domain. How many trusts would be required to enable access bidirectional access between the *Corp.contoso.com* domain and the *Fabrikam.com* and *FabAccounts2* domains?

QUESTION Can you establish a transitive trust relationship between the *Fabrikam.com* and *Contoso.com* domains?

QUESTION You want to establish a forest trust between the Contoso and Fabrikam forests. What steps must you take in the Fabrikam forest before you can establish the forest trust?

QUESTION Assume that you are able to establish a forest trust between Contoso and Fabrikam. What can you do to ensure that users from *Fabrikam.com* can only access shared resources on CPFS001?

QUESTION What can you do to ensure that users from the Fabrikam forest do not have excessive permissions in the Contoso forest?

QUESTION You have determined that only the users in the Fabrikam forest root domain require access to the *Corp.contoso.com* domain. Given this, should you implement a forest trust?

QUESTION You do not want users in the Fabrikam forest to be able to access any resources in the *Dev.contoso.com* domain. Aside from using selective authentication, how can you accomplish this using the properties of the forest trust?

LAB 6
PROTECTING DATA

This lab contains the following exercises and activities:

- Exercise 6.1: Designing and Implementing a Data Access Strategy
- Exercise 6.2: Delegating Active Directory Permissions
- Exercise 6.3: Designing and Implementing Audit Policy Settings
- Exercise 6.4: Managing Private Keys for EFS Encryption
- Lab Review Questions
- Lab Challenge 6.1: Designing a Data Access Strategy

SCENARIO

You are a network administrator responsible for the Research and Development department at Contoso Pharmaceuticals. The department has several special security requirements, which you help them to meet during your daily activities.

After completing this lab, you will be able to:

- **Design and manage groups by using the AGDLP model.**
- **Grant NTFS file and folder and Share permissions.**
- **Use special groups to manage NTFS permissions.**
- **Understand how NTFS and Share permissions interact.**
- **Delegate tasks by using the Active Directory Delegation of Control Wizard.**
- **Delegate tasks by using the Dsacls Support Tools command-line utility.**
- **Configure local and Group Policy audit policy settings.**
- **Evaluate the effectiveness of specific audit policy settings.**
- **Back up and restore private keys used for Encrypting File System (EFS).**

Estimated lesson time: 155 minutes

BEFORE YOU BEGIN

To complete this lab, you will need to have done the following:

- Performed the Before You Begin section of Lab 1, "Assessing the Need for Security."
- Created a Member Servers organizational unit (OU) and moved the Computer*yy* member server object to the OU according to the instructions in steps 3 through 7 of Lab Exercise 3.4, "Using Group Policy To Configure Automatic Update Clients," in Lab 3, "Reducing the Risk of Software Vulnerabilities."
- Performed the steps in the section titled "Verifying Group Policy Settings by Using the Group Policy Results Wizard" in Exercise 5.2, "Implementing Password and Authentication Security," in Lab 5, "Designing Active Directory Security."

> **NOTE** In this lab, you will see the characters *dd*, *pp*, *xx*, *yy* and *zz*. These directions assume that you are working on computers configured in pairs and that each computer has a number.
>
> When you see *dd*, substitute the number used for your domain. When you see *pp*, substitute the number of your partner's computer. When you see *xx*, substitute the unique number assigned to the lower-numbered (odd-numbered) computer of the pair. When you see *yy*, substitute the unique number assigned to the higher-numbered (even-numbered) computer of the pair. When you see *zz*, substitute the number assigned to the computer you are using. The following example assumes that the partner pair of computers has been assigned the names Computer05 and Computer06 and that you have been assigned Computer05.
>
> Computer*pp* = Computer06 = your partner's computer
>
> Computer*xx* = Computer05 = lower-numbered computer
>
> Computer*yy* = Computer06 = higher-numbered computer
>
> Computer*zz* = Computer05 = computer you are currently using
>
> Contoso*dd*.msft = Contoso03.msft = Active Directory directory service domain you are using

EXERCISE 6.1: DESIGNING AND IMPLEMENTING A DATA ACCESS STRATEGY

Estimated completion time: 45 minutes

In this exercise, you will create a number of domain local and global groups and then use those groups to control access to a number of folders. To complete this exercise, read the following scenario and perform the instructions that follow.

You are a network administrator working for Contoso Pharmaceuticals. You receive a memo from your manager that states the following:

"As you know, a competitor has somehow acquired some of our proprietary research data. Although the source of the leak is still being investigated, we are concerned that the leak may have occurred internally. This suspicion has prompted a review of the file and folder permissions on confidential data. We are particularly concerned about the data that is located in the \\CPRDFS01\R and D\Research Data shared folder on a server in the Research department. Access to this shared folder should be highly restricted. The \\CPRDFS01\R and D\Lab Procedures folder contains some information that should be regarded as proprietary, but not confidential. Access to this folder does not need to be as restrictive as access to the \Research Data folder. All research staff should be able to create and edit files in the \Lab Procedures folder, but should not be able to change permissions on these files. Also, they should be able to delete only their own files. No one should have Full Control permissions to objects they create in these folders. Susan Burk, our lead scientist, is an exception to these rules. Finally, we want to ensure that we do not allow general staff at Contoso to view data in the top-level R and D Folder. Susan Burk will need Full Control permissions for all files and folders within the R and D Folder.

"Is it possible to create permissions on folders so that researchers can create files, read and modify them, but not be able change permissions on those files to allow others access? I think the owner of an object can always change permissions on that object if the owner attaches to it locally, but see what you can do. At the very least, researchers should not be able to change permissions on files they create when they connect to the Research Data folder over the share, nor should they be able to delete files that they create in this folder. Also, I want the permissions on the Research Data folder to prevent researchers from reading files that they did not create. I think that we should make the default folder and share permission settings as secure as possible, and let Susan Burk, who is really in the best position to know, determine what access to the files in this folder the scientists should have. She should be able to grant that access as she feels necessary.

"You may have to create some groups in the R and D Groups OU to accomplish your task. Please create the necessary groups as required."

The folder hierarchy is shown in Figure 6-1.

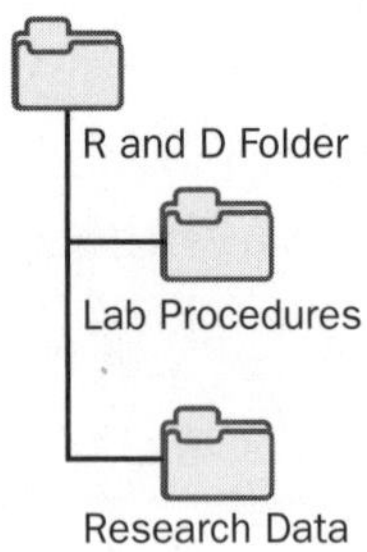

Summary of Permission Requirements for R and D Folder

- Only Sburkzz and Administrators should have full control permissions.
- Access to the R and D folder should be restricted to only members of the Research OU.
- Members of the R and D OU should not be able to modify permissions on files they or others create.
- Access to the Research Data folder should be restricted to Researchers only.
- By default, Researchers should be able to create files in the Research Data folder and read and modify those files.
- By default, Researchers should not be able to delete files they create in the Research Data folder.
- By default, Researchers should not be able to read files they did not create in the Research Data folder.

Figure 6-1 Summary of permission requirements for R and D Folder

QUESTION *Contoso Pharmaceuticals uses the Account Group/Resource Group Authorization method as its standard for providing access to resources. Given this standard, what will be your strategy for creating groups?*

QUESTION *What are the characteristics of a good group-naming strategy?*

Creating Domain Local and Global Groups

In this section, you will create and modify the membership of three domain local and two global groups in the R and D Groups OU. Following the principle of AGDLP, you will create global groups to organize users, place those global groups into domain local groups, and assign permissions to the domain local groups. You will create domain local groups based on the permissions that need to be assigned to folders. The names of the groups are as follows:

- DLG Loc*zz* R and D Admins FC. You will use this domain local group to assign Full Control permissions to all folders used by R and D.
- DLG Loc*zz* R and D Research RW. You will use this domain local group to assign Read and Write permissions to the Lab Procedures folder and Read permissions to the R and D Folder. You will also use it to assign Change share permissions to the R and D share.
- DLG Loc*zz* R and D Research W. You will use this domain local group to assign Write permissions to the Research Data folder.

- GG Loc*zz* R and D Administration. You will use this global group to organize R and D administrators and make it a member of DLG Loc*zz* R and D Admins FC
- GG Loc*zz* R and D Researchers. You will use this global group to organize R and D researchers and make it a member of DLG Loc*zz* R and D Research RW and DLG Loc*zz* R and D Research W.

Note the *zz* variable indicates your assigned computer number.

1. Log on as Contoso*dd*\Admin*zz* using **P@ssw0rd** as the password.
2. Click Start, point to Administrative Tools, and select Active Directory Users And Computers.
3. In the tree pane of Active Directory Users And Computers, expand the Location*zz*\R and D OU, and then select the R and D Groups OU.
4. Right-click the R and D Groups OU, point to New, and then select Group.
5. In the New Object – Group dialog box, type **GG Loc*zz* R and D Administration** in the Group name box, and click OK to create a global security group.

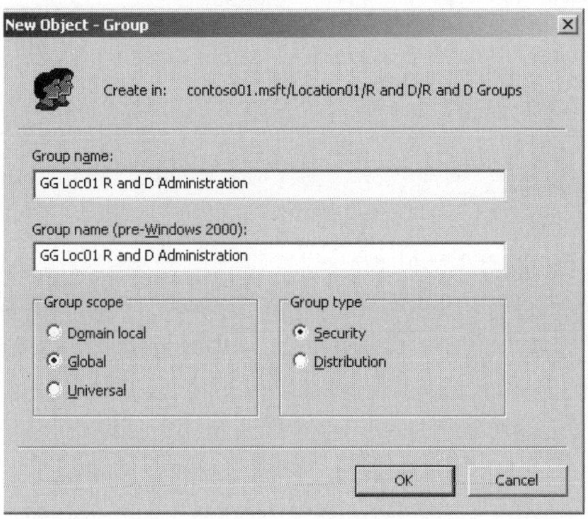

6. Repeat steps 4 and 5 to create another global group named GG Loc*zz* R and D Researchers.
7. Right-click the R and D Groups OU, point to New, and then select Group.
8. In the Group Name text box, type **DLG Loc*zz* R and D Admins FC**. In the Group Scope area, select the Domain Local option, and click OK to create a domain local security group.

9. Repeat steps 7 and 8 to create two additional domain local groups named DLG Loc*zz* R and D Research RW and DLG Loc*zz* R and D Research W.

10. In the details pane, double-click the GG Loczz R and D Administration group, click the Members tab, and click Add.

11. In the Select Users, Computers, Or Groups dialog box, in the Enter The Object Names To Select text box, type **SBurk*zz*** and click OK.

12. In the GG Loczz R and Administration Properties dialog box, click the Member Of tab, and then click Add.

13. In the Select Groups dialog box, in the Enter The Object Names To Select text box, type **DLG Loc*zz*** and then click OK.

14. In the Multiple Names Found dialog box, select the DLG Loc*zz* R and D Admins FC group, and click OK twice.

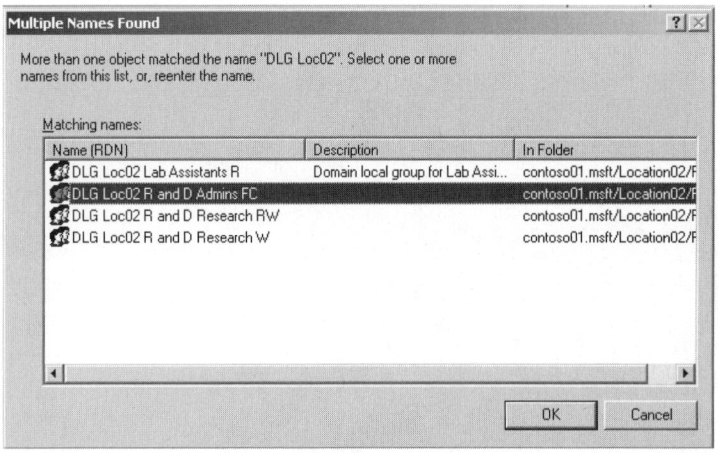

You will now add the user accounts of R and D employees to the GG Loc*zz* R and D Researchers group and make the group a member of both the DLG Loc*zz* R and D Research RW and DLG Loc*zz* R and D Research W groups. The domain local groups will be assigned permissions to resources. Members of all these groups will acquire the permissions assigned to these groups, including users who are members of groups that belong to domain local groups.

15. In the details pane of Active Directory Users And Computers, double-click the GG Loc*zz* R and D Researchers group object, click the Members tab and then click Add.

16. In the Select Users, Contacts, Computers, Or Groups dialog box, in the Enter The Object Names To Select text box, type **JGeist*zz*;SBurk*zz*** and click OK.

17. In the GG Loc*zz* R and D Researchers Properties dialog box, click the Member Of tab, and then click Add.

18. In the Select Groups dialog box, in the Enter The Object Names To Select box, type **DLG Loc*zz*** and then click OK.

19. In the Multiple Names Found dialog box, press and hold CTRL, select both the DLG Loc*zz* R and D Research groups, and then click OK twice.

    Remember that you are organizing users into global groups, making these global groups members of domain local groups, and then using the domain local groups to assign permissions to resources. You will use these domain local groups to assign the appropriate NTFS and share permissions.

20. Close Active Directory Users And Computers.

Implementing Folder and File Permissions

In this section, you will grant permissions on the R and D folders to the domain local groups you created previously. You will first create the folder structure by running a batch file.

1. Click Start, select Run, type **c:\lab manual\lab 06\createfolders.cmd**, and then click OK.

2. Open Windows Explorer and, below the C drive, right-click R and D Folder. Select Properties, and then click the Security tab. The R And D Folder Properties dialog box shows the default permissions on the folder.

    QUESTION What is the visual indication that the permissions are inherited from the parent folder?

3. On the Security tab, click Advanced. The Advanced Security Settings For R And D Folder dialog box appears.

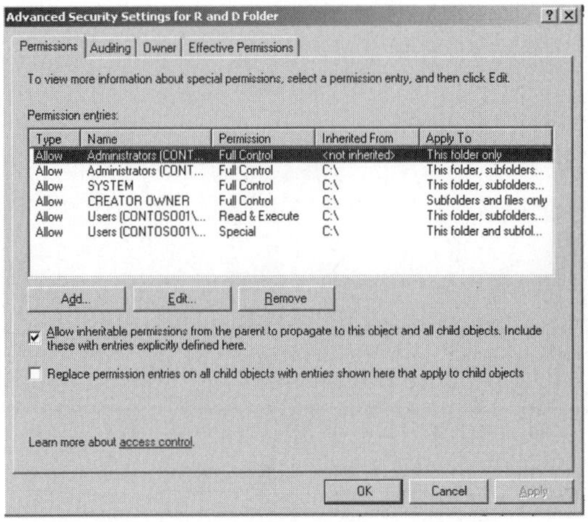

In the next step, you will replace the inherited permissions with explicit permissions on the folder.

4. Clear the Allow Inheritable Permissions From The Parent To Propagate To This Object And All Child Objects check box. The Security dialog box appears, giving you the option to copy or remove the inherited permissions.

5. In the Security dialog box, click Copy. The inherited permissions are copied to the access control list (ACL) of R and D Folder, and the Security dialog box closes. Leave open the Advanced Security Settings For R And D Folder dialog box.

   In the next step, you will remove the CREATOR OWNER object from the folder permissions.

6. In the Advanced Security Settings For R And D Folder dialog box, select the CREATOR OWNER object, click Remove, and then click OK. The R And D Folder Properties dialog box appears.

7. On the Security tab of the R And D Folder Properties dialog box, select the Users (either CONTOSOZZ\Users or COMPUTERZZ\Users) object in the Group Or User Names box, and then click Remove.

8. On the Security tab of the R And D Folder Properties dialog box, click Add.

9. In the Select Users, Computers, Or Groups dialog box, in the Enter The Object Names To Select box, type **creator owner**, and then click OK. The CREATOR OWNER group reappears.

10. With the CREATOR OWNER group selected in the Group Or User Names box, select the Allow check box for the Modify permission in the Permissions For CREATOR OWNER box. Be careful not to select the Allow check box for the Full Control permission.

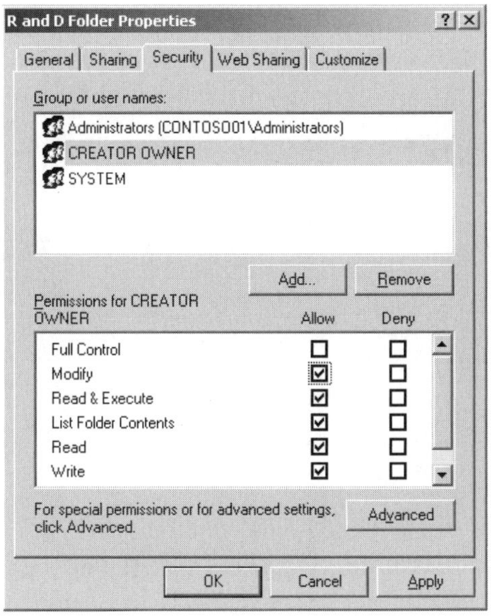

You will now grant the Full Control permission to the DLG Loc*zz* R and D Admins FC group.

11. Click Add.
12. In the Select Users, Computers, Or Groups dialog box, in the Enter The Object Names To Select text box, type **DLG Loc*zz* R and D Admins FC**, and then click OK.
13. With the DLG Loc*zz* R and D Admins FC group selected in the Group Or User Names box, select the Allow check box for the Full Control permission.

    You will now grant the DLG Loc*zz* R and Research RW group the default permissions to the folder. The reason that we are giving limited permissions here is that we do not want research staff to be able to create files and folders at this level. In a production environment, you might want to create an additional domain local group to use for this purpose. To simplify the steps in this lab somewhat, you use this group to assign the Read Only permission to the top-level folder.

14. Click Add.
15. In the Select Users, Computers, Or Groups dialog box, in the Enter The Object Names To Select box, type **DLG Loczz R and D Research RW**, and click OK.
16. On the Security tab of the R And D Folder Properties dialog box, click Advanced.

17. In the Advanced Security Settings For R And D Folder dialog box, select the Replace Permission Entries On All Child Objects With Entries Shown Here That Apply To Child Objects check box, and then click OK. The Security dialog box appears.
18. Read the information in the Security dialog box, and then click Yes.
19. Click OK to close the R And D Folder Properties dialog box.

    You will now grant the DLG Loc*zz* R and Research RW additional permissions on the Lab Procedures folder.

20. Right-click the Lab Procedures folder, select Properties, and then click the Security tab.
21. In the Group Or User Names box, select the DLG Loc*zz* R and D Research RW group, and then, in the Allow column, select the Write permission check box.
22. Click OK to close the Lab Procedures Properties dialog box.

    You will now modify the permission on the Research Data folder to restrict access further.

23. Right-click the Research Data folder, select Properties, and click the Security tab.
24. Click Advanced, clear the Allow Inheritable Permissions From The Parent To Propagate To This Object And All Child Objects check box. The Security dialog box appears, giving you the options to copy or remove the inherited permissions.
25. Click Copy, and then click OK.
26. In the Research Data Properties dialog box, in the Group Or User Names box, select the DLG Loc*zz* R and D Research RW group, click Remove, and then click Add.
27. In the Select Users, Computers, Or Groups dialog box, in the Enter The Object Names To Select box, type **DLG Loczz R and D Research W**, and then click OK.
28. With the DLG Loc*zz* R and D Research W group selected in the Group Or User Names box, clear the Allow check boxes for the Read & Execute and Read permissions, and then select the Allow check box for the Write permission. Both the Allow check boxes for the List Folder Contents and Write permissions should be selected.

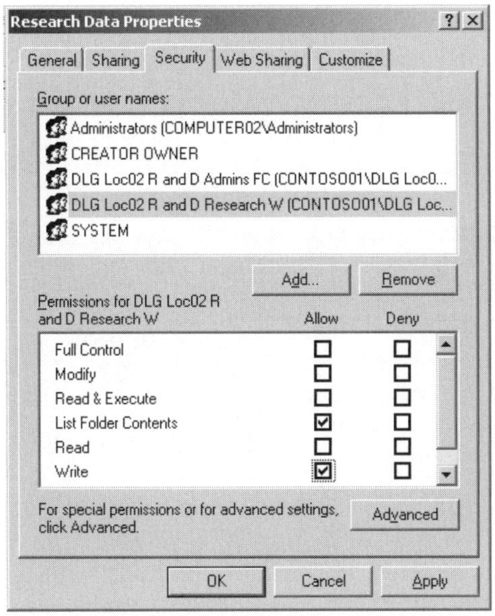

29. Click OK to close the Research Data Properties dialog box.
30. Copy the file named Confidential.txt from the \Lab Manual\Lab 06 folder to the C:\R and D Folder\Research Data folder.
31. Copy the file named Proprietary.txt from the \Lab Manual\Lab 06 folder to the C:\R and D Folder\Lab Procedures folder.

Modifying Share Permissions

In this section, you will modify the default share permission on the R and D Folder.

1. In Windows Explorer, right-click the R and D Folder, select Sharing and Security, and, on the Sharing tab, click Permissions.
2. In the Permissions For R And D dialog box, verify that the Everyone group is selected, and then click Remove.
3. Click Add.
4. From the In The Select Users, Computers, Or Groups dialog box, in the Enter The Object Names To Select text box, type **DLG Loczz** and then click OK.
5. In the Multiple Names Found dialog box, select the DLG Loc*zz* R and D Admins FC and the DLG Loc*zz* R and D Research RW groups, and then click OK.

6. In the Permissions For R And D dialog box, grant the following permissions:
   - DLG Loc*zz* R and D Admins FC: Full Control
   - DLG Loc*zz* R and D Research RW: Change and Read
7. Close all open windows and log off.

Verifying Share and NTFS Permissions

In this section, you will log on as Contoso*dd*\Jgeist*zz*, verify the NTFS and share permissions, and then modify the NTFS permission again to correct a problem with permissions on the Research Data folder.

1. Log on as Contoso*dd*\Jgeist*zz* using **P@ssw0rd** as the password.
2. Click Start, select Run, type **\\computerzz\r and d** in the Open text box, and click OK. The R and D shared folder opens.
3. Right-click within this folder, point to New, and select Text Document.

   QUESTION *Why do you receive an Unable To Create File message?*

4. Click OK to acknowledge the Unable To Create File message, and then double-click the Lab Procedures folder.
5. Right-click within this folder, point to New, select Text document, type **Test** for the file name, and then press ENTER.
6. Repeat step 5 twice to create two more text files named Test1 and Test2.

   QUESTION *Why are you able to create the files in the Lab Procedures folder?*

7. Double-click the Proprietary.txt file, make some changes to the file, and then save the file and close it.

   QUESTION *Why are you able to save changes to the Propietary.txt file?*

8. Select the Proprietary.txt file and attempt to delete the file.

   QUESTION *Why are you unable to delete the Propietary.txt file in the Lab Procedures folder?*

9. Select the Test.txt file and attempt to delete it.

> **QUESTION** Why are you able to delete the Test.txt file in the Lab Procedures folder? Where did the additional permissions come from?

10. Navigate to the top-level R and D shared folder and then double-click the Research Data folder.
11. Double-click the Confidential.txt file. An Access Is Denied message appears.

> **QUESTION** Why are you unable to open the Confidential.txt file in the Research Data folder?

12. Create a text file named Test in the Research Data folder.

> **QUESTION** Why are you able to create a file in the Research Data folder?

13. Right-click Test, select Properties, and then click the Security tab.

> **QUESTION** What is the highest Allow permission listed for the Contoso*dd*\Jgeist*zz* account? Where did this permission come from? Is it sufficient to delete the file?

> **QUESTION** Are you able to change permissions on this file?

14. Delete the Test file in the Research Data folder, and leave the folder open.

    In the next steps, you will modify the permissions granted to the CREATOR OWNER group on the Research Data. You will be using the Run As command to perform this task. Because you cannot use the Run As command with Windows Explorer, you will launch Microsoft Internet Explorer by using the Run As command.

15. On the taskbar, right-click the Internet Explorer icon, and select Run as.
16. In the Run As dialog box, log on as Contoso*dd*\Administrator using **P@ssw0rd** as the password. Internet Explorer opens.
17. In the Address box, type **c:\R and D Folder**, and then press ENTER.
18. Right-click the Research Data Folder, select Properties, click the Security tab, and then click Advanced.

19. In the Advanced Security Settings For Research Data dialog box, select the CREATOR OWNER group, and click Edit. The Permission Entry For Research Data dialog box appears.

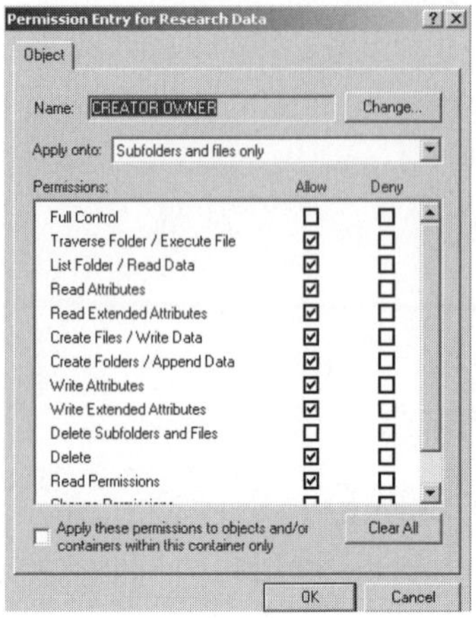

20. In the Permissions box, clear the Allow check box for the Delete permission, and click OK three times to close all the dialog boxes.

21. Close Internet Explorer.

    In the authentication context of the JGeist*zz* account, you will copy the Test1 and Test2 files you created in the Lab Procedures folder in step 6 to the Research Data folder to test NTFS permissions.

22. In Windows Explorer, click Folders on the menu bar to display the Folders tree view, and then copy the Test1 and the Test2 file from the Lab Procedures folder to the Research Data folder.

    Note that you cannot rename a file in this folder, because renaming a file requires the ability to delete the old version of the file. Although you can create a new file named New Text Document, you will not be able to change this name.

23. Attempt to delete the Test1 and the Test2 files. A message appears indicating that you cannot delete the files.

24. Click OK to close the message and then close the shared folder.

    In the next steps, you will connect to the R and D Folder on the local computer, rather than through the R and D file share, and examine the NTFS permissions on the file you created in the previous steps.

25. Open Windows Explorer, navigate to the R and D Folder, right-click the Test2 file, select Properties, and select the Security tab.

26. In the Test Properties dialog box, grant the JGeistzz account Full Control Allow permission, and close the dialog box.
27. Delete the Test2 file. You are able to delete the file.

    Do not delete the Test1 file. You will use this file in Exercise 6.3.

> **QUESTION** *What additional step(s) would you recommend to your manager for protecting the files in the Research Data folder?*

28. Close all open windows, but stay logged on as Jgeistzz for the next exercise.

EXERCISE 6.2: DELEGATING ACTIVE DIRECTORY PERMISSIONS

Estimated completion time: 30 minutes

Your manager is pleased with the work you did to secure the folders that are used by the R and D division. Your manager sends you a memo that states the following:

"Thanks for your work on securing the R and D shared folder. I am sure the new permissions will help to ease some minds around here.

"I have another couple of requests. Susan Burk, our lead scientist, says that she would like to be able to modify group memberships of the groups in the R and D Groups. (Actually, she has requested that she also have the ability to create groups, but I think that is going a bit too far and we will have to disappoint her.) She is also requesting that Jim Geist have the ability to modify the membership of the Research Assistants global group. Could you please delegate these permissions to the appropriate group and OU?

"We haven't done a proper risk analysis on granting these abilities, but I will be sure to mention the new configuration to the security team when they have their next meeting. I am sure that the change will be acceptable. Susan is our most senior scientist, and she is extremely security-conscious, as is Dr. Geist. However, I would like to hear your thoughts on the kind of risks that are created by delegating these abilities and what we might do to minimize the risk."

In the steps that follow, you will delegate the ability to modify group membership and to reset passwords to the Contosozz\SBurkzz account. As a best practice in multiple-domain environments, you should not use domain local groups to assign permissions to Active Directory objects. The reason for this is that domain local groups can't be evaluated in other domains, and a subset of the properties of all Active Directory objects are replicated in the Global Catalog. For more information on this topic, see the Microsoft Knowledge Base article "Group Type and Scope Usage in Windows," at *http://support.microsoft.com/kb/231273.*

1. Click Start, select Run, type **cmd** in the Open text box, and click OK.
2. At the command prompt, type **runas /user:Contoso*dd*\Admin*zz* "mmc dsa.msc"** and press ENTER.
3. When prompted, type your password, and press ENTER. Active Directory Users And Computers opens.
4. In the tree pane of Active Directory Users And Computers, expand the Locationzz\R and D OU, right-click the R and D Groups OU, and select Delegate Control. The Welcome To The Delegation Of Control Wizard page appears.
5. Click Next.
6. On the Users Or Groups page, click Add. Type **SBurk*zz*** in the Enter The Object Names To Select box of the Select Users, Groups Or Computers dialog box, click OK, and then click Next.
7. On the Tasks To Delegate page, select the Create A Custom Task To Delegate option, and click Next.

> **NOTE** For the task you are going to delegate, you could have selected the check box option to modify the membership of a group. However, you are going to use the custom method to specify the granular permissions that are required for the task. Permissions on Active Directory objects are not as straightforward as permissions on other types of objects, such as file or printer objects. For example, different types of objects, such as groups or users, can have different sets of permissions that are specific to the object.

8. On the Active Directory Object Type page, select the Only The Following Objects In The Folder option. Select the Group Objects check box, and click Next.

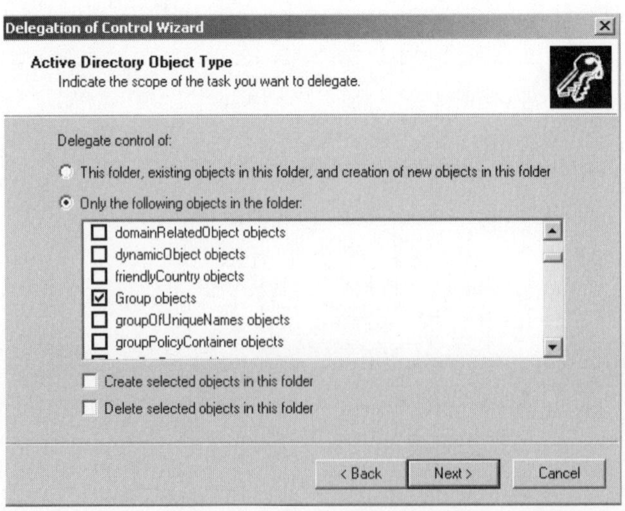

9. On the Permissions page, select the Property-Specific check box option, select the Read Members and the Write Members property permissions check boxes, and click Next.

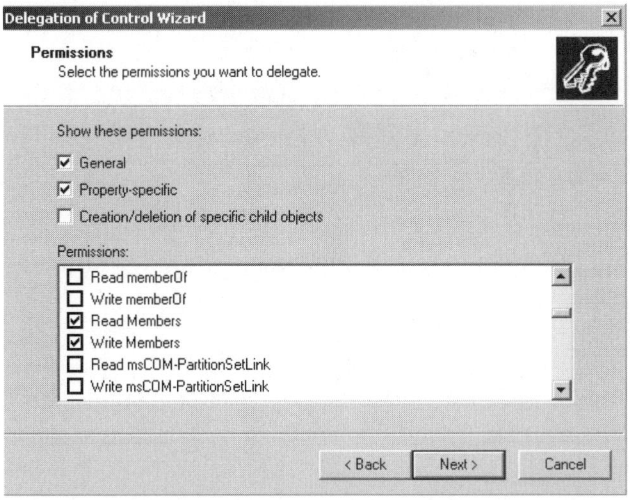

10. On the Completing The Delegation Of Control Wizard page, click Finish, and leave Active Directory Computers And Users open.

> **TIP** It is also possible to grant a user or group the permissions to manage the membership of a specific group through the Managed By tab of the properties of the group object. However, as a demonstration of the capabilities of the Support Tools Dsacls command-line tool to manage Active Directory permissions, you will use the Dsacls command to grant the JGeist01 account the ability to modify the membership of a specific group, rather than grant this ability through the graphical user interface.

11. Switch to the command prompt window; if you have closed it, open a new command prompt window.

12. At the command prompt, type **runas /user:Contosodd\Adminzz cmd** and press ENTER. Type your password when prompted, and press ENTER. A second command prompt window opens in the context of the Contoso*dd*\Admin*zz* account.

13. At the second command prompt window, type **cd\lab manual\lab 06**, and press ENTER.

14. At the second command prompt window, type **notepad lab06dsacls.cmd**, and press ENTER. Notepad opens, displaying a Dsacls command string.

15. In Notepad, examine the command string, replace the *dd* (your domain number) and *zz* (your computer number) variables with your assigned numbers as appropriate, and then save and close the file.

16. At the second command prompt window, type **lab06dsacls.cmd**, and press ENTER. The Dsacls command executes and grants the JGeist*zz* account the ability to manage the GG Loc*zz* Research Assistants group. If you edited this file correctly, you should see a message stating that the command completed successfully.

17. At the second command prompt window, scroll through the output of the Dsacls command and, on the left side, locate the line "Allow Contoso*dd*\Jgeist*zz*".

> **QUESTION** What permissions are listed for the JGeistzz account?

18. Close the second command prompt window.

Examining and Verifying Active Directory Permissions

In this section, you will examine and verify the delegated Active Directory permissions.

1. In Active Directory Users And Computers, right-click the R and D Groups OU, select Properties, click the Security tab, and then click Advanced. The Advanced Setting For R And D Groups dialog box appears.

   If you do not see the security tab, this means that the Advanced Features has not been enabled on the View menu of Active Directory Users And Computers.

2. In the Permissions Entries box, locate and select the entry for the SBurk*zz* account, click Edit, and note the permissions that are granted to the account.

> **QUESTION** What two specific permissions are granted to the SBurkzz account?

3. Click Cancel three times to close the dialog boxes.

4. In the tree pane, select the R And D Groups OU. In the details pane, right-click the GG Loc*zz* Lab Assistants group and select Properties. Click the Security tab, and click Advanced.

5. In the Permissions Entries box, locate and select the entry for the JGeist*zz* account, click Edit, and in the Permission Entry For GG Loc*zz* LabAssistants dialog box, note the permissions that are granted to the account.

   The Dsacls command was executed with the /I:T switch, rather than /I:P, which causes the permissions to be applied to sub-objects as well. In the next step, you will reconfigure the permission so that it applies to only the object.

6. In the Permission Entry For GG Loc*zz* Lab Assistants dialog box, select the Apply Onto drop-down list, and select This Object Only. Click OK three times to close the dialog boxes.

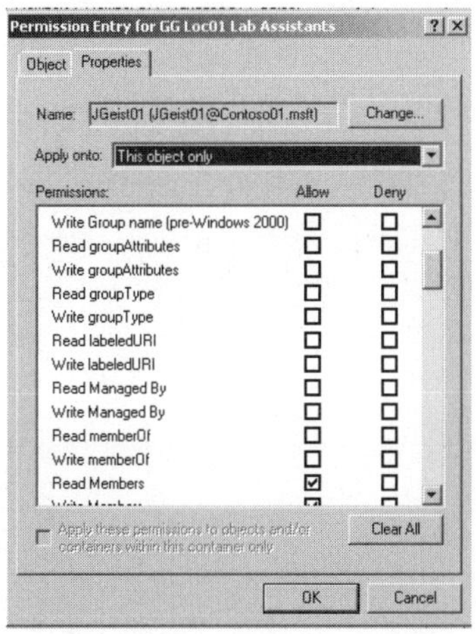

7. Close Active Directory Users And Computers.

   In the next steps, you will verify that the JGeist*zz* and the SBurk*zz* accounts can manage group membership, as configured in the previous steps.

8. Click Start, select Run, type **mmc c:\windows\system32\dsa.msc** in the Open text box, and click OK. Active Directory Users And Computers opens in the context of the JGeist*zz* account.

9. In the tree pane of Active Directory Users And Computers, select the R and D Groups OU. Right-click the GG Loc*zz* Lab Assistants group object in the details pane, select Properties, and then click the Members tab.

10. In the GG Loc*zz* Lab Assistants Properties dialog box, click Add.

11. In the Select Users, Contacts, Computers, Or Groups dialog box, in the Enter The Object Names To Select box, type **MLeezz**, and press ENTER.

12. In the GG Loc*zz* Lab Assistants Properties dialog box, click OK. The MLee*zz* account is added to the group.
13. Close Active Directory Users And Computers.
14. Switch to the command prompt window.
15. At the command prompt, type **runas /user:Contoso*dd*\SBurk*zz* "mmc dsa.msc"**, press ENTER, and use **P@ssw0rd** as the password to launch Active Directory Users And Computers in the context of the SBurk*zz* account.
16. In the tree pane of Active Directory Users And Computers, select the R and D Group OU. Right-click the GG Loc*zz* R and D Researchers group object in the details pane, select Properties, and then click the Members tab.
17. In the GG Loc*zz* R and D Researchers Properties dialog box, click Add.
18. In the Select Users, Contacts, Computers, Or Groups dialog box, in the Enter The Object Names To Select box, type **TBremerzz**, and press ENTER.
19. In the GG Loc*zz* Researchers Properties dialog box, click OK. The TBremer*zz* account is added to the group.
20. Close all open windows.

QUESTION What kinds of risks or vulnerabilities are introduced by delegating the ability to manage group membership?

QUESTION List at least two strategies you might implement to reduce the risks that delegating the ability to manage groups introduces.

EXERCISE 6.3: DESIGNING AND IMPLEMENTING AUDIT POLICY SETTINGS

Estimated completion time: 40 minutes

Your manager sends you a memo that states the following:

"Thanks for the recommendations you made regarding strategies to reduce risks introduced by delegating tasks to managers in the R and D divisions. I think one of the most effective ways of reducing the risk here is to audit for changes to those group accounts, so that there is an audit trail for administrative activities. We should probably let the managers know we are going to audit those groups for administrative activity–this will make them more accountable for their actions.

"Would you please enable auditing as appropriate for the R and D groups? Also, I think we should enable auditing of the R and D Folder. However, in both cases, we want to be careful that the security logs do not run out of room. We don't want to lose any events in the security logs. I am not sure what the best approach here is, so I am counting on your advice and good judgment.

"As you know, we haven't really been paying much attention to auditing, but we do need to take it more seriously. I think there is some setting or settings you have to enable if you want to audit file and Active Directory access. I can't remember what the setting is, but I am sure you will know.

"One final thing: We really should be auditing for failed logon activity and other critical events, such as system shutdown and startup, on both the domain controllers and the member workstations and servers. Can you please also configure auditing for those events?"

In this exercise, you will examine the default audit settings for domain controllers and member servers. You will then make a number of changes to those settings and then test and review the results of those settings.

Examining Default Audit Settings

In this section, you will examine the default audit settings of the domain controller (Computer*xx*) and member server (Computer*yy*) in your domain by viewing the Group Policy results you generated in Exercise 5.2 of Lab 5.

1. Log on as Contoso*dd*\Admin*zz*.
2. Click Start, point to Administrative Tools, and select Group Policy Management.
    a. If you see an Internet Explorer dialog box warning you about content being blocked, click Add.
    b. In the Trusted Sites dialog box, verify that the Require Server Verification (Https:) For All Sites In This Zone check box is cleared, click Add, and then click Close. The Group Policy Management Console appears.
3. In the tree pane of the Group Policy Management Console, expand the Group Policy Results node, and select Computer*xx*.
4. In the details pane, select the Settings tab and, if necessary, click Show All to display the settings.

5. In the details pane, scroll to the section titled "Local Policies/Audit Policy," and record the current settings in this table.

Table 6-1 **Default Domain Controller Audit Policy Settings**

Policy	Setting	Winning GPO
Audit Account Logon Events		
Audit Account Management		
Audit Directory Service Access		
Audit Logon Events		
Audit Object Access		
Audit Policy Change		
Audit Privilege Use		
Audit Process Tracking		
Audit System Events		

6. In the tree pane of the Group Policy Management Console, under the Group Policy Results node, select Computer*yy*, and view the Group Policy settings for the member server.

> **QUESTION** *Are there any Group Policy settings that define audit settings for the member server?*

7. Click Start, select Run, type **mmc %windir%\system32\secpol.msc** in the Open text box, and click OK. The Local Security Settings Console appears.

8. In the tree pane of the Local Security Settings Console, expand the Local Policies node, and select Audit Policy.

   Note that, on the domain controller, you will see audit policy settings that are defined in the Default Domain Controllers Policy. On the member server, you will see audit policy settings that are defined on the local computer.

9. On Computer*yy*, note the audit policy settings.

> **QUESTION** *What two audit policies are configured?*

> **QUESTION** *Given the current configuration of the audit logon policies on both computers, what changes would you have to make to leverage the audit policy settings to act as a simple but effective intrusion-detection mechanism? If you left the audit account settings as is, what kind of event might indicate a successful intrusion?*

10. In the Local Security Settings console, right-click Audit Account Logon Events and select Help. The help file for the setting appears.

11. Using the help files for the audit settings and the information in Chapter 6 of the textbook, "Protecting Data," answer the following questions about audit settings.

> **QUESTION** What audit setting has to be enabled to audit access to an object that has a System Access Control List (SACL)?

> **QUESTION** You want to record audit information about the account that is used to perform activities, such as perform a remote shutdown, change the system time, or take ownership of objects. What audit setting should you enable?

> **QUESTION** What is a disadvantage of auditing for success on the Audit Privilege Use setting?

> **QUESTION** You want to determine who altered the membership of a group in Active Directory. What audit setting should you enable?

> **QUESTION** You want to determine when the Security log was cleared. What audit setting is responsible for tracking this?

> **QUESTION** What audit setting is responsible for tracking domain logons and logoffs?

> **QUESTION** Why might it be important to consolidate the Security logs from multiple domain controllers?

12. Close all open windows.

    In the steps that follow, you will examine the default log settings on your computer and your partner's computer and answer questions regarding their configuration.

13. Click Start, select Run, type **eventvwr** in the Open text box, and click OK. Event Viewer opens, connected to the local computer.

14. Minimize Event Viewer.

15. Click Start, select Run, type **eventvwr** in the Open text box, and click OK. A second instance of Event Viewer opens, connected to the local computer.

16. In the second instance of Event Viewer, in the tree pane, right-click Event Viewer (Local), and select Connect To Another Computer.
17. In the Select Computer dialog box, in the Another Computer box, type **Computer*pp***, and click OK. The second instance of Event Viewer connects to your partner's computer.
18. In the second instance of Event Viewer, in the tree pane, right-click Security, and select Properties. The properties of the Security log on your partner's computer are displayed.
19. Note the settings in the Log size area of the Security Properties dialog box.
20. Switch to the first instance of Event Viewer, and view the properties of the Security log.

> **QUESTION** What is the default size for the Security log on the domain controller and the member server?

> **QUESTION** What will happen when the maximum log size is reached on both computers? What risk does this setting possess for organizations that want to use audit logs for forensic purposes?

> **QUESTION** If the log file size setting was set to Do Not Overwrite Events, what risk would this pose to organizations that wished to use audit logs for the purposes of intrusion detection?

21. Close the Security Properties dialog box.
22. In the instance of Event Viewer for your local computer, in the tree pane, select Security to show security events in the details pane. Right-click Security, and select Clear All Events.
23. In the Event Viewer dialog box, in response to the prompt to save the Security log, click No.
24. Double-click the single entry in the details pane of the Security log and view the details. Notice that the category for the event is System Event and that this event appears on the member server as well as the domain controller, even though the Audit system events policy is not enabled on the member server. Also notice that the name of the user who cleared the log file is included in the log entry.

> **QUESTION** What might you want to double check when you see a System event 517?

In the next steps, you will attempt to view the Security log in the authentication context of a user who does not have sufficient rights to view it.

25. Click Start, select Run, type **runas /user:Contoso*dd*\Student*zz* eventvwr** in the Open text box, and click OK. When prompted, type **P@ssw0rd**, and press ENTER. A third instance of Event Viewer opens. Notice that the log file sizes are not displayed in the details pane.
26. In the third instance of Event Viewer, in the tree pane, select Security. An Access Is Denied message appears.
27. Click OK to acknowledge the message, and then close the third instance of Event Viewer.
28. Switch to the first instance of Event Viewer where you are connected to your local computer, right-click Security, and select Refresh.
29. Scroll through the entries in the Security log. Notice that there is no event to indicate the failed attempt to view the Security log.

> **QUESTION** *The ability to read the Security log is determined by whether a security principal has been assigned the Manage Audit And Security Log user right. By default, only Administrators and Exchange Administrators have been assigned this right. Based on this information, what audit setting should you enable to detect failed attempts to view the Security log?*

Configuring and Examining Security Audit Events

In this section, you will make a few changes to the audit settings of your computer, generate security-related events by performing a number of actions on your computer, and then examine the events in Event Viewer.

> **NOTE** *Because of the different computer configurations, the steps you perform will differ, depending on the computer you have been assigned. Make sure you read the steps carefully to ensure that you are performing the steps that are appropriate for your assigned computer.*

Steps 1 through 3 should be performed on the domain controller (Computer*xx*). If you are sitting at the member server (Computer*yy*), proceed to step 4.

1. Click Start, point to Administrative Tools, and select Group Policy Management.
2. In the tree pane of the Group Policy Management Console, expand the Domain Controllers node, right-click Default Domain Controllers Policy, and select Edit.

3. In the tree pane of the Group Policy Object Editor, under Computer Configuration, expand the Windows Settings\Security Settings\Local Policies node, and select Audit Policy. Proceed to step 6.

   Perform steps 4 and 5 on only the member server (Computeryy).

4. Click Start, point to Administrative Tools, and select Local Security Policy.

5. In the tree pane of the Security Settings console, expand Local Policies, and select Audit Policy.

   Both students should perform the following steps:

6. In the details pane, double-click Audit Account Logon Events. In the Audit Account Logon Events Properties dialog box, select the Failure check box, and then click OK.

7. Configure or verify the following audit policy settings:

Policy	Policy Setting
Audit Account Logon Events	Success, Failure
Audit Account Management	Success
Audit Logon Events	Success, Failure
Audit Object Access	Success, Failure
Audit Policy Change	Success, Failure
Audit Privilege Use	Failure
Audit System Events	Success, Failure

8. Close the Group Policy Object Editor and the Group Policy Management Console or the Security Settings Console, depending on your assigned computer.

9. Open a command prompt window, type **gpupdate /target:computer /force**, and press ENTER.

   You will now configure auditing on the Research Data folder that you configured in Exercise 6.1.

10. Open Windows Explorer, navigate to the R and D Folder. Right-click the Research Data folder and select Properties. Click the Security tab, and then click Advanced.

11. In the Advanced Security Settings For Research Data dialog box, click the Auditing tab.

12. On the Auditing tab, click Add.

13. In the Select User, Computer, Or Group, in the Enter The Object Name To Select box, type **everyone**, and then click OK.

14. In the Auditing Entry For Research Data dialog box, in the Access box, select the Successful and Failed check boxes for Full Control access, and then click OK.

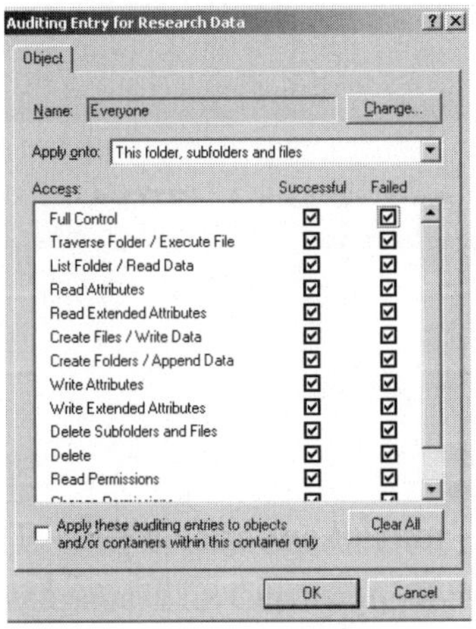

15. Click OK twice to close the remaining open dialog boxes.

16. On the taskbar, right-click the Internet Explorer icon, and select Run As.

17. In the Run As dialog box, log on as Contoso*dd*\JGeist*zz*. Internet Explorer opens. Click OK to acknowledge any messages that may appear informing you about Internet Explorer security settings.

18. In the Address text box, type **C:\R and D Folder**, and press ENTER. Internet Explorer displays the local R and D Folder.

    To make the Security log easier to read, you will clear the log before attempting to access the Research Data folder.

19. Switch to the first instance of Event Viewer (the instance connected to your local computer), or open Event Viewer if you previously closed it.

20. Right-click Security, select Clear All Events, and click No to acknowledge you do not want to save the log.

21. Switch to Internet Explorer, and double-click the Research Data folder.

22. Double-click the Test1 file you created in Exercise 6-1, and then close the file.

23. Double-click the confidential document in the folder, and click OK to acknowledge the Access Is Denied message.

24. Click the Internet Explorer back button to navigate to the R and D Folder.

25. Double-click the Lab Procedures folders, and then double-click the Proprietary text file. Close the file.

26. Close Internet Explorer and switch to the local computer instance of Event Viewer.

27. In the tree pane, select Security, and press F5 to refresh the events in the details pane. You see many Success Audit entries for the JGeist*zz* account and a few Failed Audit entries.

> **QUESTION** *Briefly describe the risks associated with the auditing configuration on the Research Data folder. What would you do to minimize these risks?*

28. Double-click the top entry in the details pane of the Security log, and examine the details in the Event Properties box.

29. Click the down arrow on the Event Properties drop-down box, and view the successive entries.

> **QUESTION** *Why do you not see any entries for the access of the Proprietary text file?*

In the next steps, you will examine audit entries related to the Audit account management audit policy setting.

30. Click Start, select Run, type **runas /user:Contoso*dd*\JGeist*zz* "mmc dsa.msc"** in the Open text box, and click OK. When prompted, type **P@ssw0rd** at the command prompt, and press ENTER. Active Directory Users And Computers opens in the context of the JGeist*zz* account.

31. In the tree pane of Active Directory Users And Computers, navigate to the Location*zz*\R and D OU and select the R and D Groups OU.

    In the next step, the student sitting at the domain controller will clear the Security log. Wait until both you and your lab partner have completed step 30 and the Security log has been cleared before proceeding with step 32.

32. On Computer*xx*, switch to the first instance of Event Viewer, and clear the Security log without saving it.

33. In the details pane of Active Directory Users And Computers, double-click the GG Loc*zz* Lab Assistants group, click the Members tab, and remove the MLee*zz* account.

34. Switch to the instance of Event Viewer that is connected to Computer*xx*, and refresh the event details in the Security log. You should see a number of entries for the JGeist*xx* and JGeist*yy* accounts.

35. Double-click the JGeist*xx* and JGeist*yy* entries and examine the event details.

> **QUESTION** In the scenario, the manager states, "There is some setting or settings you have to enable if you want to audit file and Active Directory access." Why is this statement only partially true?

36. Close all open windows and log off.

EXERCISE 6.4: MANAGING PRIVATE KEYS FOR EFS ENCRYPTION

Estimated completion time: 20 minutes

The research scientists make extensive use of EFS to protect confidential files that are stored on laptops that are issued to them. One of the researchers needs help in backing up his private EFS encryption key. Your manager sends you the following memo:

"We have purchased a new laptop for Jim Geist and need to migrate his data to it. A number of files on his current laptop are encrypted with EFS. Although we have a number of recovery agents that could recover his EFS data, he prefers to configure the laptop himself to read the EFS data. He needs some help, however. Could you please show him how to export and import his personal EFS key?"

In the following exercise, you will configure EFS and then examine the steps that are required to maintain a backup of the key used for EFS.

1. Log on as Contoso*dd*\JGeist*zz*.
2. Click Start, select Run, type **explorer** in the Open text box, and click OK.
3. In Windows Explorer, create a folder named C:\EFS Test.
4. Right-click EFS Test, select Properties, and click Advanced.
5. In the Advanced Attributes dialog box, in the Compress or Encrypt attributes area, select the Encrypt Contents To Secure Data check box, and then click OK to close the dialog boxes.
6. In the EFS Test folder, create a text file named EncryptedFile. Note that the file and the folder are color-coded to indicate EFS encryption.
7. Open the file and type some text into it and then save it.

   In the following steps, you will verify that others cannot access the file.

8. On the taskbar, right-click the Internet Explorer icon, select Run As, and log on as Contoso*dd*\Admin*zz*.
9. In the Address box, type **c:\efs test**, press ENTER, and then double-click EncryptedFile.txt. You receive an Access Is Denied message.
10. Click OK to acknowledge the message and then close Notepad and Internet Explorer.

    In the next steps, you will examine and export the private key used to encrypt files.

11. Click Start, select Run, type **mmc** in the Open text box and click OK.
12. On the Console1 console, select Add/Remove Snap-In from the File menu.
13. In the Add/Remove Snap-In dialog box, click Add.
14. In the Add Standalone Snap-In, in the Available Standalone Snap-Ins list, select Certificates, click Add, and then click Close.
15. In the Add/Remove Snap-In dialog box, click OK.
16. From the File menu, select Save As.
17. In the Save As dialog box, select Desktop from the Save In drop-down list, type **Certificates** in the File Name text box, and click Save. The name of the console changes to Certificates.
18. In the Certificates console, in the tree pane, expand Certificates–Current User, expand Personal, and then select Certificates.
19. In the details pane, right-click the Jgeist*zz* certificate and select Properties.

QUESTION What purpose is listed for the certificate?

20. Click Cancel.
21. Right-click the Jgeist*zz* certificate, point to all tasks and select Export. The Certificate Export Wizard appears.
22. On the Welcome To The Certificate Export Wizard page, click Next.
23. On the Export Private Key page, select Yes, Export The Private Key, and click Next.
24. On the Export File Format page, select the Delete The Private Key If The Export Is Successful check box, and click Next.
25. On the Password page, type **P@sswr0rd** in the Password and Confirm Password text boxes, and then click Next.

26. On the File To Export page, type **MyEfsCert** in the File Name text box and click Next.
27. On the Completing The Certificate Export Wizard page, click Finish, and click OK to acknowledge the The Export Was Successful message.
28. Right-click the Jgeist*zz* certificate, select Delete, and click Yes to acknowledge the message that you will not be able to decrypt files.

    For the change to take effect, it is necessary to log off and log on again.
29. Close all open windows. When prompted, save the Certificates console. Log off, and log on again as Contoso*dd*\Jgeist*zz*.
30. Open Windows Explorer, navigate to the C:\EFS Test folder, and double-click EncryptedFile. You receive an Access Is Denied message. Click OK to close this message.
31. Close Notepad.
32. On the desktop, double-click the Certificates console you created earlier.
33. In the tree pane, right-click the Personal node, point to All Tasks, and select Import. The Certificate Import Wizard appears.
34. On the Welcome To The Certificate Import Wizard page, click Next.
35. On the File To Import page, click Browse.
36. In the Open dialog box, from the Files Of Type drop-down list, select Personal Information Exchange (*.pfx;*.p12). In the list of files, select MyEfsCert, and click Open.
37. On the File To Import page, click Next.
38. On the Password page, type **P@ssw0rd** in the Password box, select the Mark This Key As Exportable check box, and click Next.

    > **NOTE** *Do not select the check box option Enable Strong Key Protection. The exercise will fail if you choose this setting.*
39. On the Certificate Store page, click Next.
40. On the Completing The Certificate Import Wizard page, click Finish, and then click OK.
41. In the tree pane of the Certificates console, expand the Personal folder, and select Certificates. You should see your restored certificate in the details pane.
42. Open Windows Explorer, navigate to the EFS Test folder, and double-click EncryptedFile. The file opens as before.
43. Close all open windows and log off.

LAB REVIEW QUESTIONS

Estimated completion time: 20 minutes

1. You want to prevent users from changing permissions on files that they own, but they still need to be able to create and modify files. What permissions should you grant the users?
2. You do not wish users to have Full Control Allow permissions on files that they create. What can you do to ensure that users do not have Full Control permissions on these files?
3. What are users' effective permissions when NTFS and Share permissions are combined?
4. Your organization uses delegation extensively. What can you do to reduce the risk that delegation introduces?
5. Every day, an automated process exports log files from computers on your network and places them in a central location. What special considerations should you give to the locations where the log files are stored?
6. Why is it a good idea to audit successful and failed attempts to read the Security audit log?
7. In reviewing your audit logs, you notice a number of account lockout events (Event ID 539). However, the users whose accounts were locked out have not made requests to the Help Desk to have the lockout removed. Why haven't the users contacted the Help Desk, and what other information should you be paying attention to in analyzing the account lockout audit entries?
8. Why is it often advisable to limit the audit information that is generated for successful or failed attempts to access a file or folder?
9. You have given your users instructions for backing up the keys used for file encryption. What other special instructions should you provide to these users?

LAB CHALLENGE 6.1: DESIGNING A DATA ACCESS STRATEGY

Estimated completion time: 40 minutes

You are a network administrator for Contoso Pharmaceuticals. The company has provided a new server to host data from the Finance department. An administrator has created the top-level folder structure for the Finance department data, and you have been asked to create the data protection strategy for the finance department data. Your manager sends you an e-mail with the requirements for access to the finance department data. The e-mail states the following:

"We need you to design a data access and protection strategy for the Finance department data. As you know, the Finance department has recently been undergoing an internal restructuring. We have completed the OU design to accommodate this new structure and are in the process of implementing a new server to host the Finance department data. We have created the top-level folder design for the Finance department. We now need you to help us design the group objects and assign file and share permissions we will grant to those groups.

"If you look on the new server, you will see that folders for the Finance department reflect the four new divisions: Payroll, Accounts Payable, Accounts Receivable, and General Accounting. The new OU structure for the Finance department reflects these four divisions as well.

"According to meetings I have had with the Finance department, their data access has to meet the following requirements:

- All Finance directors must be able to read all data from other divisions.
- The division directors, team leads, and staff need to be able to read and modify files in their own division, but not in other divisions.
- No one except the Finance administrators should be able to change permissions on files.

"When you are designing the group and permission strategy, please keep in mind that we want to follow the AGDLP method for providing access to the data. Also, we want to prevent the possibility that unauthorized administrators can alter the permissions on files. If you are unfamiliar with who occupies what role in the Finance department, you will find that we are storing that information in Active Directory, which you can easily view in the description of the account objects in the Finance department OU."

Instructions

To complete this lab challenge, examine the objects in the Location*zz*\Finance OU and the folder structure under the Finance Folder on the C drive of your computer. Then, working with your lab partner, design a group strategy, which employs the AGDLP strategy and uses informative names. Then determine the NTFS and share permissions to grant each group. In devising the data access strategy for the Finance department, consider any additional actions you might take to reduce the risk of unauthorized changes to group membership or file permissions. If necessary, consult Chapter 6 of the textbook. When you are finished your design, if time permits, implement your design on your computers. At the end of the exercise, your instructor will take up your results as a class discussion.

LAB 7

HARDENING SERVERS

This lab contains the following exercises and activities:

- Exercise 7.1: Working with Security Templates
- Exercise 7.2: Using Security Templates To Configure Group Policy Objects
- Exercise 7.3: Configuring and Securing DNS Servers
- Lab Review Questions
- Lab Challenge 7.1: Designing a Secure DNS Infrastructure

SCENARIO

You are a network administrator for Contoso Pharmaceuticals. You have been assisting the recently formed security team with its analysis of and recommendations for the current infrastructure. In this lab, you will continue your work with the security team, assisting with analyzing computer security configuration settings, and configuring the Domain Name System (DNS) infrastructure to improve security.

After completing this lab, you will be able to:

- **Use the Security Templates and the Security Configuration and Analysis tools to modify, create, and implement security templates.**
- **Use the Security Configuration And Analysis tool to compare a current computer configuration against a security template.**
- **Use the Security Configuration and Analysis tool to document computer settings.**
- **Import security templates into a Group Policy object (GPO).**
- **Understand when it is appropriate to use the Security Configuration and Analysis tool to configure computer settings and when it is appropriate to use Group Policy.**
- **Use the Secedit command-line tool to generate a rollback template.**
- **Use security templates to disable services and configure permissions on services.**
- **Use Microsoft Network Monitor to analyze DNS query and zone transfer traffic.**

- **Mitigate common DNS threats.**
- **Configure standard zone transfers.**
- **Understand the effects of disabling recursion.**
- **Configure forwarding.**
- **Design a secure DNS infrastructure.**

Estimated lesson time: 125 minutes

BEFORE YOU BEGIN

To complete this lab, you will need to have done the following:

- Created a Member Servers organizational unit (OU) and moved the Computer*yy* member server object to the OU as instructed in steps 3 through 7 of Lab Exercise 3.4, "Using Group Policy To Configure Automatic Update Clients," in Lab 3, "Reducing the Risk of Software Vulnerabilities."

> **NOTE** In this lab, you will see the characters *dd*, *pp*, *xx*, *yy* and *zz*. These directions assume that you are working on computers configured in pairs and that each computer has a number.
>
> When you see *dd*, substitute the number used for your domain. When you see *pp*, substitute the number of your partner's computer. When you see *xx*, substitute the unique number assigned to the lower-numbered (odd-numbered) computer of the pair. When you see *yy*, substitute the unique number assigned to the higher-numbered (even-numbered) computer of the pair. When you see *zz*, substitute the number assigned to the computer that you are currently using. The following example assumes that the partner pair of computers has been assigned the names Computer05 and Computer06 and that you have been assigned Computer05.
>
> Computer*pp* = Computer06 = your partner's computer
>
> Computer*xx* = Computer05 = lower-numbered computer
>
> Computer*yy* = Computer06 = higher-numbered computer
>
> Computer*zz* = Computer05 = computer you are using
>
> Contoso*dd*.msft = Contoso03.msft = Active Directory directory service domain you are using

EXERCISE 7.1: WORKING WITH SECURITY TEMPLATES

Estimated completion time: 30 minutes

You are a network administrator for Contoso Pharmaceuticals. Although you and your team are very security-conscious, there is a lack of standardization in the environment, especially regarding the security configuration of computers that occupy similar roles. This lack of standardization has bothered you for some time, so you are pleased when your manager sends you the following e-mail:

"You are no doubt aware of the big security review going on here. The security team needs some assistance documenting the configuration of the servers throughout the company, and you will be joining the team. Currently, one of the goals of the team is to document how the current configuration of our servers differs from some security templates they are evaluating for deployment.

"The templates the security team is evaluating come from the Microsoft Windows Server 2003 Security Guide. I am not sure if you are aware of this guide. If you are interested, you should download a copy of it from *http://www.microsoft.com/technet/security/prodtech/Win2003/W2003HG/SGCH00.mspx*. My understanding is that even the NSA's policy is that the "High" security settings described in the guide track closely with the guidelines the NSA has historically recommended. In any event, the guide consists of security guidance and a number of tools and templates.

"The templates themselves represented recommended configurations for various server roles, such as domain controller, file server, bastion host, and so on. For each of these roles, the guide provides a legacy client, enterprise client, and high-security template.

"What we want to do is compare the current configuration of our servers with a couple of those templates, so we can do a further threat and risk analysis and develop our own standard baselines based on those templates and the specific requirements of our business.

"You will be working directly with the security team to document the server configurations and compare the server configurations with a number of security templates."

Configuring an MMC for Use To Manage Templates and Security Settings

In this section, you will use the Security Templates and the Security Configuration And Analysis tools to compare and document security configurations. You will first create a custom Microsoft Management Console (MMC) that contains both tools. Then you will use the tools to copy security templates and analyze the security templates against your current computer configuration. You will not apply any templates in this section.

1. Log on as Contoso*dd*\Admin*zz* using **P@ssword** as the password.
2. Open Windows Explorer, navigate to C:\Lab Manual\Lab 07, and copy the Security Templates folder to C:\Security Templates.

   This folder contains the security templates from the Windows Server 2003 Security Guide. The folder also contains a Microsoft Excel spreadsheet file that lists the configuration settings for each template.
3. Close Windows Explorer.
4. Click Start, select Run, type **mmc** in the Open text box, and click OK.
5. In Console1, select File, and select Add/Remove Snap-In.
6. In the Add/Remove Snap-In dialog box, click Add.
7. In the Add Standalone Snap-In dialog box, from the Available Standalone Snap-Ins list, select Security Configuration And Analysis, and then click Add.
8. In the Add Standalone Snap-In dialog box, from the Available Standalone Snap-Ins list, select Security Templates, click Add, and then click Close. Both the Security Configuration And Analysis and the Security Templates snap-ins appear in the Add/Remove Snap-In dialog box.
9. In the Add/Remove Snap-In dialog box, click OK.
10. In Console1, select File, and select Save As.
11. In the Save As dialog box, select Desktop from the Save In drop-down list, type **Security Configuration Toolset** in the File Name text box, and click Save. The name of the console changes to Security Configuration Toolset.
12. In the Security Configuration Toolset console tree, right-click Security Templates. Select New Template Search Path. If the option to select a

New Template Search Path is dimmed, verify that you have selected the Security Templates node.

13. In the Browse For Folder dialog box, expand My Computer, expand Local Disk (C:), select the Security Templates folder, and then click OK.
14. In the Security Configuration Toolset console tree, expand Security Templates, and then expand the C:\Security Templates folder.

    Because you should not modify the default templates, we will create copies of the High Security – Domain, High Security – Domain Controller, and the High Security – Member Server Baseline templates in steps 15 and 16.

15. Right-click the High Security – Domain Controller template, select Save As, type **ContosoHS-DC** in the File Name text box, and click Save.
16. Repeat step 15 to save the High Security – Domain template as ContosoHS – Domain and the High Security – Member Server Baseline template as ContosoHS – MSB.

Using Security Configuration and Analysis To Compare Template and Computer Settings

In this section, you will compare your computer's security settings with those defined in various templates. In steps 1 through 8, we will compare the settings in the ContosoHS – Domain template with the current computer configuration. Normally, we compare the settings in this template file with the settings on only a domain controller. The reason for this is that Account Policies for the domain can be specified only once for the domain. However, if you performed Exercise 5-2 and are sitting at the member server, you will have made some changes to the Account Policy settings of the member server. Because this template defines Account Policy settings, it is useful to use this template to compare Account Policy settings.

1. In the Security Configuration Toolset console, right-click Security Configuration And Analysis, and select Open Database.
2. In the Open Database dialog box, type **CP-HS-Domain** in the File Name text box, and then click Open. You can use the Open Database dialog box to create a new database or open an existing database. In this step, you are creating a new database to store the settings contained in a security template.

3. In the Import Template dialog box, select C:\Security Templates from the Look In drop-down list, select ContosoHS-Domain.inf, and then click Open.

> **NOTE** In the next step, make sure that you select Analyze Computer Now and do *not* select Configure Computer Now. If you were to select Configure Computer Now, this would result in applying the template's settings to your computer. You will not apply settings in this lab exercise by using Security Configuration And Analysis. Normally, you should use Security Configuration And Analysis only to configure settings *not* defined by Group Policy. Instead, you will apply settings by using Group Policy. Moreover, some of the settings in the various templates result in highly secure configurations that may cause problems with future lab exercises.

4. In the Security Configuration Toolset console, right-click Security Configuration And Analysis, and select Analyze Computer Now.
5. In the Perform Analysis dialog box, accept the default path and file name for the error log file, and click OK. The Analyzing System Security Progress box opens briefly.
6. When the analysis completes, expand Security Configuration And Analysis, expand Account Policies, and select Password Policy. Depending on the computer at which you are working and whether you performed Exercise 5.2, the graphic in the lab manual might differ from what you see on your computer.

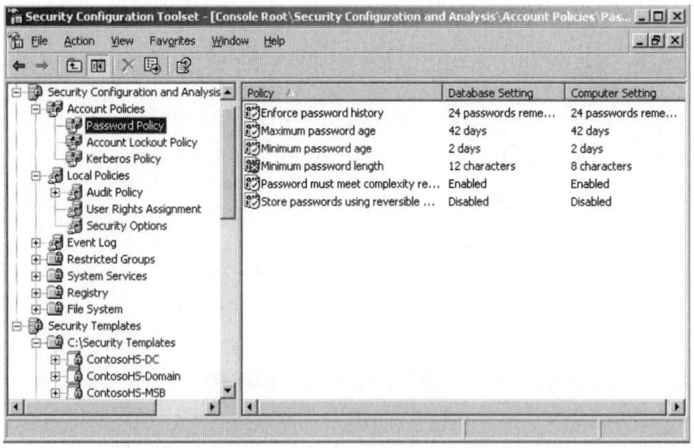

7. In the tree pane, select Account Lockout Policy and note that one or more policy settings contains a red "X" icon to indicate a discrepancy between the Computer Setting and the Database Setting.

QUESTION *Which column, the Database Setting or the Computer Setting, indicates the settings of the ContosoHS – Domain template?*

8. In the tree pane, select a number of other nodes and spend a few moments examining the discrepancies between the Database Settings and the Computer Settings. Note that many database settings are listed as Not Defined or Not Analyzed. The reason for this is that the ContosoHS-Domain.inf template primarily, but not exclusively, contains settings related to Account Policy.

   In the remaining steps, you will compare your current computer settings against a template that is specific to the computer role of your assigned computer. Pay attention to the instructions in the steps to ensure that you compare your computer settings with the appropriate template.

9. In the tree pane, right-click Security Configuration And Analysis, and Select Open Database.
10. In the Open Database dialog box, in the File Name box, enter either of the following names, depending on your computer role:
    a. On Computer*xx* (the domain controller), type **CP-HS-DC**.
    b. On Computer*yy* (the member server), type **CP-HS-MSB**.
11. Click Open, and select the following template depending on your computer role.
    a. On Computer*xx*, select the ContosoHS-DC.inf template file, and click Open.
    b. On Computer*yy*, select the ContosoHS-MSB.inf template file, and click Open.
12. In the console tree, right-click Security Configuration And Analysis, select Analyze Computer Now, and click OK in the Performing Analysis dialog box. The Analyzing System Security progress box opens briefly.
13. In the console tree, expand Local Policies, and select Security Options.
14. In the details pane, examine the Database Setting and Computer Setting columns, and answer the following question:

    QUESTION *What are the meanings of the red "X," green check, and exclamation-point visual flags?*

15. In the details pane, double-click the entry Audit: Shutdown System Immediately If Unable To Log Security Audits, select the Disabled option button, and click OK. Note that the visual flag for the setting becomes a green check.

    QUESTION *Briefly explain why enabling the setting Audit: Shutdown System Immediately If Unable To Log Security Events may itself represent a security vulnerability.*

16. In the console tree, select System Services, and note the descriptions in the Startup and Permission columns.
17. In the details pane, double-click Telnet, and note the value for the Service startup mode in the Telnet Properties dialog box.
18. Click Start, select Run, type **cmd** in the Open text box, and click OK.
19. At the command prompt, type **sc qc TlntSvr**, press ENTER, and note that the START_TYPE for the Telnet Service is the same as the Service Startup Mode listed in the Security Configuration And Analysis tool.
20. Close the command prompt window.
21. In the Telnet Properties dialog box, click Edit Security, and note the permissions in the Database Security For Telnet dialog box.
22. Move the Database Security For Telnet dialog box so that you can view the Telnet Properties dialog box, and then in the Telnet Properties dialog box, click View Security.
23. Compare the permissions in the Last Analyzed Security For Telnet with the permissions in the Database Security For Telnet.

    In the Last Analyzed Security For Telnet, on the domain controller, you will see an unknown object with a security identifier (SID) listed as S-1-5-32-547. As a point of information, this SID represents the Power Users group, which exists on stand-alone and member servers, but not on domain controllers. Note that the member server correctly displays the Power Users group.

24. Click Cancel to close the Database Security For Telnet, Last Analyzed Security For Telnet, and Telnet Properties dialog boxes. Leave the Security Configuration Toolset console open for the next section.

Documenting Differences Between Templates and Computer Configuration

In this section, you will document the difference between a security template and the computer configuration in a delimited file that you could export to a database or spreadsheet.

1. In the Security Configuration And Analysis console tree, select and then right-click Audit Policy. Select Export List.
2. In the Export List dialog box, verify that Text (Tab Delimited) (*.txt) is selected in the Save As Type drop-down list, type **Audit Policy** in the File Name text box, and click Save.
3. Repeat step 2 and export the User Rights Assignment and the Security Options settings to tab delimited text files named User Rights.txt and Security Options.txt respectively.
4. Open Windows Explorer, navigate to My Documents and double-click to open each of the text files you just created.

> **QUESTION** *Why do you want to export these settings as tab delimited, rather than as comma-delimited files?*

5. Close all instances of Notepad, and close Windows Explorer. Minimize the Security Configuration Toolset console.

EXERCISE 7.2: USING SECURITY TEMPLATES TO CONFIGURE GROUP POLICY OBJECTS

Estimated completion time: 30 minutes

You have completed your documentation showing the differences between server configurations and the high-security templates from the Microsoft Windows Server 2003 Security Guide. The team leader for the security team sends you the following e-mail:

"Thanks for your work documenting server configurations against the security templates. We have done some analysis of the computer configurations and the security templates, but have not finished. The current configuration of many of the computers is pretty solid, but we have noticed that the member servers and the domain controllers receive their computer settings through a number of group policies.

"What we would like to do is create a single template each for the member servers and domain controllers based on the current configurations of these computers. We will make a few changes to the security templates. Then, we will apply the security template settings in a single GPO linked to the appropriate OU. After we have done this, we would like to unlink the redundant GPOs from the OUs.

"One way to create a security template that is based on the current configuration is to use the Secedit /Generaterollback command."

Using Secedit to Create a Rollback Security Template

In this section, you will create a security template rollback file by using the command-line tool Secedit with the /Generaterollback option. The primary purpose of the Generaterollback option is to create an easy way to reverse changes that you apply through the Security Configuration And Analysis tool or the Secedit command. However, we can also use the /Generaterollback option to create a baseline security template that is based on the current configuration of a computer.

Note that some of the instructions will differ, depending on your assigned computer. Please pay close attention to the instructions in the steps that follow. In this section, you will see the use of an asterisk (*) in the instructions. The asterisk is used as a placeholder to indicate the portion of the name that is specific to your computer's assigned role.

1. Open a command prompt window.
2. At the command prompt, type **cd My Documents\Security\Database** and press ENTER.
3. Depending on your assigned computer, carefully type the following command, and press ENTER:
    a. On Computer*xx*, type **Secedit /generaterollback /db CP-HS-DC.sdb /cfg "C:\Security Templates\ContosoHS-DC.inf" /rbk CP-DCrollback.inf /log CP-DCrollback.log**.
    b. On Computer*yy*, type **Secedit /generaterollback /db CP-HS-MSB.sdb /cfg "C:\Security Templates\ContosoHS-MSB.inf" / rbk CP-MSrollback.inf /log CP-MSrollback.log**.

    You are notified that rollback is not supported for file and registry security.

4. Press Y when prompted to continue, and then press ENTER. The rollback template is generated. This file contains your computer's current security configuration settings.
5. Close the command prompt window, open Windows Explorer, and navigate to the My Documents\Security\Database folder.
6. Copy the *rollback.inf file to C:\Security Templates.
7. Navigate to the C:\Security Templates folder, and rename the *rollback.inf security template file as follows:
    a. On Computer*xx*, rename the file to CP-DCbaseline.inf.
    b. On Computer*yy*, rename the file to CP-MSbaseline.inf.
8. Maximize the Security Configuration Toolset console, expand the Security Templates node in the console tree, and select the *baseline.inf file you just renamed. If the file does not appear in the console, right-click Security Templates and select Refresh.
9. In the console tree, under the *baseline node, expand Account Policies, and select Password Policy, Account Lockout Policy, and Kerberos Policy. Notice that the settings within each of these policies are all listed as Not Defined. The reason for this is that in a domain environment, you can specify these policies only once for the entire domain. These policies are defined in a GPO that is linked to the domain, usually the Default Domain Policy.
10. In the console tree, expand Local Policies, and select Audit Policy, User Rights Assignment, and Security Options and examine the settings.
11. In the console tree, right-click Security Configuration And Analysis, and select Open Database.
12. In the Open Database dialog box, type **CP-DCBaseline** or **CP-MSBaseline**, depending on the role of your assigned computer, in the File name text box, and click Open.
13. In the Import Template dialog box, select the CP-DCBaseline.inf or the CP-MSBaseline.inf file, depending on the file name you created in step 7, and click Open.
14. Right-click Security Configuration And Analysis, select Analyze Computer Now, and click OK in the Perform Analysis dialog box.
15. When the analysis completes, examine the database and computer settings in Account Policies and Local Policies.

Modifying Security Templates

In this section, you will modify the baseline security template and then use the baseline template as the basis for a GPO.

1. In the console tree, under the Security Templates node, expand the CP-DCBaseline or the CP-MSBaseline security template (depending on your assigned computer role), expand Local Policies, and select User Rights Assignment.
2. In the details pane, double-click Shut Down The System.
3. In the Template Security Policy Setting dialog box, ensure that the Define These Policy Settings In The Template check box is selected.
4. Select Backup Operators, and then click Remove.
5. On Computer*yy*, select Power Users, and then click Remove; on Computer*xx*, select Print Operators, and then click Remove.
6. Click OK to close the Template Security Policy Setting dialog box.
7. In the console tree, select Security Options, and then, in the details pane, double-click Interactive Logon: Do Not Display Last User Name.
8. In the Interactive Logon: Do Not Display Last User Name dialog box, click Enabled, and then click OK.

   In the details pane, notice that Enabled appears to the right of Do Not Display Last User Name.

9. In the console tree, select Security Options, and then, in the details pane, double-click Interactive Logon: Message Text For Users Attempting To Log On.
10. In the Interactive Logon: Message Text For Users Attempting To Log On dialog box, ensure that the Define This Policy Setting In The Template check box is selected. In the text box, type **Unauthorized access is prohibited. If you are not an authorized user, do not attempt to log on.**, and then click OK.

    QUESTION Why is it a good idea to include a warning for unauthorized users who attempt to log on using stolen or cracked credentials?

11. In the details pane, double-click Interactive Logon: Message Title For Users Attempting To Log On.

12. In the Interactive Logon: Message Title For Users Attempting To Log On dialog box, ensure that the Define This Policy Setting In The Template check box is selected, type **LEGAL NOTICE: Authorized Users Only**, and then click OK.

    In the details pane, notice that the message settings that you defined appear.

13. In the console tree, select System Services, and then in the details pane, double-click Telnet.
14. In the Template Security Policy Setting dialog box, ensure that the Define This Policy Setting In The Template check box is selected and that the Startup Mode is set to Disabled, and then click Edit Security.
15. On Computer*xx*, in the Security For Telnet dialog box, in the Group Or User Names box, select the Account Unknown (S-1-5-32-547) object, and click Remove. Click OK.
16. On Computer*xx*, in the Security For Telnet dialog box, in the Group Or User Names box, select the Power Users object, click Remove, and click OK.
17. In the Telnet Properties dialog box, click OK.
18. Right-click the CP-DCBaseline or the CP-MSBaseline security template, and select Save to save your changes.
19. Close all open windows. When you are prompted to save the console settings for the Security Configuration Toolset console, click Yes.

Importing Security Templates into GPOs

In this section, you will create a GPO, import the security template settings into the Group Policy, and then remove the links for redundant GPOs.

1. Click Start, point to Administrative Tools, and select Group Policy Management.
2. Perform either of the following steps, depending on your assigned computer:
    a. On Computer*xx*, in the console tree, expand the Domain Controllers OU, right-click the Domain Controllers OU and select Create And Link A GPO Here. Type **DC Baseline GPO** for the name, and click OK.

   b. On Computeryy, in the console tree, expand the Member Servers OU, right-click the Member Servers OU and select Create And Link A GPO Here. Type **MS Baseline GPO** for the name, and click OK.

3. Right-click the * Baseline GPO, and select Edit.
4. In the Group Policy Object Editor, in the console tree, navigate to Computer Configuration\Windows Settings. Right-click Security Settings, and select Import Policy.
5. In the Import Policy dialog box, select either the CP-DCBaseline or the CP-MSBaseline security template, depending on your assigned computer, and click Open. The Group Policy Management Console imports the settings in your custom security template into your new GPO.
6. Close the Group Policy Object Editor.

   Because there are numerous Group Policies linked to the OU, you must configure the order of Group Policy precedence to ensure that the settings in the new GPO will be applied in the case of a conflict between settings.

7. In the console details pane, select the * Baseline GPO object, and click the double up-arrow to move the Group Policy to the top of the list.

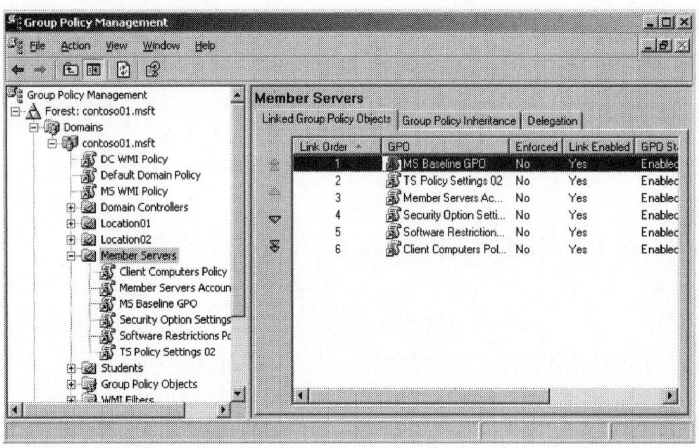

8. In the console tree, under the Domain Controllers OU or the Member Servers OU, right-click all the extra GPO links, except for the Default Domain Controllers Policy link or the * Baseline GPO link, and select Link Enabled to disable this setting.

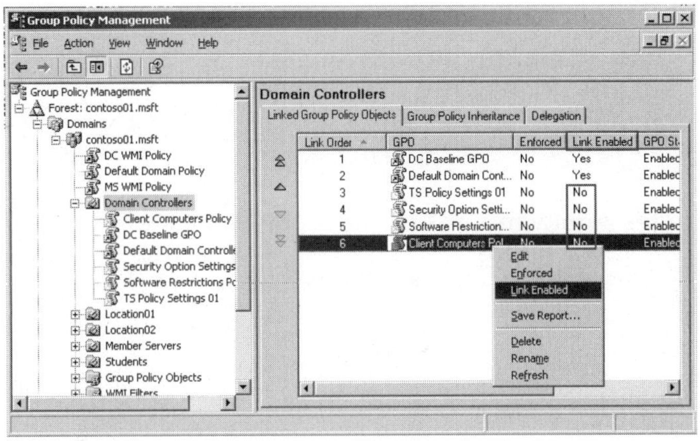

Only two GPO links should be enabled on the Domain Controllers OU, the Default Domain Controllers Policy and the DC Baseline GPO. Only one link should be enabled on the Member Servers OU, the MS Baseline GPO. Note that the Link Enabled column displays whether the link is enabled or not.

9. Open a command prompt window.
10. At the command prompt, type **gpupdate /target:computer /force**, and press ENTER.
11. When the refresh of the computer policy completes, close all open windows, save any settings or files if prompted, and log off.
12. In the Welcome To Windows dialog box, press CTRL+ALT+DEL. The logon message that you implemented in the Group Policy appears.
13. Click OK. The Log On To Windows dialog box appears. Notice that the User Name text box is empty.
14. Log on as Contoso*dd*\Admin*zz*.

> **IMPORTANT** Because the current configuration is not optimal for a lab environment on test computers, unlink the *Baseline GPO to restore the computers to a basic configuration. You must unlink the * Baseline GPO for Lab 9, "Designing a Public Key Infrastructure," to work correctly. Please make sure you complete the remaining steps in this section to unlink the GPO.

15. Click Start, point to Administrative Tools, and select Group Policy Management.
16. In the console tree, under the Domain Controllers OU or the Member Servers OU, right-click all the extra GPO links, except for the Default

Domain Controllers Policy link, and select Link Enabled to disable these Group Policies.

Make sure that the value in the Link Enabled column displays "No" to indicate that the * Baseline GPO is not enabled.

17. Open a command prompt window.
18. At the command prompt, type **gpupdate /target:computer /force**, and press ENTER.
19. Close all open windows.

EXERCISE 7.3: CONFIGURING AND SECURING DNS SERVERS

Estimated completion time: 50 minutes

The security team at Contoso Pharmaceuticals has asked you to review the configuration of the DNS servers that are used for name resolution on the internal network and the Internet. In particular, the security team is concerned about the presence of vulnerabilities that would allow an attacker to "footprint" any DNS records by performing a complete zone transfer, revealing all the DNS records stored in a particular zone. Also, the security team would like your recommendations regarding the rules they should implement on the firewall to allow specific DNS traffic. One of your concerns regarding DNS name resolution is the presence of a forest trust with an external organization. The forest trust requires that you be able to resolve DNS records of the external organization.

Analyzing DNS Traffic

In this section, you will use Microsoft Network Monitor to gain an understanding of DNS traffic. The version of Network Monitor you will use is the one that ships with Microsoft Windows Server 2003. This version of Network Monitor has several limitations. The primary limitation is that it uses the Network Driver Interface Specification (NDIS) local-only mode, rather than promiscuous mode. This means that it can capture traffic that occurs only between itself and other hosts. It cannot capture all traffic on a particular segment (which in any event might be of limited use on a switched network segment). However, this can also be an advantage in that this version of Network Monitor does not require a network adapter that is capable of promiscuous mode. Other limitations include an inability to edit and transmit frames and an inability to add additional protocol parsers, for example, to capture and analyze wireless network traffic. A full version of Network Monitor ships with Microsoft Systems Management Server (SMS).

> **NOTE** A number of the steps that follow require coordination with your lab partner. Please note the instructions where you are asked to wait for your partner before proceeding and note the instructions where only one person is asked to do something.

1. Click Start, point to Administrative Tools, and select Network Monitor.
2. In the Microsoft Network Monitor dialog box, click OK to acknowledge that you have to specify a network on which to capture data.
3. In the Select A Network dialog box, expand Local Computer, select Local Area Connection, and click OK. Microsoft Network Monitor opens.

   The student assigned to the member server (Computer*yy*) will now open a command prompt window and prepare a number of commands to execute. Perform steps 4 through 10 *only* on Computer*yy*. Just before the student assigned to Computer*yy* executes the prepared commands, you will both start capturing traffic in Network Monitor for analysis.

4. On Computer*yy*, open a command prompt window.
5. Open a second command prompt window.
6. In the second command prompt window, type **nslookup**, and press ENTER. Nslookup enters interactive mode.
7. At the Nslookup prompt, type **ls –d contoso*dd*.msft**, but do *not* press ENTER.
8. Switch to the first command prompt window, type **ping computer*xx*.contoso*dd*.msft**, and press ENTER to generate some traffic between the two computers. This step may be necessary to eliminate any possible Server Message Block traffic from the capture.
9. At the first command prompt window, type **ipconfig /flushdns**, and press ENTER to clear the local DNS resolver cache.
10. At the first command prompt window, type **ping computer*xx*.contoso*dd*.msft**, but do *not* press ENTER.

    Both students should perform the following step.

11. Switch to Network Monitor, and, from the Capture menu, select Start. Network Monitor starts to capture data.

    When both students have started capturing data, the student working at Computer*yy* will execute the prepared commands to generate DNS traffic.

12. On Computer*yy*, switch to the first command prompt window, and press ENTER to ping computer*xx*.contoso*dd*.msft.

13. Switch to the second command prompt window, and press ENTER to perform a DNS zone transfer of records from computer*xx*.contoso*dd*.msft.

    Both students should perform the following steps.

14. From the Capture menu of Network Monitor, select Stop And View. The Capture: 1 (Summary) window appears.

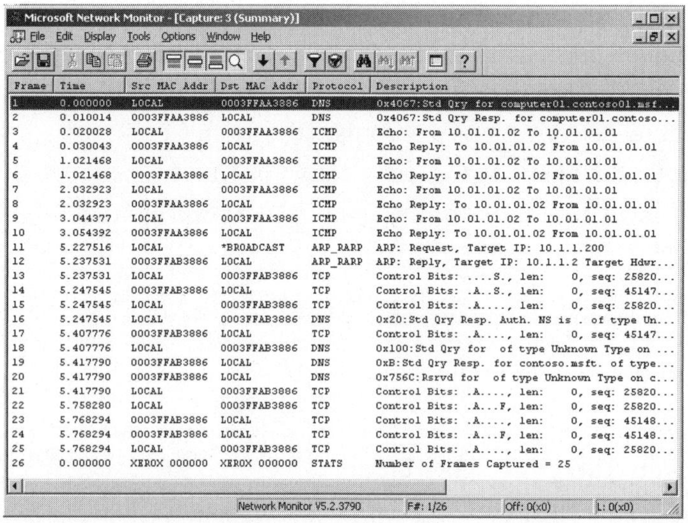

In the following steps, you will examine the details of the DNS traffic. If you have difficulty finding the data in the steps that follow, you can open a prepared capture named Lab07Dns.cap in the C:\Lab Manual\Lab 07 folder. To open the file, in the Microsoft Network Monitor console, select Open from the File menu, navigate to the C:\Lab Manual\Lab 07 folder, select the Lab07Dns.cap file, and select Open.

15. In the capture summary window, double-click the first frame that lists DNS in the Protocol column. The Detail and Hex panes open.

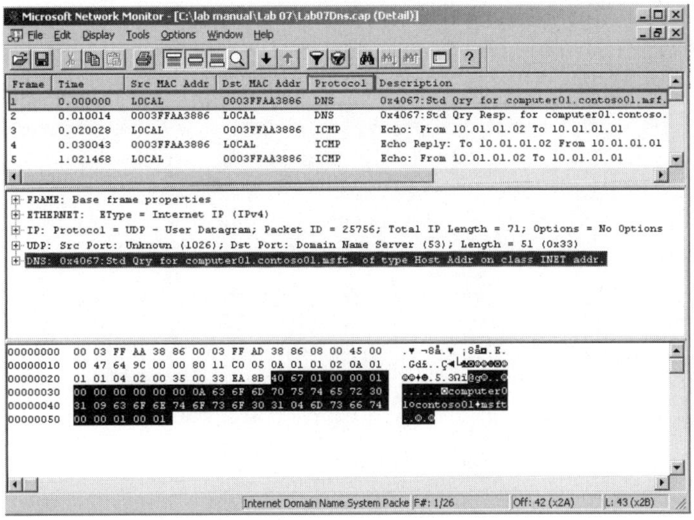

16. In the Detail pane, expand the UDP header, and answer the following questions.

> **QUESTION** What are the source and destination ports listed for the DNS query? Hint: Examine the Src Port and Dst Port information in the first line of the UDP header.

17. In the Summary pane (the top pane), select the DNS frame immediately below the first DNS frame.

> **QUESTION** What are the source and destination ports that are listed in this frame?

18. In the Detail pane, expand the DNS header and note the data that is included in the response to the DNS query. You should see the IP address of Computer*xx* in the DNS\DNS: Answer Section portion of the frame.

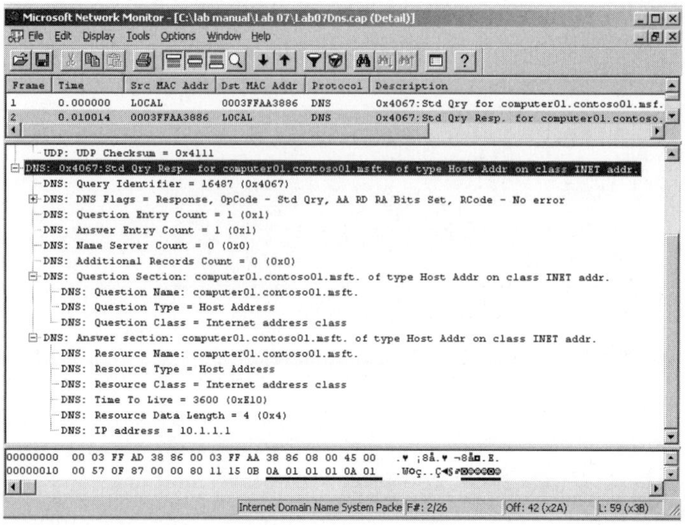

19. In the Summary pane, locate and select the first DNS frame immediately below the frames that list ICMP in the Protocol column.

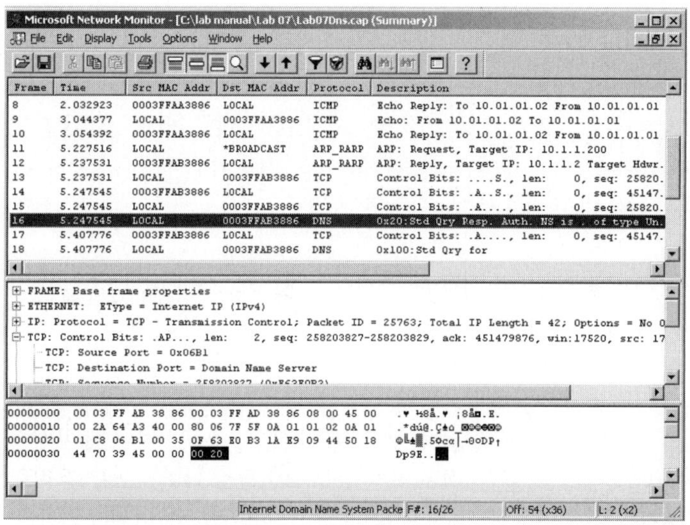

QUESTION What protocol and destination port are used for this DNS traffic?

20. Press the DOWN ARROW on the keyboard and examine the frames immediately below.

QUESTION What frame(s) list the zone transfer traffic from instructor01.contoso.msft? Hint: Look for frames that refer to a query of "type SOA" in the Description column.

QUESTION What is the length of the frame that lists the zone transfer traffic? (Optionally, what is the maximum size of a UDP packet?)

QUESTION *Why does the DNS configuration of instructor01.contoso.msft represent a security vulnerability?*

21. Close Network Monitor. If you are prompted to save entries in the address database or to save the capture, click No.
22. On Computeryy, close the command prompt windows.

Auditing DNS Server Configuration

In this section, you will review the configuration of your DNS server and examine a number of settings that you will change in a subsequent section.

Because there is only one DNS server per student pair, both students will perform different steps to configure the DNS server. Make sure that if there is more than one student per pair of computers that you follow the instructions in this section and subsequent sections regarding the identity of the student who should perform specific steps.

1. Click Start, point to Administrative Tools, and select DNS.
2. On Computeryy, in the Connect To DNS Server dialog box, select The Following Computer option, type **computer*xx*** in the text box, and click OK. The dnsmgmt - [DNS] console opens.
3. In the DNS console, select Help Topics from the Help menu. You will use the DNS help file to help guide you through parts of this lab exercise.
4. In the Microsoft Management Console containing the DNS help files, click the Search tab, type "**securing the dns server service**" (include the quotes in the query string) and click List Topics. Three topics are shown in the Select Topic box.
5. In the Select Topic box, double-click the Security Information For DNS topic and answer the following questions by reviewing the contents of this topic and the Securing The DNS Server Service topic.

   QUESTION *What is footprinting, and what can you do to mitigate the threat?*

   QUESTION *What is redirection, and how is this threat mitigated?*

6. Minimize the Microsoft Management Console containing the DNS help file to refer to it as necessary throughout the lab exercise.

In the next few steps, you will review the configuration of your DNS server.

7. In the DNS console tree, right-click Computer*xx*, select Properties, and then click the Advanced tab.

   QUESTION What is the default setting for Secure Cache Against Pollution?

   QUESTION What would be the effect if you were to select the Disable Recursion (Also Disable Forwarders) check box? For example, what DNS records would be returned by the DNS server in response to a DNS query?

8. Click the Root Hints tab.

   QUESTION What is the purpose of the root hints?

9. Click the Forwarders tab.

   Note that the Forwarders tab contains an entry that points to the IP address of the instructor's computer. Because of this configuration and some additional configuration on the instructor's computer, you are able to resolve names to IP addresses in the classroom lab.

10. Click Cancel to close the Computer*xx* Properties dialog box.
11. In the DNS console tree, expand Computer*xx*, expand Forward Lookup Zones, and select Contoso*dd*.msft. You will see a number of DNS records in the details pane. These records include the Start of Authority (SOA) and the Name Server (NS) record, along with Host (A) records.
12. Right-click the Host (A) record for Computer*zz*, select Properties, and click the Security tab.

    QUESTION What does the presence of the Security tab tell you about the zone type?

13. Click Advanced, and then click the Owner tab.

    QUESTION What object is listed as the current owner of the DNS record? Is there a difference between the owner of the record for the even-numbered and odd-numbered computers?

14. Click Cancel, and then click Cancel again to close the Computer*zz* Properties dialog box.
15. In the DNS console tree, right-click Contoso*dd*.msft, and select Properties.

    Note that, on the General tab, the zone type is Active Directory Integrated and that Dynamic Updates is configured as Secure only.
16. Click the Zone Transfers tab.

    Note that, on the Zone Transfers tab, the setting is to allow zone transfers to any server. This configuration is part of the lab setup and is not the default configuration for DNS. The default configuration of DNS on Microsoft Windows Server 2003 does not allow zone transfers to any host.
17. Leave the Zone Transfers tab visible for the next section.

Securing Zone Transfer Traffic

In this section, you will make a number of configuration changes to the DNS server to secure zone transfer traffic. You will also configure a secondary zone that contains your partner domain's DNS zone information. Your partner domain is the one with which you established a forest trust in "Exercise 5.3: Establishing a Forest Trust with Selective Authentication." However, if there are an odd number of student domains, it is preferable for one student pair to double up with another student pair and perform the labs on an even number of domains. If you have an odd number of domains, your instructor will provide instructions on which two student pairs should sit together for the remaining steps in this exercise.

If you did not perform Exercise 5.3 or if you removed the forest trust, your instructor will assign you another partner pair to work with in this lab exercise. Before proceeding, enter the partner domain information in the following table. Refer to the table when you encounter instructions that use the *pd*, *px*, and *py* variables. For example, if you are partnered with the Contoso05.msft domain and you are asked to ping computer*py*.contoso*pd*.msft, you would type **ping computer10.contoso05.msft**.

Partner Name Variables	Fully Qualified Domain Name (FQDN)
Partner domain: Contoso*pd*.msft	Example: Contoso16.msft
Domain controller in partner domain: Computer*px*.contoso*pd*.msft	Example: Computer31.contoso16.msft
Member server in partner domain: Computer*py*.contoso*pd*.msft	Example: Computer32.contoso16.msft

1. On Computer*yy*, open a command prompt window, type **nslookup**, and press ENTER.
2. At the nslookup prompt, type **ls -t contoso*dd*.msft**, and press ENTER to verify that Computer*xx* still responds to zone transfer requests from your computer.

   In the next steps, you will reconfigure the zone transfer settings so that Computer*xx* will respond to zone transfer requests from only computer*px*.contoso*pd*.msft (the domain controller of your partner domain). You will first use Nslookup to determine the IP address of the domain controller in the partner domain.
3. On Computer*xx*, open a command prompt window, type **nslookup**, and press ENTER.
4. On both computers, at the Nslookup prompt, type **set querytype=ns**, and press ENTER.
5. At the Nslookup prompt, type **contoso*pd*.msft**, and press ENTER, and record the Internet Protocol (IP) address of computer*px*.contoso*pd*.msft.
6. Leave the Nslookup prompt open.
7. On Computer*xx*, switch to the DNS console, and on the Zone Transfers tab, select the Only To The Following Servers option, type the IP address from step 5 in the IP Address box, click Add, and then click Apply.
8. On Computer*yy*, at the Nslookup prompt, type **ls -t contoso*dd*.msft**, and press ENTER to verify that Computer*xx* does not respond to requests from your computer.

   Wait until the students in your partner domain have completed step 8 before proceeding.

9. On both computers, at the Nslookup prompt, type **server computer*px*.contoso*pd*.msft** , and press ENTER.

10. At the Nslookup prompt, type **ls -d contoso*pd*.msft**, and press ENTER to verify that Computer*px* will respond to zone transfer requests from Computer*xx*. Note that this command will fail on Computer*yy*.

11. On Computer*xx*, switch to the DNS console, and, on the Zone Transfers tab, click Notify.

12. In the Notify dialog box, verify that the Select The Following Servers option is selected. In the IP Address text box, enter the IP address from step 5, click Add, and then click OK.

> **QUESTION** The default setting for Notify is for any server listed in the Name Servers tab. Is this an appropriate setting for an Active Directory–Integrated zone? Briefly explain your answer.

13. On both computers, in the Contoso*dd.msft* Properties dialog box, click OK.

    Perform steps 14 through 19 on Computer*yy*.

14. On Computer*yy*, in the DNS console, right-click Forward Lookup Zones, and select New Zone. The New Zone Wizard appears.

15. On the Welcome To The New Zone Wizard page, click Next.

16. On the Zone Type page, select Secondary Zone, and click Next.

17. On the Zone Name page, type **contoso*pd*.msft** in the Zone Name text box, and click Next.

18. On the Master DNS Servers page, type the IP address from step 5 in the IP Address text box and click Add. Click Next.

19. On the Completing The New Zone Wizard Page, click Finish.

20. On both computers, in the DNS console tree, select the Contoso*pd*.msft forward lookup zone. You should see the DNS records from your partner's domain zone. Do not proceed with the next section until you can see the records from your domain partner's zone.

> **QUESTION** Assume that you are using standard DNS zone transfer mechanism to replicate between a primary and secondary DNS server. Should you take further steps to protect this traffic?

Disabling Recursion

In this section, you will examine the effect of disabling recursion on your DNS server. These steps should be performed on Computer*xx*.

1. On Computer*xx*, in the DNS console tree, right-click Computer*xx*, select Properties, and then click the Advanced tab.
2. In the Server Options box, select the Disable Recursion (Also Disables Forwarders) check box, and click Apply.
3. On both computers, open another command prompt window. Type **ping instructor01.contoso.msft** and press ENTER. The Ping command fails.
4. Type **ping computer*py*.contoso*pd*.msft**, and press ENTER. The Ping command is successful.

> **QUESTION** *Why does the Ping command fail for the instructor computer and succeed for the domain partner computer?*

5. On Computer*xx*, switch to the DNS console, and, in the Server Options box on the Advanced tab, clear the Disable Recursion (Also Disables Forwarders) check box, and click Apply.

> **QUESTION** *In what situation(s) would it be useful to disable recursion on a DNS Server?*

Configuring Forwarding

In this section, you will configure your DNS with the IP address of a DNS forwarding server that can perform name resolution. You will first delete the secondary zone you created previously. Perform steps 1 through 8 on Computer*yy*.

1. On Computer*yy*, switch to the DNS console, and, in the console tree, select the Contoso*pd*.msft secondary zone (be careful not to select your own zone), and press DELETE.
2. In the DNS dialog box prompting you for confirmation to delete the zone, click Yes.
3. In the DNS console, right-click Computer*xx*, select Properties, and click the Forwarders tab.
4. On the Forwarders tab, click New.

5. In the New Forwarders dialog box, type **contoso*pd*.msft**, and click OK.

6. With the Contoso*pd*.msft zone selected in the DNS domain box, type the IP address of computer*px*.contoso*pd*.msft in the Selected domain's forwarder IP address list, and click Add.

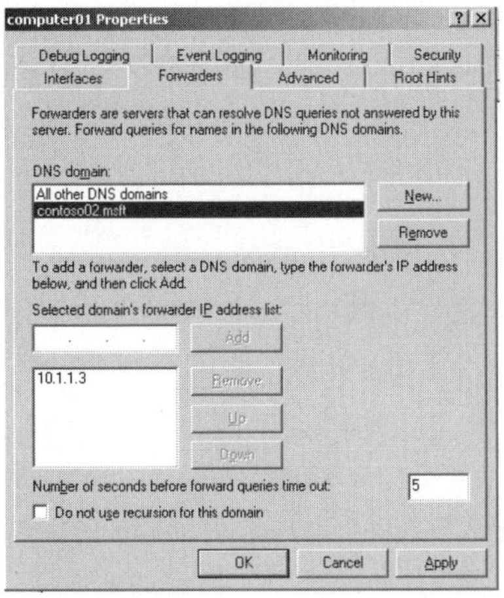

7. In the DNS domain box, select All Other DNS domains, and then, under the Selected Domain's Forwarder IP Address List, click Remove to remove 10.1.1.200 as a forwarder.

8. Click Apply.

9. On both computers, switch to a command prompt window and type **ping instructor01.contoso.msft**, and press ENTER. The Ping command fails.

10. Type **ping computer*py*.contoso*pd*.msft**, and press ENTER. The Ping command is successful.

11. On Computer*yy*, switch to the DNS console, and, in the Forwarders tab, ensure that All Other Domains is selected in the DNS domain box, type **10.1.1.200** in the Selected domain's forwarder IP address list, click Add, and then click Apply.

12. Switch to a command prompt, and type **ping instructor01.contoso.msft**, and press ENTER. The Ping command is successful.

    Make sure that you can ping the instructor's computer by using its FQDN before you perform step 13.

13. Close all open windows and log off.

LAB REVIEW QUESTIONS

Estimated completion time: 15 minutes

1. You have a number of servers in a screened subnet that are configured as members of a workgroup. What tools or tools should you use to deploy security configuration settings?
2. You need to perform a security analysis of a number of computers during off hours. What tool should you use?
3. You have an Active Directory domain. All computers are configured with a Windows 2000 or later operating system. In what circumstances would you use Security Configuration and Analysis to configure security settings?
4. You have configured a number of settings on a member server by using Secedit. The Active Directory object for the member server is placed in an OU that has a number of group policies linked to it. In addition, group policies are linked to the domain and the site. In case of a conflict between the computer setting and a Group Policy setting, what Group Policy setting will take precedence? What is the order of Group Policy processing?
5. You have implemented Active Directory–Integrated DNS zones. A network administrator tells you that you should configure the DNS notify settings to ensure timely replication of DNS changes between DNS servers. What's wrong with his statement?
6. You have implemented a Standard Primary zone on a DNS Server in the screened subnet. During the configuration of the zone, you enabled dynamic updates. What vulnerabilities did you introduce with this setting?
7. You have implemented an Active Directory forest and have established a forest trust with an external organization. Your internal clients must be able to resolve names in the external forest. Your corporate security policy states that the DNS service on domain controllers should not be capable of providing Internet name resolution. How would you configure the DNS service on your domain controllers?

LAB CHALLENGE 7.1: DESIGNING A SECURE DNS INFRASTRUCTURE

Estimated completion time: 50 minutes

You are a network administrator for Contoso Pharmaceuticals and have recently been transferred temporarily to the Contoso security team. Yesterday, a serious security incident occurred and the CIO calls you to a meeting regarding the incident. At the meeting, he states the following:

"I know you are aware that our Web site was unavailable for most of the day yesterday and that, furthermore, most of our staff in the head office had little or no Internet access. I don't even want to think about the losses, not just in terms of lost business and productivity, but the damage to our reputation and the loss of confidence in us with our business partners and customers. In terms of impact, this ranks right up there. In fact, we did a quick ad hoc threat and risk analysis after the event with our security consultant and the risk rating is extremely high.

"Let me give you some background. At around 8:00 A.M., the two DNS servers in our screened subnet were flooded with bogus queries from a variety of locations. Obviously, somebody or some group with a grudge against us set up a number of zombie servers to launch the attack–it has all the characteristics of being a well-thought, coordinated attack carried out by motivated and knowledgeable individuals. Anyway, our DNS servers became so busy they could not respond to legitimate queries from both internal users wanting to access the Internet and from customers and business partners wishing to access our Web site. From there, things just got worse. The upstream router connecting us with the ISP suffered a denial of service as well.

"I don't have to tell you just how serious this situation is, nor do we need to do another risk and threat analysis before we act. We know that the DNS and the routing infrastructure now represent a serious vulnerability.

"What I would like you to do is draw up a new DNS infrastructure design that provides as much confidentiality, integrity, and availability as possible. I have some thoughts on the issue.

"First, users on the internal network should not be performing DNS queries to resolve Internet addresses. We have a server running Microsoft Internet Security and Acceleration (ISA) Server, and I don't understand why so many computers are not configured as Web proxy or Firewall clients.

"Second, the Active Directory domain controllers should not be able to resolve Internet names at all, nor should they be accessible from the Internet.

"Third, on the DNS servers that are exposed to the Internet, we need to find some way of preventing bogus queries from bringing them to their knees.

"Fourth, we need to improve both availability and fault tolerance of the DNS servers that are authoritative for the contoso.com domain. Perhaps our ISP could play a role here.

"Fifth, I really think we should consider a separation of DNS roles.

"Sixth, determine what services should be running on the DNS servers in the screened subnet.

"Finally, consider how we might implement any security configurations.

"I know it is not our style to just slap in a bunch of hardware, but I think we can justify a pretty significant expenditure if we can come up with a reasonable plan to implement quickly. When we are done, we will do a formal threat and risk analysis to see what the residual risk is after the implementation. Let me know what you come up with as soon as you can."

To complete this lab challenge, consider the following network diagram in Figure 7-1 showing the current DNS infrastructure of Contoso Pharmaceuticals. Then, working with your lab partner or in small groups assigned by your instructor, devise a secure DNS infrastructure that meets the CIO's goals and that provides as much confidentiality, integrity, and availability to the DNS infrastructure as possible. You should be as specific as possible. When performing this lab challenge, consider the following:

- What additional DNS servers will be required, if any.
- Where the DNS servers should be placed.
- The role of the DNS server, for example, whether it provides Internet name resolution, or whether it provides name resolution for the zones for which it is authoritative.
- The DNS configuration, given a particular role.
- The firewall rules that should be put in place to accommodate or restrict DNS traffic.
- The startup settings for system services that should be enabled or disabled as a baseline for DNS servers. (You do not have to list all the services that should be disabled, but you should try to list at least five or more services that have a default startup setting as manual or automatic and should be set to disabled.)

- The mechanism(s) for implementing security configuration settings.
- Whether to implement other services, such as Active Directory to improve security, with due consideration for the risks involved in implementing those services.

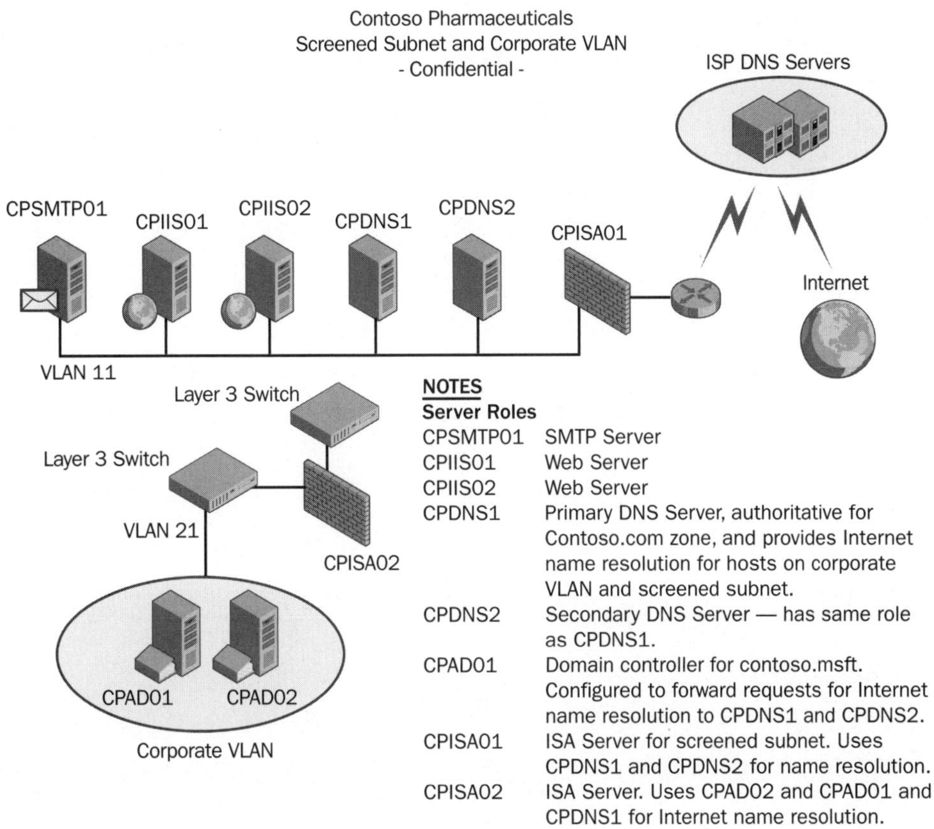

Figure 7-1 Contoso network diagram

To assist you in determining what system services to enable or disable, a Word file named W2K3_SystemServices.doc is provided for you in the \Lab Manual\Lab 07 folder. This file provides information on the default startup values for system services on Windows 2003 Server domain controllers, member servers, and standalone servers.

> **TIP** *Consider the tools and security templates you used in the lab to derive a list of system service startup values for a high-security environment.*

When you are finished discussing a possible design, your instructor will review the results with the class.

LAB 8

HARDENING CLIENT COMPUTERS

This lab contains the following exercises and activities:

- Exercise 8.1: Enforcing Software Restrictions
- Exercise 8.2: Configuring Internet Explorer Security Settings
- Exercise 8.3: Using Advanced Security and Group Policy Features and Settings
- Lab Review Questions
- Lab Challenge 8.1: Designing Client Computer Security

SCENARIO

As network administrator for Contoso Pharmaceuticals, you have been asked to review and implement security settings to harden client operating systems. You must ensure that the environment for users and the computers that they use has the appropriate level of security, according to Contoso's security-policy requirements.

Contoso's Acceptable Use Policy prohibits the downloading of and storing of audio and video files. You are responsible for determining the technological controls that would, at the very least, discourage the downloading and storing of audio and video files. Contoso Acceptable Internet Use policy prohibits users from making configuration changes to Microsoft Internet Explorer that would, among other things, allow users to bypass Microsoft Internet Security and Acceleration (ISA) Server 2004 for Internet access or adding external Web sites to the Trusted or the Intranet zones. Finally, Contoso has several security policies that are to be followed by administrators. These policies specify requirements for the configuration of users' desktops. In general, these policies specify that the security of client computers follows the principle of least privilege, in that users are allowed only the minimum access to the desktop and the network that their tasks require.

After completing this lab, you will be able to:

- **Enforce software restrictions by using certificate rules, hash rules, and path rules.**
- **Import Microsoft Office and other administrative templates for use in Group Policies.**
- **Extend the Security Configuration Editor (SCE) with additional security-related settings.**
- **Configure loopback processing of Group Policies.**
- **Create Windows Management Interface (WMI) queries to filter Group Policy processing.**
- **Use the WMIC command prompt.**
- **Configure representative settings for client security.**
- **Use Internet zones to enhance security.**

Estimated lesson time: 125 minutes

BEFORE YOU BEGIN

To complete this lab, you will need to have done the following:

- Created a Member Servers organizational unit (OU) and moved the Computer*yy* member server object to the OU as instructed in steps 3 through 7 of Lab Exercise 3.4, "Using Group Policy to Configure Automatic Update Clients," in Lab 3, "Reducing the Risk of Software Vulnerabilities."
- Performed the steps in the "Before You Begin" section of Lab 4, "Designing a Management Infrastructure," to create user accounts and to grant the Domain Users group the right to log on locally to the domain controller.

NOTE In this lab, you will see the characters *dd*, *pp*, xx, yy, and zz. These directions assume that you are working on computers configured in pairs and that each computer has a number.

When you see *dd*, substitute the number used for your domain. When you see *pp*, substitute the number of your partner's computer. When you see xx, substitute the unique number assigned to the lower-numbered (odd-numbered) computer of the pair. When you see yy, substitute the unique number assigned to the higher-numbered (even-numbered) computer of the pair. When you see zz, substitute the number assigned to the computer at which you are currently using. The following example assumes that the partner pair of computers has been assigned the names Computer05 and Computer06 and that you have been assigned Computer05.

Computer*pp* = Computer06 = your partner's computer

Computerxx = Computer05 = lower-numbered computer

Computeryy = Computer06 = higher-numbered computer

Computerzz = Computer05 = computer you are using

Contoso*dd*.msft = Contoso03.msft = Active Directory domain you are using

EXERCISE 8.1: ENFORCING SOFTWARE RESTRICTIONS

Estimated completion time: 30 minutes

As a result of lawsuits that have imposed extremely punitive penalties on companies that stored copyright-protected audio and video files, Contoso Pharmaceuticals has formed a committee to reexamine its Acceptable Use Policy. As a member of the committee, you have been asked to determine whether it is possible to use Group Policy or some other mechanism to enforce a new acceptable-use policy to restrict the use of specific software, such as software that is used for peer-to-peer file sharing.

In this exercise, you will examine the feasibility of using software restriction policies to enforce the company's proposed acceptable-use policy.

Examining Software Restriction Policy Settings

In this section, you will examine the various settings for software restriction policies to develop a better understanding of how you might design software restrictions for a specific environment. In the next section, you will create a software restriction policy.

1. Log on as Contoso*dd*\Admin*zz* using **P@ssw0rd** as the password.
2. Click Start, point to Administrative Tools, and select Group Policy Management.
3. Depending on your assigned computer, perform either of the following steps:
    a. On Computer*xx*, in the console tree, navigate to the Domain Controllers OU, right-click the Domain Controllers OU, select Create And Link A GPO Here, type **Software Restrictions Policy** *zz*, and then click OK.
    b. On Computer*yy*, in the console tree, navigate the Member Servers OU, right-click the Member Servers OU, select Create and Link a GPO Here, type **Software Restrictions Policy** *zz*, and click OK.
4. In the console tree, right-click the Software Restrictions Policy *zz* Group Policy link, and select Edit.
5. In the Group Policy Object Editor console, in the tree pane, browse to \Computer Configuration\Windows Settings\Security Settings, right-click Software Restriction Policies, and then select New Software Restriction Policies. You now see additional objects in the tree console and details pane. You use these objects to define a software restriction policy and its rules.

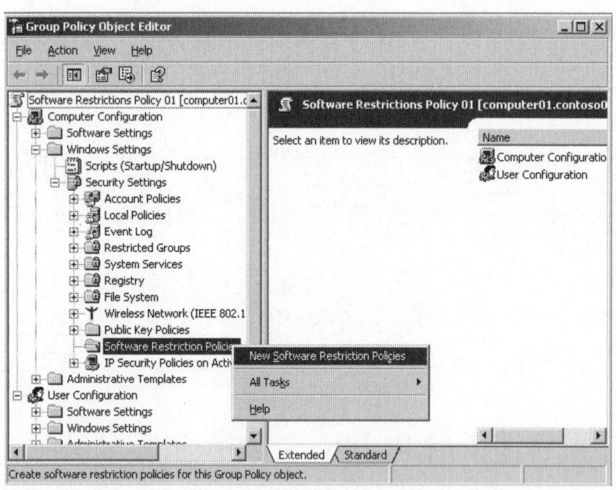

6. In the console tree, select Security Levels, and, in the details pane, double-click Disallowed, note the description, and then double-click Unrestricted, and note the description. Click Cancel.

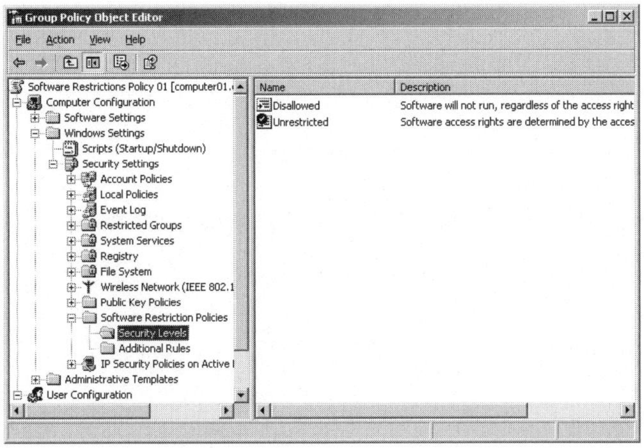

QUESTION What are the two security levels? What is the default level?

QUESTION Why would you use each security level?

7. In the details pane, right-click one of the security levels, and select Help. The Microsoft Management Console appears, showing the Help files containing information on Software Restriction Policies. Use the Help files to answer the following question and subsequent questions in the lab exercise.

QUESTION What is the relationship between the default security levels and software restriction policy rules?

8. Switch to the Group Policy Object Editor, and select Additional Rules in the console tree.

QUESTION What type of paths do these four rules use?

QUESTION Is it possible to use wildcards for the path rules? If so, what wildcards are supported?

QUESTION Can you use environment variables in path rules?

9. In the Group Policy Object Editor console tree, select Software Restriction Policies, and then, in the details pane, double-click Enforcement.

QUESTION What setting would you choose if you did not want the policy to apply to users who were local administrators of their computers?

QUESTION What special consideration would you have to take into account if the default security level were set to Disallowed?

10. Click Cancel.
11. In the details pane, double-click Designated File Types and note the files that are considered executable files, and then click Cancel.
12. In the details pane, double-click Trusted Publishers.

QUESTION What is meant by the term "Trusted Publishers?"

QUESTION What settings in the Trusted Publishers Properties dialog box might affect the performance of the computer?

13. Click Cancel.

Creating a Software Restriction Policy

1. In the Group Policy Object Editor tree console, right-click Additional Rules, and then select New Certificate Rule.
2. In the New Certificate Rule dialog box, click Browse.
3. In the Open dialog box, in the Look In drop-down list, navigate to C:\Lab Manual\Lab 08, select MSN app.cer, and click Open.

   You are adding an Authenticode certificate issued to Microsoft Corporation. These steps are intended as a demonstration only of the Certificate Rule settings. You would use a Certificate Rule to permit or deny users to run particular applications that use authenticode technology and certificates. For example, a number of spyware applications are notorious for prompting users in Internet Explorer to trust software from a particular vendor. Often, users will click Yes to trust the software from a particular vendor after having seen the same authenticode dialog box a number of times.
4. In the Security Level drop-down box, select Unrestricted.
5. Click Details. The Certificate dialog box appears.
6. In the Certificate dialog box, click the Details tab, select Critical Extensions Only in the Show drop-down list, and select Key Usage.

QUESTION What purposes are listed for the Key Usage?

7. Click OK, and then click Cancel to close the New Certificate Rule dialog box without creating a rule.
8. In the Group Policy Object Editor tree console, right-click Additional Rules, and then select New Hash Rule.
9. In the New Hash Rule dialog box, click Browse.
10. In the Open dialog box, select the Look In drop-down list, browse to C:\Program Files\Windows Media Player, select Wmplayer.exe, and then click Open.
11. In the New Hash Rule dialog box, ensure that Disallowed is selected from the Security Level drop-down list, as shown below, and then click OK. This rule prevents users from using the Windows Media Player application. Because you have created a hash rule, users will not be able to run the Windows Media Player from any location on their hard disks or even a network share.

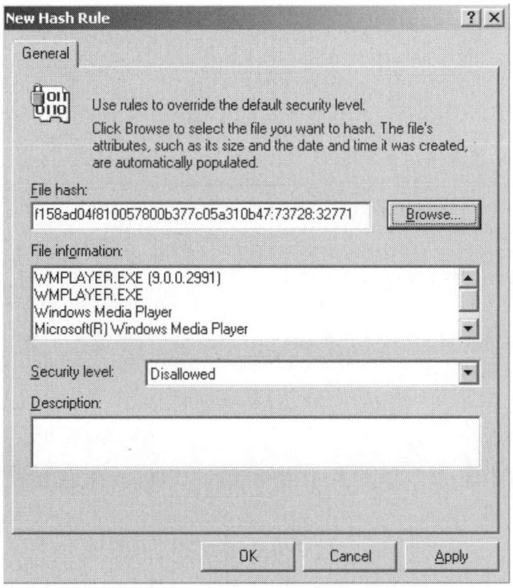

12. In the Group Policy Object Editor tree console, right-click Additional Rules, and then select New Path Rule.
13. In the New Path Rule dialog box, type **vod.cmd** in the Path box, ensure that Disallowed is selected from the Security Level drop-down list, and then click OK. This rule will prevent users from running the executable file, vod.com. Because you haven't provided a specific path, the

rule will be applied regardless of where the file is located. You might use a path rule such as this if you have a virus that spawns an executable file that has the same name, but adds or removes random bits and places itself in a variety of locations.

14. In the Group Policy Object Editor tree console, select Software Restriction Policies, and then, in the details pane, double-click Enforcement.
15. In the Enforcement Properties dialog box, select the All Users Except Local Administrators option, and then click OK.
16. Close the Group Policy Object Editor console.
17. Click Start, select Shut Down, select Restart in the What Do You Want Your Computer To Do drop-down list, type **Restart to apply software restriction policy** in the Comment text box, and then click OK.

    Software restriction policies represent a rare instance when it is necessary to restart the computer for Windows Server 2003 to apply the policy.

18. After the computer restarts, log on as Contoso*dd*\Jgeist*zz* using **P@ssw0rd** as the password. Because you have configured the policy to apply to all users but administrators, you must log on as a non-administrative user to view the effect of the software restriction policy.
19. Click Start, select Run, type **wmplayer.exe** in the Open box, and then click OK.

    QUESTION What message did you receive?

20. Click OK to close the Wmplayer.exe dialog box.
21. Click Start, select Run, type **cmd /k "c:\lab manual\lab 08\vod.cmd"**, and then click OK.

    QUESTION Are you able to run the batch file?

22. Close the command prompt window, log off, and then log on as Contoso*dd*\Admin*zz*.
23. Click Start, select Run, type **wmplayer.exe** in the Open box, and then click OK.

    The Welcome To The Windows Media Player 9 Series page opens.

24. Close the Welcome To The Windows Media Player 9 Series page.

25. Click Start, click Run, type **cmd /k "c:\lab manual\lab 08\vod.cmd"**, and press ENTER. The batch file invokes Notepad, and shows the permissions on the C: drive.
26. Close Notepad and the command prompt window.

EXERCISE 8.2: CONFIGURING INTERNET EXPLORER SECURITY SETTINGS

Estimated completion time: 30 minutes

As network administrator for Contoso Pharmaceuticals, you have been asked to examine some Group Policy settings with the aim of mitigating vulnerabilities that exist for the client computers in the company. In particular, management wants to mitigate vulnerabilities related to Internet Explorer settings. Management also wants to ensure that the security settings for Internet Explorer adequately implement technological controls to ensure conformance with the Internet Acceptable Use Policy. This policy stipulates that users will not attempt to bypass access controls or weaken Internet Explorer security. You will first compare and contrast various Internet Explorer settings.

Examining Internet Explorer Security Settings

In this section, you will examine a number of Internet Explorer settings related to browser security. You will first remove the Internet Explorer Enhanced Configuration for the Administrators group. You will then compare the Internet Explorer security settings that are applied to members of the Administrators group with the settings applied to users.

1. Ensure you are logged on as Contoso*dd*\Admin*zz*.
2. Click Start, select Control Panel, and then select Add Or Remove Programs.
3. In the Add Or Remove Programs dialog box, click Add/Remove Windows Components.
4. In the Windows Components Wizard, select the Internet Explorer Enhanced Security Configuration option, and then click Details.
5. In the Subcomponents Of Internet Explorer Enhanced Security Configuration dialog box, clear the For Administrator Groups check box, and then click OK.

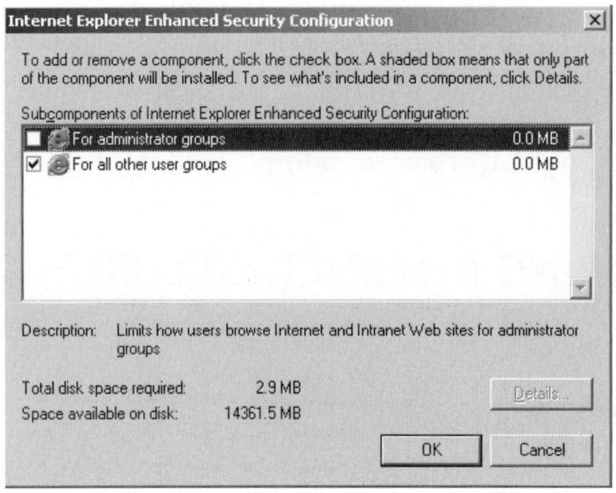

6. On the Windows Components page, click Next, and then click Finish.
7. Close the Add Or Remove Programs dialog box.

   Before proceeding, make sure that no windows are open on your desktop.

8. Open Internet Explorer.

   A message appears, indicating that the Internet Explorer Enhanced Security Configuration is not enabled. Leave this message displayed in your browser.

9. On the taskbar, right-click the Internet Explorer icon, and select Run As.
10. In the Run As dialog box, select the The Following User option, and then log on as Contoso*dd*\ Jchen*zz* using **P@ssw0rd** as the password.

    When Internet Explorer opens, it attempts to connect to the Microsoft Web site. To prevent this page from loading in the browser, on the Internet Explorer toolbar, click Stop.

11. Right-click the taskbar, and then select Tile Windows Vertically.
12. In both instances of Internet Explorer, from the Tools menu, select Internet Options, and then click the Advanced tab.
13. Position the Internet Options dialog boxes so that they are side by side.

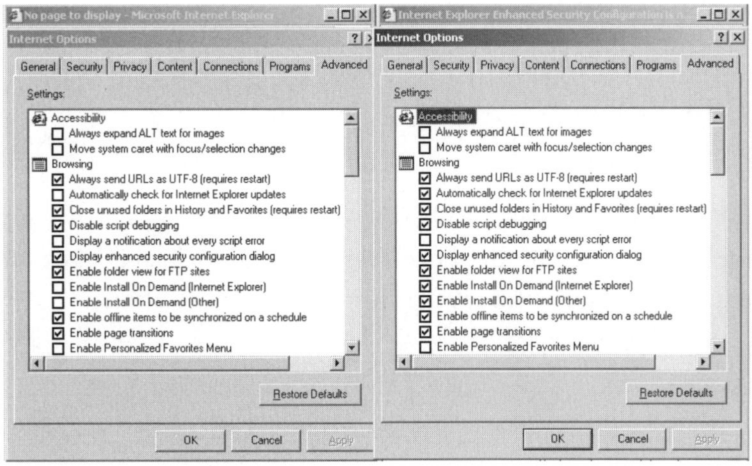

14. Scroll through the option settings in both Internet Options dialog boxes, note the differences, and then answer the following questions.

    To view brief explanations for any of these settings, click the question mark in the upper-right corner of the dialog box, drag the mouse cursor to the option setting, and then click it.

    QUESTION What happens when Check For Server Certificate Revocation (Requires Restart) is enabled?

    QUESTION What is the effect of selecting the Enable Install On Demand (Internet Explorer) option?

15. In both Internet Options dialog boxes, select the Security tab, and then compare the respective security-level settings for each Web content zone.

    QUESTION What is the difference in security-level settings for the Internet and Trusted Sites zones between both instances of Internet Explorer?

16. In the instance of Internet Explorer that is enabled for Enhanced Security, select Local Intranet, and then click Custom Level; in the Settings dialog box, scroll to the bottom and locate the settings for User Authentication.

    Note the settings.

    QUESTION What is the setting for User Authentication Logon?

17. Click Cancel to close the Security Settings dialog box.
18. In the same browser instance, on the Security tab, select Local Intranet, and then click Sites.
19. In the Local Intranet dialog box, select the Include All Local (Intranet) Sites Not Listed In Other Zones check box, and then click OK.
20. On the Security tab, ensure that Local Intranet is still selected, click Custom Level, and review the settings for User Authentication.

> **QUESTION** What is the setting for User Authentication Logon?

21. Click Cancel.
22. Select the Internet zone, and then click Custom Level.

    Note the settings.

> **QUESTION** What is the setting for User Authentication Logon?

> **QUESTION** If the setting were changed to Automatic Logon With Current Username And Password, what would happen when a user connected to a site that required NTLM authentication?

23. Click Cancel to close the Security Settings dialog box.
24. Click Cancel to close both Internet Options dialog boxes, and then close both instances of Internet Explorer.

Implementing Internet Explorer Security Settings

In this section, you will implement representative security settings that are found in the User Configuration portion of the Group Policy settings.

1. Click Start, point to Administrative Tools, and select Group Policy Management.
2. In the Group Policy Management console tree, navigate to the Location*zz* OU, right-click the Sales OU, and select Create And Link A GPO Here.
3. In the New GPO dialog box, in the Name text box, type **Sales Employees Policy** ***zz***, and then click OK.
4. In the details pane, right-click the GPO link you just created, and select Edit.

5. In the Group Policy Object Editor, navigate to User Configuration\ Windows Settings, and then select and expand Internet Explorer Maintenance.

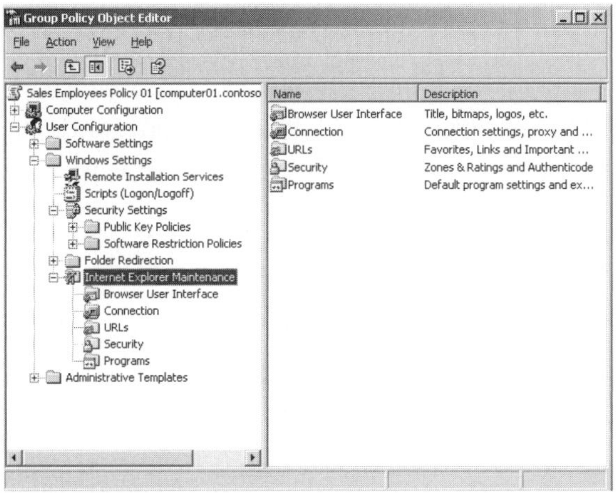

6. In the console tree, under Internet Explorer Maintenance, select Connection, and in the details pane, double-click Proxy Settings.

7. In the Proxy Settings dialog box, select the Enable Proxy Settings check-box, type **10.1.1.200** in the Address Of Proxy box, and type **8080** in the Port box, and then click OK.

   In many environments, access to the Internet occurs through a Proxy server, such as ISA Server 2004. When you configure Proxy server settings, you are in effect enabling a Web proxy client that can be authenticated for authorization to access the Internet or Web sites on the Internet. Configuring a Group Policy setting for the Proxy server settings on Internet Explorer reduces the administration required to configure the Web Proxy client settings on each computer.

8. In the console tree, under Internet Explorer Maintenance, select URLs, and in the details pane, double-click Important URLs.

9. In the Important URLs dialog box, select the Customize Home Page URL check-box, type **http://computer*zz*** in the Home Page URL box, and then click OK.

10. In the console tree, under Internet Explorer Maintenance, select Security, and, in the details pane, double-click Security Zones And Content Ratings.

11. In the Security Zones And Content Ratings dialog box, select the Import The Current Security Zones And Privacy Settings option. An

Internet Explorer Enhanced Security Configuration dialog box appears.

12. Click Continue.
13. In the Security Zones And Privacy area, click Modify Settings. The Internet Properties dialog box appears.
14. In the Internet Properties dialog box, select the Internet zone, and, in the Security Level For This Zone area, move the slider bar to High.
15. Click OK twice to close the Internet Properties and the Security Zones And Content Ratings dialog boxes.
16. In the Group Policy Object Editor console tree, navigate to User Configuration\Administrative Templates\Windows Components, select Internet Explorer, and then select the Standard tab.

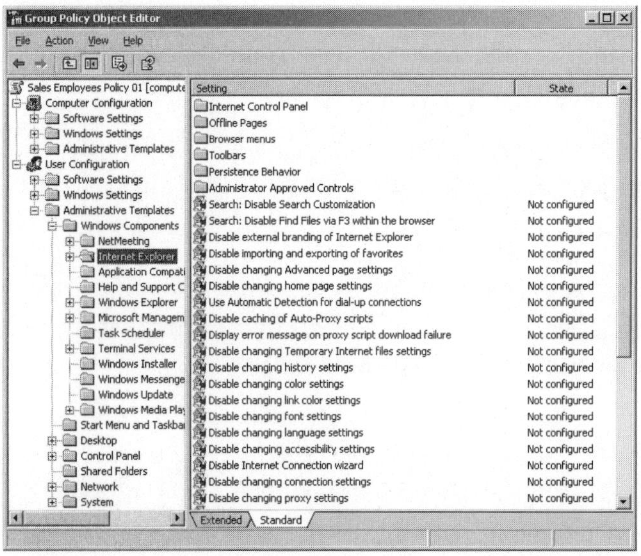

17. In the details pane, double-click Disable Changing Proxy Settings.
18. On the Disable Changing Proxy Settings Property page, select the Enabled option, and then click OK.

    It is sometimes desirable to prevent users from changing Proxy settings so that you can ensure that access to the Internet occurs through a Proxy server that authenticates, authorizes, and logs user access.

19. In the Group Policy Object Editor console tree, navigate to User Configuration\Administrative Templates, and then select Start Menu And Taskbar.

20. In the details pane, double-click Remove Run Menu From Start Menu, select the Enabled option, and click OK.
21. Close all open windows and log off.
22. Log on as Contoso*dd*\CPhilips01 using **P@ssw0rd** as the password.
23. Click Start.

QUESTION *Does the Run command appear on the Start menu?*

24. Open Internet Explorer, and click OK to acknowledge the Internet Explorer dialog box informing you that Internet Explorer's Enhanced Security Configuration is enabled.
25. From the Tools menu, select Internet Options, and, in the Internet Options dialog box, select the Connections tab.
26. On the Connections tab, click LAN Settings.

QUESTION *Can you change the proxy server settings?*

27. Close all open windows and log off.

EXERCISE 8.3: USING ADVANCED SECURITY AND GROUP POLICY FEATURES AND SETTINGS

Estimated completion time: 50 minutes

You are continuing your work in designing a secure environment for users and client computers at Contoso Pharmaceuticals. In this exercise, you will look at advanced features and settings, including using administrative templates, implementing loopback processing, and creating Windows Management Interface (WMI) queries.

Importing Administrative Templates for Use in Group Policy

In this section, you will import administrative templates to apply Group Policy settings that are specific to Office applications.

1. Log on as Contoso*dd*\Admin*zz*.
2. Open Windows Explorer and copy the C:\Lab Manual\Lab 08\Administrative Templates to C:\Administrative Templates.

NOTE In a production environment, you would normally copy administrative and security template files to a secure location accessible only to administrators.

3. Click Start, point to Administrative Tools, and select Group Policy Management.
4. Depending on your assigned computer, perform either of the following steps:
   a. On Computer*xx*, in the console tree, navigate to the Domain Controllers OU, right-click the Domain Controllers OU, select Create And Link A GPO Here, type **Client Computers Policy** ***zz***, and then click OK.
   b. On Computer*yy*, in the console tree, navigate the Member Servers OU, right-click the Member Servers OU, select Create And Link A GPO Here, type **Client Computers Policy** ***zz***, and then click OK.
5. Right-click the Client Computers Policy *zz*, and select Edit.
6. In the console tree of the Group Policy Object Editor, expand Computer Configuration, right-click Administrative Templates, and select Add/Remove Templates.
7. In the Add/Remove Templates dialog box, click Add.
8. In the Policy Templates dialog box, in the Look In drop-down box, browse to C:\Administrative Templates, select Office10.ADM, click Open, and then, in the Add/Remove Templates dialog box, click Close. In the console tree, expand Administrative Templates. You now see the Microsoft Office XP folder in the console tree.
9. In the console tree, expand Microsoft Office XP, select the Security Settings folder, and, in the details pane, double-click Word: Macro Security Level.
10. In the Word: Macro Security Levels dialog box, select the Enabled option, select Medium from the Security Level drop-down list, and then click OK.

    This setting allows the user to choose whether to run potentially unsafe macros. If the Security Level is set to High, only digitally signed macros from trusted sources are allowed to run and unsigned macros are not allowed to run.
11. Examine the other settings in the details pane.

Examining Internet Explorer Settings in the Computer Configuration Console Tree

In this section, you will examine the Internet Explorer policy settings in the Computer Configuration console tree to compare with the Internet Explorer configuration settings in the User Configuration console tree you worked with earlier in this lab.

1. In the console tree, navigate to Computer Configuration\Administrative Templates\Windows Components, and select Internet Explorer.
2. In the details pane, double-click Security Zones: Use Only Machine Settings and select the Enabled option. Click Apply, click the Explain tab, and then read the explanation for this setting.
3. Click Next Setting to read the next explanation to review the remaining settings in the Internet Explorer folder.

> **QUESTION** What two ways are available for you to prevent users from changing Internet Explorer zone settings?

4. Close all open windows.

Extending the Security Configuration Editor (SCE)

The Security Configuration Editor (SCE) toolset is responsible for providing the Security Settings portion of the console tree for different snap-ins, such as the Group Policy Object Editor, Security Configuration And Analysis, Security Templates, Local Security Policy, and others. It contains the security template settings for account policies, lockout policies, registry settings, file settings, and others. For environments in which it is necessary to configure and manage custom security settings that do not appear under the Security Settings portion of the console and which would otherwise have be configured by using the Registry Editor, it is possible for you to extend the SCE to provide access to these settings in tools that you use to manage security settings for Group and Local Policies.

In this section, you will extend the SCE to provide access to the security settings that are referenced in both the Windows XP Security Guide, which is available at *http://go.microsoft.com/fwlink/?LinkId=15159*, and the Threats and Countermeasures: Security Settings in Windows Server 2003 and Windows XP guide, which is available at *http://go.microsoft.com/fwlink/?LinkId=14839*. The SCE settings you will extend to the security consoles are taken from the Windows XP Security Guide.

> **NOTE** Please pay attention to the following steps to avoid making errors. If you make a mistake copying and pasting text between the Notepad files you work with, you can press CTRL+Z to undo the change.

1. Click Start, select Run, type **%systemroot%\inf** in the Open text box, and click OK.
2. In the Inf folder, scroll down the list of files, locate the Sceregvl.inf file, right-click the Sceregvl.inf file, select Copy, and then press CTRL+V to create a backup copy of the file.
3. Double-click the Sceregvl.inf file. Notepad opens showing the content of the file.
4. Minimize Notepad.
5. In Windows Explorer, navigate to C:\Lab Manual\Lab 08, and double-click the SCE-Additions.txt file. Notepad opens showing the custom SCE settings.
6. With the mouse, select the lines of text including and directly beneath the line that contains the text "MSS Values." Make sure you include ";" at the beginning of the first line and that you highlight only that section of text.

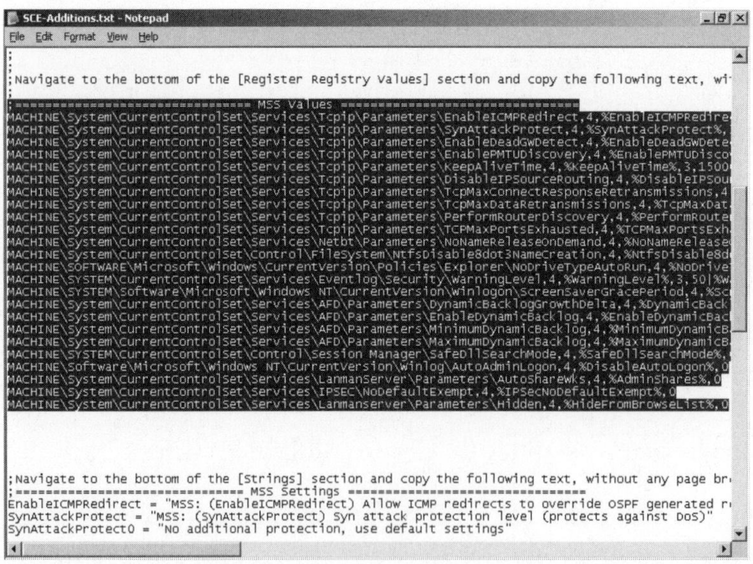

7. Press CTRL+C to copy the selected text to the clipboard.
8. Switch to the instance of Notepad containing the Sceregvl.inf settings, scroll to the end of the [Register Registry Values] section of the file, and, on a new line, press CTRL+V to copy the text into the file.

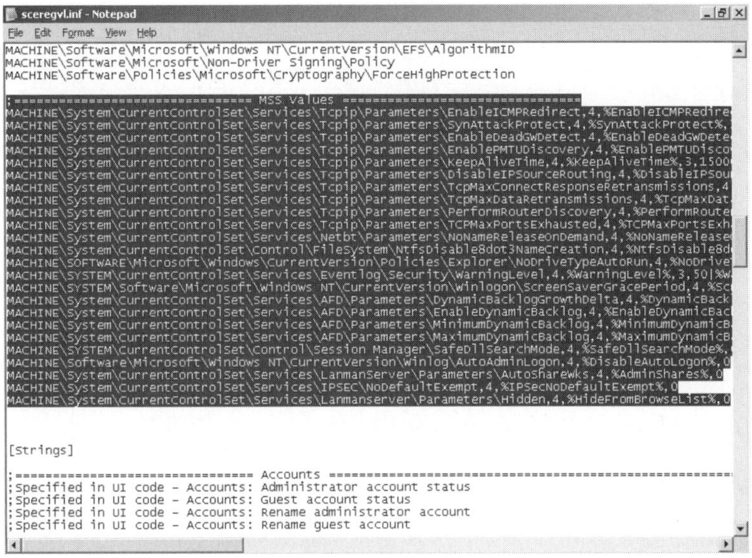

9. Switch to the instance of Notepad containing the custom SCE settings, select the text in the section that begins with a line containing the text "MSS Settings," and press CTRL+C.

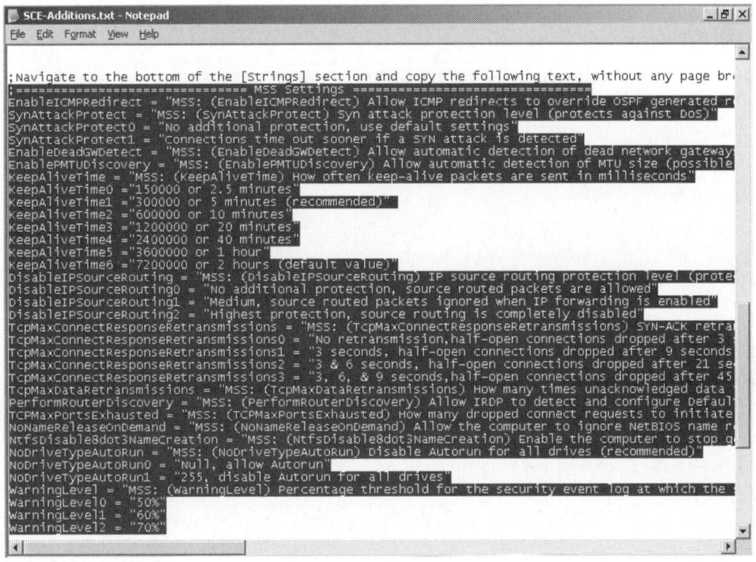

10. Switch to the instance of Notepad containing the Sceregvl.inf settings, scroll to the bottom of the [Strings] section (there may be a lot of white space between the [Register Registry Values] and the [Strings] section, and, on a new line, press CTRL+V.

11. Save and close the Scergvl.inf file, and then close SCE-Additions.txt without saving it (if prompted to do so).

12. Click Start, select Run, type **regsvr32 scecli.dll** in the Open text box, and click OK. The Scecli.dll is reregistered, and the RegSvr32 message box appears, indicating the successful registration of the Scecli.dll file.
13. Click OK to acknowledge the message.
14. Click Start, select Run, type **gpedit.msc** in the Open text box, and click OK. The Group Policy Object Editor opens.
15. In the console tree of the Group Policy Object Editor, navigate to Computer Configuration\Windows Settings\Security Settings\Local Policies, and select Security Options. The details pane shows custom settings grouped by the string "MSS:" in the Policy column.

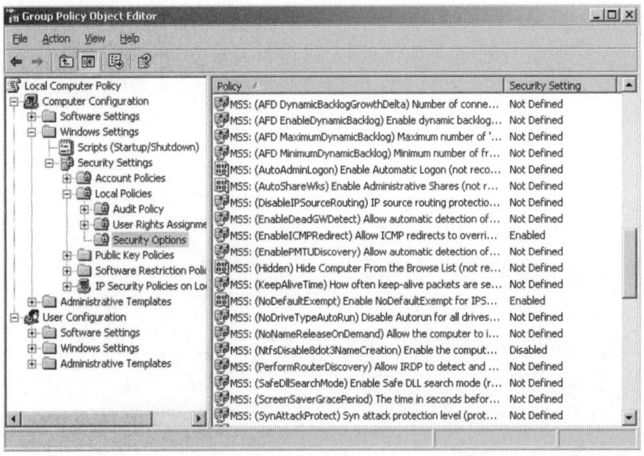

16. Examine the custom MSS settings, and then close the Group Policy Object Editor.

    In a later section, you will make representative changes to these and other security settings.

Using Loopback Processing

In this section, you will configure loopback processing to ensure that users who log on to particular computers, such as kiosks, receive Group Policies based on the location of the computer object in Active Directory, rather than the location of their user object.

1. Click Start, point to Administrative Tools, and select Group Policy Management.

2. Depending on your assigned computer, perform either of the following steps:

    a. On Computer*xx*, in the console tree, navigate to the Domain Controllers OU, right-click the Domain Controllers OU, select Create And Link A GPO Here, type **Loopback Policy *zz***, and click OK.

    b. On Computer*yy*, in the console tree, navigate the Member Servers OU, right-click the Member Servers OU, select Create And Link A GPO Here, type **Loopback Policy *zz***, and then click OK.

3. Right-click Loopback Policy *zz*, and select Edit.

4. In the Group Policy Object Editor console tree, navigate to Computer Configuration\Administrative Templates, expand System, and select Group Policy.

5. In the details pane, double-click User Group Policy Loopback Processing Mode.

6. In the User Group Policy Loopback Processing Mode Properties dialog box, select the Explain tab and read the description of the setting.

7. Click the Setting tab, select the Enabled option, and, from the Mode drop-down list, select Merge, and click OK.

8. In the Group Policy Object Editor console tree, navigate to User Configuration\Administrative Templates\Windows Components, expand Internet Explorer, and select Internet Control Panel.

9. In the details pane, double-click Disable The Security Page, select the Enabled option, and then click OK.

10. Repeat step 9 to enable the Disable The Connections Page setting.

11. In the Group Policy Object Editor console tree, navigate to the User Configuration\Administrative Templates\Start Menu And Taskbar node.

12. In the details pane, enable the policy setting to Remove Help Menu From The Start Menu.

13. In the Group Policy Object Editor console tree, navigate to User Configuration\Administrative Templates\System node.

14. In the details pane, enable the setting Prevent Access To Registry Editing Tools.

15. Close the Group Policy Object Editor.

In steps 16 through 19, we will configure permissions on the Group Policy object (GPO) so that the Group Policy does not apply to the Domain Admins group. Follow the instructions carefully.

16. In the Group Policy Management console tree, double-click Loopback Policy *zz*, click OK to acknowledge the Group Policy Management Console dialog box, and then, in the details pane, click the Delegation tab.

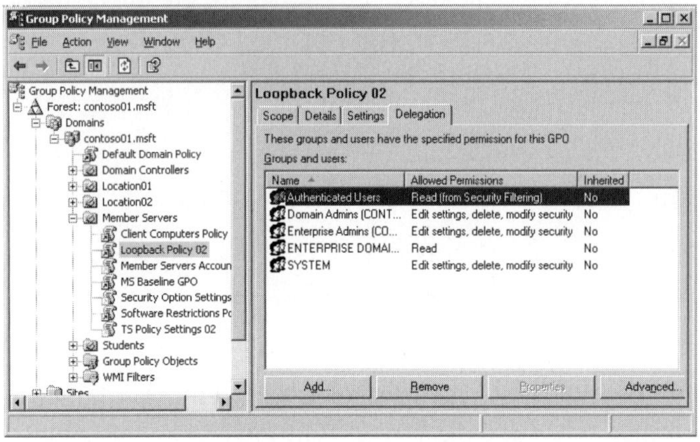

17. Click Advanced. The Loopback Policy *zz* Security Settings dialog box appears.

18. In the Group Or User Names box, select Domain Admins (CONTOSO*DD*\Domain Admins), in the Permissions For Domain Admins box, select the Deny check-box for the Apply Group Policy permission, as shown below, and click OK. A Security dialog box appears.

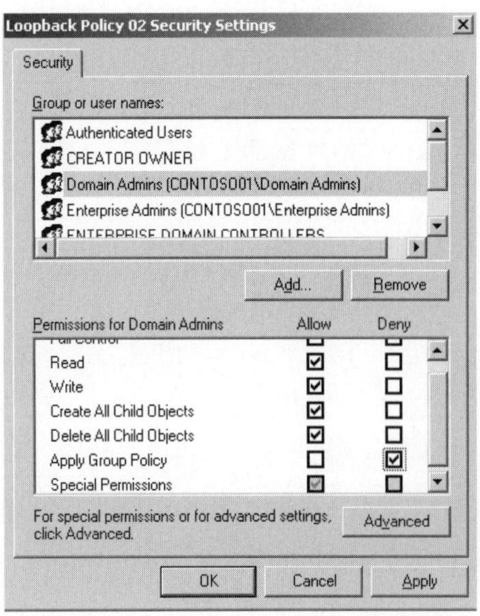

19. In the Security dialog box, read the message, and click Yes.
20. Close the Group Policy Management console.
21. Open a command prompt window, type **gpupdate /target:computer /force**, and press ENTER.
22. Log off and then log on as Contoso*dd*\Cphilips*zz*.
23. Click Start.

> **QUESTION** *Do you see the Help menu on the Start menu? Why or why not?*

24. On the Start menu, select Search.
25. In the Search Results dialog box, type **regedt32** in the All Or Part Of A File Name box, click Search, and click Stop when the Regedt32 executable file appears in the search results area.
26. Double-click Regedt32.

> **QUESTION** *Were you able to launch Regedt32? Why or why not?*

27. Click OK to close the Registry Editor message box, and close the Search Results dialog box.
28. Open Internet Explorer and click OK to close the message box informing you that Microsoft Internet Explorer's Enhanced Security Configuration is enabled. From the Tools menu, select Internet Options.

> **QUESTION** *Do you see the Security or the Connection tabs? Why or why not?*

29. Log off and then log on as Contoso*dd*\Admin*zz*. Examine the Start Menu and Internet Options dialog box within Internet Explorer. Note that the Admin*zz* account is not affected by the loopback policy.

    The loopback policy is fairly restrictive, and you should remove it before proceeding. In the step below, you will remove the policy.

30. Open the Group Policy Management console, and, in the console tree, expand Group Policy Objects, right-click Loopback Policy *zz*, select Delete, and click OK to confirm that you want to delete the policy.

31. Close all open windows, but remain logged on as Contoso*dd*\Admin*zz* for the next section.

Using WMI Filtering to Apply Group Policy

In this section, you will use WMI to filter Group Policy. First, you will examine a few WMI aliases by using the Windows Management Interface Console (WMIC) command-line utility. Then, by using the WMIC utility, you will derive a WMI query to use to filter a GPO.

1. Open a command prompt window, type **wmic**, and press ENTER. You see a message asking you to wait while WMIC is installed. After a few minutes, the WMIC prompt appears in the default role (root\cli).
2. At the WMIC prompt, type /?, and press ENTER. After a few moments, the WMIC help appears.
3. Review the information on the first screen, and then press any key to continue. The next screen shows the WMIC aliases that are available to query for information. Keep pressing any key to step through the help screens until the end.
4. At the WMIC prompt, type **nic** /?, and press ENTER. A list of the verbs that can be used with the alias appears.
5. Type **nic list** and press ENTER. A list of the data for the alias appears.
6. Scroll to the right and observe the data and values that are output for the command.
7. Type **nicconfig list**, press ENTER, and observe the output.
8. Type **logicaldisk list**, press ENTER, and observe the output.

QUESTION *How much free space is available on your C drive?*

9. Type **qfe list**, press ENTER, and note the output.

QUESTION *What hotfix ID is shown as installed?*

10. Type **computersystem list**, press ENTER, and observe the output. In particular, note the values for CreationClassName and Domain.
11. Type **computersystem get domainrole**, and press ENTER. The command returns a number.

12. Record the number in the output of the command in step 11 and compare it with the number that your partner received.
13. At the WMIC prompt, type **exit**, and press ENTER.
14. Leave the command prompt window open.
15. Open the Group Policy Management Console (GPMC).

    In the following steps, you will create a Group Policy and link it to the domain. Then, you will use a WMI filter so that this policy is applied either to the domain controllers or member servers in your domain.

16. Depending on your assigned computer, perform either of the following steps:
    a. On Computer*xx*, in the console tree, under the Domains node, right-click Contoso*dd*.msft, select Create And Link A GPO Here, type **DC WMI Policy**, and then click OK.
    b. On Computer*yy*, in the console tree, under the Domains node, right-click Contoso*dd*.msft, select Create And Link A GPO Here, type **MS WMI Policy**, and then click OK.
17. Right-click the policy you just created, and select Edit.
18. In the Group Policy Object Editor, navigate to Computer Configuration\Windows Settings\Security Settings\Local Policies, and select Security Options.
19. In the details pane, double-click MSS: (WarningLevel) Percentage Threshold For The Security Event Log At Which The System Will Generate A Warning, select the Define This Policy Setting check box, and then do the following:
    a. On Computer*xx*, select a value of 80% from the drop-down list.
    b. On Computer*yy*, select a value of 90% from the drop-down list.
20. Click OK, and then close the Group Policy Object Editor.

> **QUESTION** *When you and your partner have completed step 20, there will be three GPOs linked to the domain. In the absence of any filtering, in the case of a conflict between GPOs, what determines the effective Group Policy setting that will be applied?*

21. In the Group Policy Management console tree, right-click WMI filters, and select New. The New WMI Filter dialog box appears.

22. In the New WMI Filter dialog box, depending on your assigned computer, perform either of the following steps:

    a. On Computerxx, in the Name text box, type DC WMI Filter. Click Add, and in the Query text box, type **Select * from Win32_ComputerSystem where DomainRole** = "*n*" (where *n* is the number you recorded in step 12). Click OK, and then click Save.

    b. On Computeryy, in the Name text box, type MS WMI Filter. Click Add, and in the Query text box, type **Select * from Win32_ComputerSystem where DomainRole** = "*n*" (where *n* is the number you recorded in step 12). Click OK, and then click Save.

23. In the Group Policy Management console tree, select the WMI filter you just created, and, in the details pane, in the GPOs That Use This WMI Filter box, right-click anywhere in the box, and select Add. The Select GPO dialog box appears.

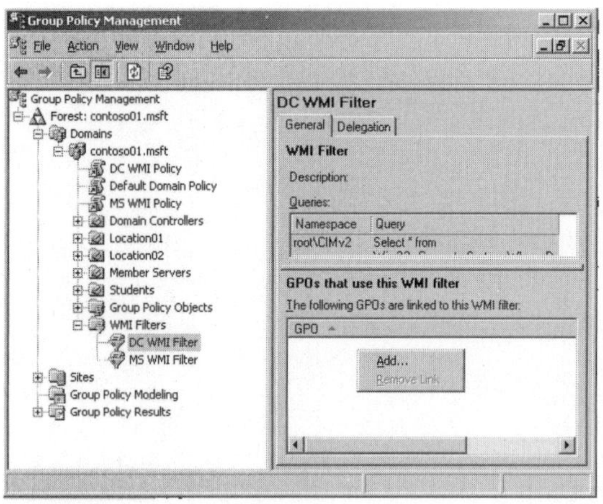

24. In the Select GPO dialog box, select the GPO you created in steps 16 through 20 (DC WMI Policy or MS WMI Policy), and click OK. The WMI Filter is linked to the GPO.

25. Close the Group Policy Management console.

26. Switch to the command prompt window you left open in step 14, type **gpupdate /target:computer /force**, and press ENTER.

    In the next steps, you will run a batch file that invokes the Gpresult command to determine if the WMI filtering was applied correctly.

27. At the command prompt, type **"c:\lab manual\lab 08\gptest.cmd"** (with the quotes), and press ENTER. The command will take a few

moments to run. When it completes, Notepad opens, displaying the output of the Gpresult command.

28. In Notepad, toward the top of the document, note the GPOs that were applied and the GPOs that were denied. The output should show that one WMI filter resulted in a GPO's being applied to your computer and that another WMI filter resulted in a GPO's being denied.

29. Close Notepad, close all open windows, and log off.

LAB REVIEW QUESTIONS

Estimated completion time: 15 minutes

1. A virus outbreak has occurred in your company. The virus always creates a file with the name Innocuous.exe. You have many computers on which to update the virus signature definition files. Moreover, you are short-staffed and are having difficulty getting to the computers that need this file cleaned off in a timely manner. What should you do?

2. You want to prevent an older version of software from running, but you want to allow a newer version of the software to run. What kind of software restriction rule should you use?

3. Briefly explain why loopback processing might be desirable in environments that have high security requirements for kiosks?

4. You have a group of users that sometimes connect to the network using wireless network adapters. When they connect to the wireless network, you want to implement different security configuration settings. How would you accomplish this?

5. Windows 2000 computers ignore WMI filters. Consequently, WMI-filtered Group Policies are always applied to them. Explain how you might use Group Policy precedence to create a workaround for this when you want to use WMI filters to apply different Group Policies to Windows XP and Windows 2000 computers, respectively.

LAB CHALLENGE 8.1: DESIGNING CLIENT COMPUTER SECURITY

Estimated completion time: 30 minutes

As network administrator for Contoso Pharmaceuticals, you have been asked to design an OU strategy for managing the security configuration setting of the servers and client computers that are used by the Research and Development department. Currently, the Research and Development (R and D) department consists of a departmental OU and two child OUs. The OUs are shown in Figure 8-1.

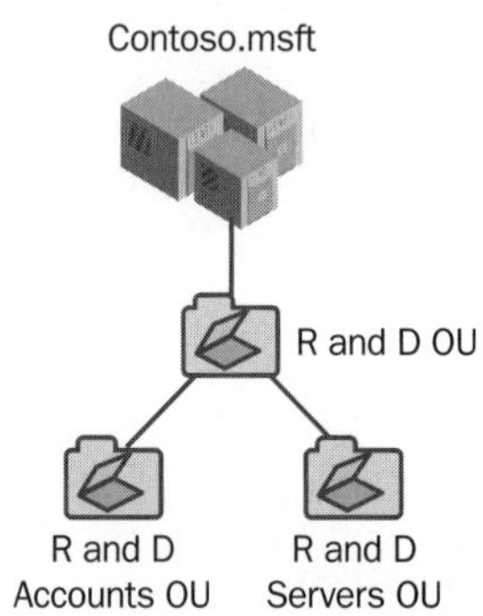

Figure 8-1 Research and Development OUs

Your manager explains the issues that are driving the redesign of the R and D OU.

"We have been examining the management of computer security settings within the R and D department. Not to put too fine a point on it, it is a difficult situation to manage. Currently, all the client computer account objects are located in the R and D Accounts OU, along with the user account objects. We have been using both local computer policy settings and a number of GPOs linked to the Accounts OU and filtered according to group.

"For example, the computers that are used by the lab assistants are placed in a single group and the GPOs are filtered to apply or not apply to this group of computers, as appropriate. The situation is similar for computers used by the scientists, administrative support staff, and other groups. Adding further complication is the fact that there is a mixture of Windows 2000 Professional and

Windows XP with Service Pack 1 within the department. We also have a mixture of different laptop and desktop computers. Some of these, depending on what they are used for, require a very high degree of security.

"The issue came to a head when a lab assistant was discovered printing a document on an unsecured printer outside the lab. The R and D admins thought that they had applied the appropriate policies to force users of the lab computers to print only to secured printers within the lab. The computers within the lab need to be locked down. When R and D staff use these computers, they should have access to only a very restricted desktop that removes access to most applications. Also, we have to find a way to deal separately with client computers that contain highly sensitive data.

"We have been looking at a number of predefined templates in the Windows XP Security guide. And, we think that, as a baseline for all computers in the R and D department, we should apply something equivalent to the Enterprise Client baseline template to all client computers in the R and D OU. At the same time, however, we don't want to affect the security settings for the computer objects in the R and D Servers OU.

"From there, we have to take into account the following requirements:

- The desktop and the laptop computers have different security requirements.
- The Windows 2000 and Windows XP computers have different security settings.
- We have a number of client computers that have very high security requirements because they can contain confidential data. These computers are all desktops running Windows XP with Service Pack 2.
- The computers in the lab need to be highly secure. Furthermore, with the exception of administrators, users logging on to these computers need to have a very restricted desktop, regardless of where the account object resides.
- The management of Group Policies needs to be simplified."

To complete the lab challenge, work with your lab partner or in small groups assigned by your instructor to design the OUs for the R and D department to manage computer and user security configurations. When you have completed the lab challenge, your instructor will review the results with the entire class. Consider the following questions to help you perform this lab challenge.

QUESTION Could WMI be used to filter computers based on their type, operating systems, or roles? Would WMI be useful for this scenario?

QUESTION What would you do to ensure that a user has a very restricted desktop when logging on to a lab computer?

QUESTION Would you create a separate OU for just the Windows XP computers that have very high requirements?

LAB 9

DESIGNING A PUBLIC KEY INFRASTRUCTURE

This lab contains the following exercises and activities:

- Exercise 9.1: Installing and Configuring a Stand-Alone Root Certification Authority (CA)
- Exercise 9.2: Publishing CRL and AIA Information to Active Directory for an Offline Stand-Alone Root CA
- Exercise 9.3: Installing an Enterprise Subordinate CA
- Exercise 9.4: Managing Computer and User Certificates
- Lab Review Questions
- Lab Challenge 9.1: Designing a Public Key Infrastructure

SCENARIO

You are a security administrator for Contoso Pharmaceuticals. Planned improvements to the network infrastructure require the implementation of an enterprise CA. You need to install the enterprise certification authority (CA) to support the automatic enrollment of user certificates. You also need to take advantage of several advanced features of certificate services on Microsoft Window Server 2003 Enterprise Edition.

Contoso Pharmaceuticals has some stringent security requirements for the CA hierarchy that require you to configure an offline stand-alone root CA in addition to the enterprise CA.

After completing this lab, you will be able to:

- **Configure a Capolicy.inf file to install a root CA.**
- **Publish the root CA Certificate Revocation List Distribution Point (CDP) and Authority Information Access (AIA) locations to Active Directory directory service.**
- **View CDP and AIA information in Active Directory.**

- **Update the CDP and AIA locations in the root CA certificate.**
- **Use the Certutil.exe command-line tool to perform diagnostic and configuration tasks related to the management of CAs.**
- **Use the PKI Health tool to validate the CDP and AIA locations.**
- **Install a subordinate enterprise CA.**
- **Understand role-based permissions.**
- **Configure version 2 certificate templates.**
- **Configure permissions on version 2 certificate templates for autoenrollment.**
- **Configure a Group Policy object (GPO) for autoenrollment.**
- **Design a CA hierarchy.**

Estimated lesson time: 160 minutes

BEFORE YOU BEGIN

> **IMPORTANT** Because of the limitations of the lab environment, many of the steps and procedures presented here do not follow best practices for implementing a public-key infrastructure (PKI). For example, you should not install an offline root CA on a member server, but on a stand-alone server instead. For a comprehensive presentation of best practices for PKIs, please see the white paper "Best Practices for Implementing a Windows Server 2003 Public Key Infrastructure," which is available for download from the Microsoft Web site at *http://www.microsoft.com/technet/prodtechnol/windowsserver2003/technologies/security/ws3pkibp.mspx.*

To complete this lab, you will need to have done the following:

- Created a Member Servers organizational unit (OU) and moved the Computer*yy* member server object to the OU, as instructed in steps 3 through 7 of Lab Exercise 3.4, "Using Group Policy To Configure Automatic Update Clients," in Lab 3, "Reducing the Risk of Software Vulnerabilities."
- Performed the steps in the Before You Begin section of Lab 4, "Designing a Management Infrastructure," to create user accounts and to grant the Domain Users the right to log on locally to the domain controller.
- Have unlinked any Group Policy objects you created in Lab 7, "Hardening Servers," as specified in the instructions at the end of Exercise 7.2, "Using Security Templates to Configure Group Policy Objects."

> **NOTE** In this lab, you will see the characters *dd*, *pp*, *xx*, *yy*, and *zz*. These directions assume that you are working on computers configured in pairs and that each computer has a number.

When you see *dd*, substitute the number used for your domain. When you see *pp*, substitute the number of your partner's computer. When you see xx, substitute the unique number assigned to the lower-numbered (odd-numbered) computer of the pair. When you see yy, substitute the unique number assigned to the higher-numbered (even-numbered) computer of the pair. When you see zz, substitute the number assigned to the computer that you are using. The following example assumes that the partner pair of computers has been assigned the names Computer05 and Computer06 and that you have been assigned Computer05.

Computer*pp* = Computer06 = your partner's computer

Computerxx = Computer05 = lower-numbered computer

Computeryy = Computer06 = higher-numbered computer

Computerzz = Computer05 = computer you are using

Contoso*dd*.msft = Contoso03.msft = Active Directory domain you are using

EXERCISE 9.1: INSTALLING AND CONFIGURING A STAND-ALONE ROOT CERTIFICATION AUTHORITY (CA)

Estimated completion time: 50 minutes

You plan to install the root CA for the CA hierarchy. Before you install the root CA, however, you must first define the requirements for the root CA and implement those requirements in a Capolicy.inf file. You will use the Capolicy.inf file to install the root CA.

Defining and Documenting Stand-Alone Root CA Requirements

In this section, you will consider several questions that will help you to determine the requirements for a stand-alone root CA that you will configure later in this lab exercise.

1. Log on to your computer as Contoso*dd*\Admin*zz*.

   If necessary, use the Microsoft Windows Server 2003 help files or Internet resources (if available), as well as the course textbook, to answer the following questions. The responses to these questions will help you define the configuration of the root CA you will install.

   TIP For quick access to the Certificate Services help file, in the Open box of the Run command, type **%systemroot%\help\cs.chm**, and then press ENTER.

QUESTION For maximum security, you want to remove the computer that is the stand-alone root CA from the network and store it in a secure vault. How should you configure this computer? For example, should you configure it as a member of a workgroup or as a member of a domain? If you choose an inappropriate configuration, what problems could result?

QUESTION The CA name consists of the common name and the distinguished name suffix. The distinguished name can be defined as the Lightweight Directory Access Protocol (LDAP) distinguished name of the forest root domain. What is the LDAP distinguished name of your forest root domain?

QUESTION Is the common name the same as the NetBIOS computer name? If not, what should be the common name for the root CA? Indicate a common name that would be appropriate to a CA for the Contoso*dd*.msft domain.

QUESTION The validity period for a CA defines how often it must reissue certificates. A CA checks to ensure that new certificates it issues fall within the CA's validity period. If a CA has a validity period of one year, it can issue certificates that are valid for a period of up to a year. On an offline CA, you want to minimize the frequency with which you have to bring it online to reissue certificates. What should be the validity period of the offline CA?

QUESTION Where should you store the certificate database and log files? For example, would you store them on a file allocation table (FAT) volume?

QUESTION Aside from configuring NTFS permissions on the database and logs, what else should you do to help you verify appropriate access to these files and detecting inappropriate access?

QUESTION What is a certification revocation list (CRL)? Where can it be located?

QUESTION The Certificate Revocation List Distribution Point (CDP) and the Authority Information Access (AIA) are optional extensions to X.509 v 3 certificates. The CDP provides information about the location(s) of the CRL that can be checked to verify the validity of a nonexpired certificate. The AIA provides information on the location(s) that can be checked to determine the validity of the CA that issued the certificate. Given that a root CA provides its own self-signed certificate, is it necessary to provide information about the CDP or AIA for the root CA?

QUESTION What is a Capolicy.inf file? What is it used for, and when should it be installed?

2. Open Microsoft Windows Explorer, navigate to C:\Lab Manual\Lab 09, and double-click the Rfc2527.txt file. Notepad opens, showing the contents of the Request For Comments (RFC): 2527, Internet X.509 Public Key Infrastructure: Certificate Policy and Certification Practices Framework.
3. Scroll to section 2, Definitions, and read the definitions for Certificate Policy and Certification Practice Statement (CPS).
4. Read sections 3.5 and 3.6 of the RFC and answer the following question.

   QUESTION Is the CPS a legal document? If so, what purpose, or purposes, does it serve?

5. Close Notepad.

Modifying a Capolicy.inf File

In this section, you will modify a Capolicy.inf file that you will install before installing Certificate Services on Computeryy.

You use a Capolicy.inf file to configure several important settings on the self-signed root CA certificate, such as the key length, certificate validity period, the CRL and AIA publishing locations, certificate policies, and a Certification Practice Statement (CPS). A Capolicy.inf (or a Policy.inf file) is also used to define the basic constraints, name constraints, issuance policy constraints, and the application policy constraints that are discussed in Chapter 9 of the textbook, "Designing a Public Key Infrastructure." For example, if you wanted to prevent a CA from issuing SubCA certificates, which allow the creation of another CA lower in the hierarchy of the certificate chain, you could set the path value to 0 in the basic constraints section of the Capolicy.inf file. This would restrict the CA to issuing only end-entity certificates.

Constraints are central to implementing qualified subordination. For example, assume that you have a decentralized certificate administrative model, where regional administrators are responsible for issuing certificates to users at their location. By implementing name constraints, you can ensure that the CAs in the specific regions create certificates that include only allowed names, such as Europe.contoso.com, and not, for example, Asia.contoso.com.

You must configure and place the Capolicy.inf file in the %Systemroot% folder before the installation of the CA, or upon the renewal of the keys. The \Lab Manual\Lab 09 folder on the Student CD-ROM contains examples of the Capolicy.inf and Policy.inf files. These files are from the appendixes of the white paper, *Planning and Implementing Cross-Certification and Qualified Subordination Using Windows Server 2003*, available at *http://www.microsoft.com/technet/prodtechnol/windowsserver2003/technologies/security/ws03qswp.mspx*.

Both students can perform these steps, but you will use the file only on Computeryy for the installation of the root CA later.

1. If necessary, open Windows Explorer, and navigate to C:\Lab Manual \Lab 09 folder.
2. Right-click Capolicy.inf, select Properties, ensure that the Read-Only check box is cleared, and then click OK.
3. Double-click Capolicy.inf. Notepad opens.
4. Under the [Legal Policy] section, in the text string that begins with "OID=", replace *y* with the number representing the last octet of your Internet Protocol (IP) address.
5. Under the [Legal Policy] section, in the text string that begins with "URL=", replace *xx* with the assigned number of the domain controller in your domain (the odd-numbered computer). Do not specify the number assigned to the member server.
6. Under the [Certsrv_Server] section, set the following values:
   a. CRLPeriodUnits=26
   b. CRLPeriod=weeks
   c. CRLDeltaPeriodUnits=0
   d. CRLDeltaPeriod=days

   QUESTION For how long is the certificate for the root CA valid?

   QUESTION What is the publication interval for the base CRL? Why is this interval such a relatively long one?

7. Save the file and close Notepad.

Installing a Stand-Alone Root CA

In this section, the student sitting at the odd-numbered computer, Computeryy, will copy the Capolicy.inf file to the %Systemroot% folder and then install a stand-alone root CA. You will need to use the Windows Server 2003 installation CD that accompanies the course materials. At some point during the installation, you might be prompted to insert this CD.

> **NOTE** These steps should be performed *only* by the student sitting at the member server in the domain (Computeryy). The other student should observe the process of installing a stand-alone CA. In the next exercise, students will alternate to perform several configuration tasks.

1. In Windows Explorer, copy the C:\Lab Manual\Lab 09\Capolicy.inf file to the root of the C:\Windows folder.

    IMPORTANT You must place this file at the root of the C:\Windows folder. Make sure that only the student sitting at Computeryy performs this step.

2. Click Start, point to Control Panel, and select Add Or Remove Programs.
3. In the Add Or Remove Programs dialog box, click Add/Remove Windows Components.
4. In the Windows Components Wizard, in the Components box, select the Certificate Services check box.
5. In the Microsoft Certificate Services message box stating that you cannot change the computer's name or domain membership after installing Certificate Services, click Yes to verify that you want to continue.
6. On the Windows Components page, click Next.
7. On the CA Type page, select the Stand-Alone Root CA option, select the Use Custom Settings To Generate The Key Pair And CA Certificate check box, and then click Next.

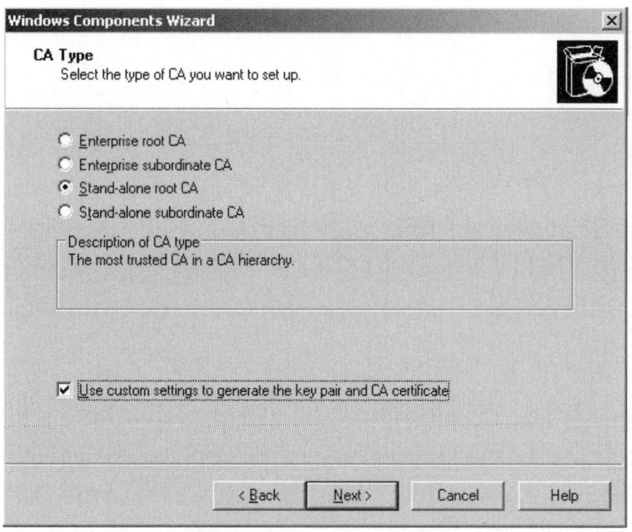

8. On the Public And Private Key Pair page, select the following options:
    a. In the CSP box, verify that Microsoft Strong Cryptographic Provider is selected.
    b. In the Hash Algorithm box, verify that SHA-1 is selected.

c. From the Key Length drop-down list, select 4096. Click Next.

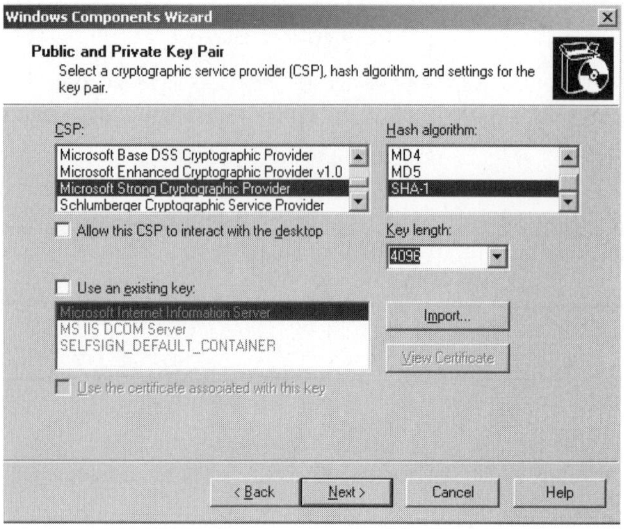

NOTE For reasons of interoperability, you should generally not select a Key Length greater than 4096. This increases certificate and certificate chain sizes and may not be supported by all applications and protocols. For example, some smart cards may not be able to store all the data from a large-keyed PKI. However, you should not select a size less the 2048.

In the next step, you will configure a common name and enter a validity period. The common name (CN) identifies the CA. Because of LDAP limitations, you should not make the CN longer than 64 characters and preferably not longer than 51 characters. We are configuring a long validity period of 20 years for this CA to reduce the administrative overhead of frequent CA certificate renews, although longer periods are common. The CA's certificate should be renewed when half of this period has expired and you should generate a new key pair for every other renewal.

9. On the CA Identifying Information page, in the Common Name text box, type **Contoso*dd*RootCA** (where *dd* is the two-digit number for your domain), verify that DC=contoso*dd*,DC=msft appears in the Distinguished Name Suffix box, type **20** in the Validity box, and then click Next. The Cryptographic Key Generation page appears.

10. When the cryptographic key generation process completes, you next see the Certificate Database Settings page. Click Next to accept the default database configuration settings.

The Microsoft Certificate Services dialog box appears with a message about stopping Internet Information Services (IIS). On a production stand-alone offline root CA, you do not need to install IIS. If you were installing a stand-alone root CA on a computer on which IIS was not installed, you would see a warning message that IIS was not installed and that Web enrollment would be unavailable for the CA.

11. In the Microsoft Certificate Services message box, click Yes to continue. You now see the Configuring Components page.
12. If prompted, insert the Windows Server 2003 Enterprise Edition CD and, on the Welcome To Microsoft Windows Server 2003 screen, click Exit.
13. On the Completing The Windows Components Wizard page, click Finish.
14. If you had to insert the Windows Server 2003 Enterprise Edition installation CD during the installation, remove it.
15. Close the Add Or Remove Programs dialog box.

Verifying Installation of Stand-Alone Root CA

In these steps, you will verify the installation of the stand-alone root CA.

1. On both computers, click Start, select Run, type **cmd** in the Open text box, and then click OK.
2. At the command prompt, type **certutil –dump**, and then press ENTER.

   Note that public key information for the stand-alone root CA is displayed in the output of the command on both computers.

   QUESTION Where is the information stored that is output from the certutil –dump command?

   QUESTION If you had installed certificate services on a stand-alone server, would you be able to view public key information on the domain controller at this point?

3. At the command prompt, type **certutil –cainfo**, and then press ENTER.

   Note that information for the CA appears on only the member server.

4. On both computers, click Start, select Run, type **dssite.msc**, and then click OK. Active Directory Sites And Services opens.

5. From the View menu, select Show Services Node.
6. In the console tree of Active Directory Sites And Services, expand Services, expand Public Key Services, and select AIA. The details pane shows the Contoso*dd*RootCA Certification Authority object.

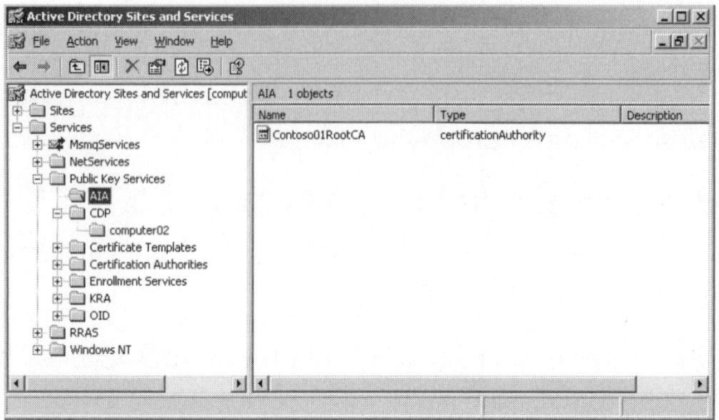

QUESTION Is the CA certificate currently trusted by all computers in the domain?

7. In the console tree, expand CDP, select Computer*yy*, and, in the details pane, note the object.

   If you had installed the root CA on a stand-alone server, you would have to publish this information to Active Directory by using the Certutil –dspublish command.

In the next step, you will remove the certificate information from Active Directory to simulate the configuration of an offline stand-alone root CA that is configured on a server that is a member of a workgroup and not an Active Directory domain.

1. On Computer*xx*, switch to the command prompt window, type **certutil –dsdel contoso*dd*rootca**, and then press ENTER.
2. On both computers, switch to Active Directory Sites And Services, press F5 to refresh the display, and note that the certificate information has been removed from Active Directory.
3. Close all open windows.

EXERCISE 9.2: PUBLISHING CRL AND AIA INFORMATION TO ACTIVE DIRECTORY FOR AN OFFLINE STAND-ALONE ROOT CA

Estimated completion time: 30 minutes

In this exercise, you will perform the steps that would be required if you were configuring an offline stand-alone root CA and publishing the CRL and AIA information to Active Directory. As you learned in the previous exercise, some CRL and AIA information is initially published to Active Directory when you install a stand-alone root CA on a member server. However, when your security requirements define the need for an offline root CA, you should install the CA on a computer that is not a member of the domain. In this case, you must manually publish information to Active Directory to ensure that the root CA is trusted by all the computers in the domain.

Examining and Modifying the CRL and AIA Settings

In this section, you will examine the CRL and AIA settings on the stand-alone root CA, and then you will modify the CRL and AIA by using a batch file.

1. On both computers, click Start, point to Administrative Tools, and select Certification Authority. The Certification Authority console opens normally on Computer*yy*, but opens with an error on Computer*xx*.
2. On Computer*xx*, in the Microsoft Certificate Services message box, click OK.
3. On Computer*xx*, in the Certification Authority console tree, right-click Certification Authority (Local), and select Retarget Certification Authority.
4. On Computer*xx*, in the Certification Authority dialog box, select the Another Computer option, type **Computer*yy*** in the text box, and then click Finish.
5. On both computers, in the Certification Authority console tree, expand Contoso*dd*RootCA, right-click Revoked Certificates, and select Properties.

> **QUESTION** What is the CRL publication interval? Where was this defined during setup?

6. Click Cancel to close the Revoked Certificates Properties dialog box.
7. On both computers, in the Certification Authority console tree, right-click Contoso*dd*RootCA, and select Properties.
8. Click the Extensions tab in the Contoso*dd*RootCA Properties dialog box.
9. Make sure that the Select Extension drop-down list displays CRL Distribution Point (CDP), and then select the entries in the CRL distribution list to review them.

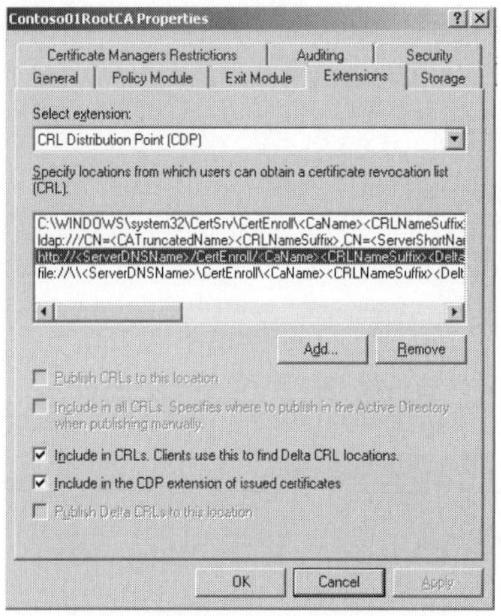

QUESTION What are the three types of locations from which you can retrieve the CRL?

10. In the Select Extension drop-down list, select Authority Information Access (AIA), and review the AIA list.
11. In the Contoso*dd*RootCA Properties dialog box, click the Auditing tab, and review the default audit settings. Note that none of the audit settings is enabled.
12. Click Cancel to close the Contoso*dd*RootCA Properties dialog box, but leave the Certification Authority console open.

    Only the student sitting at Computer*yy* should perform steps 13 through 21.

13. On Computer*yy*, open Windows Explorer, navigate to the C:\Lab Manual\Lab 09 folder, right-click the ModifyAIAandCDP.cmd file, and select Edit.

    In the next step, the student sitting at Computer*yy* prepares the batch file to map the namespace of Active Directory to the offline CA's registry configuration. On a member server, this step is unnecessary.

14. In the file, search for the string "dc=contoso*dd*,dc=msft" (without the quotes), and replace *dd* with the assigned number of your domain.

In the next step, the student sitting at Computer*yy* will prepare the batch file to update the CA with information on the location of the CDP and AIA.

15. In the file, search for the two instances of the string "computer*xx*", and replace *xx* with the assigned number of the domain controller (the odd-numbered computer).

16. Save the file, and then double-click to execute the file.

17. In Windows Explorer, right-click the SetValidityPeriodRootCA.cmd file, and then select Edit.

The commands in the file set a new validity period for certificates that the CA issues.

18. Review the commands in the file and then close it without saving.

19. Double-click the SetValidityPeriod.cmd file to execute it.

You now need to publish the updated information.

20. Switch to the Certification Authority console, right-click Revoked Certificates, point to All Tasks, and select Publish. You now see the Publish CRL dialog box.

21. In the Publish CRL dialog box, click OK.

22. On both computers, in the Certification Authority console tree, right-click Contoso*dd*RootCA and select Refresh. Right-click Contoso*dd*RootCA again, and then select Properties.

23. In the Contoso*dd*RootCA Properties dialog box, click the Extensions tab, and review the updated CDP and AIA information. Click Cancel to close the Contoso*dd*RootCA Properties dialog box.

Note that the file type has been removed as a method to retrieve information.

It is now necessary to copy the CRL and the CTL from the stand-alone root CA to the server specified as the location for the CDP (Computer*xx*). Only the student sitting at the odd-numbered computer, Computer*xx,* should perform steps 24 through 33.

24. On Computer*xx*, open Windows Explorer, and navigate to the C:\Intetpub\Wwwroot folder.

25. Create a folder named CertData beneath the Wwwroot folder.

    You will now copy the CRL and CTL files from Computer*yy* to the C:\Inetpub\Wwwroot\Certdata folder.

26. Click Start, select Run, type **\\computer*yy*\admin$\system32\certsrv\certenroll** in the Open text box, and then click OK.

27. In the CertEnroll folder, press CTRL+A to select all the files, and then press CTRL+C to copy the files to the clipboard.

28. In Windows Explorer, navigate to C:\Inetpub\wwwroot\certdata, and press CTRL+V to copy the files into the CertData folder.

29. In Windows Explorer, navigate to the C:\Lab Manual\Lab 09 folder, and then copy the LegalPolicy folder to the C:\Inetpub\wwwroot folder. In addition to other folders and files, you should now see both a CertData and a LegalPolicy folder within the Wwwroot folder.

    You now need to publish the CRL and AIA information to Active Directory.

30. On the odd-numbered computer, Computer*xx*, open a command prompt window, type **cd\inetpub\wwwroot\certdata**, and then press ENTER.

31. At the command prompt, type **certutil -dspublish -f contoso*dd*rootca.crl**, and then press ENTER.

32. At the command prompt, type **certutil -dspublish -f computer*yy*.contoso*dd*.msft_contoso*dd*rootca.crt RootCA**, and then press ENTER.

    For both commands, make sure you see a message indicating that the –dsPublish command completed successfully.

33. Type **gpupdate /force**, and then press ENTER.

    Both students should perform the following steps:

34. Click Start, select Run, type **dssite.msc** in the Open box, and then click OK to open the Active Directory Sites And Services console.

35. If necessary, from the View menu, select Show Services Node, and then verify that the CRL and AIA information has been published to Active Directory under the Public Key Services node by examining the details of the CDP and AIA nodes.

36. Click Start, select Run, type **certmgr.msc** in the Open box, and then click OK.

37. In the console tree of the Certificates – Current User console, expand Trusted Root Certification Authorities, and select Certificates.

38. In the details pane, double-click the Contoso*dd*RootCA certificate.

    On the even-numbered computer, you might see two instances of this certificate. You can double-click either instance.

39. Click Issuer Statement in the Certificate dialog box..

40. In the Disclaimer dialog box, click More Info. Internet Explorer opens, showing the Certificate Practice Statement that is downloaded from Computer*xx*.

41. Close all open windows. If you are prompted to save any of the windows, click No.

EXERCISE 9.3: INSTALLING AN ENTERPRISE SUBORDINATE CA

Estimated completion time: 25 minutes

After successfully installing the root CA, you need to install the enterprise subordinate CA. To do this, you must request a SubCA certificate from the root CA. In this exercise, you will install the enterprise subordinate CA and verify its installation. Perform steps 1 through 15 on only the odd-numbered computer for your domain, Computer*xx*.

1. Click Start, point to Control Panel, and select Add Or Remove Programs.
2. In the Add Or Remove Programs dialog box, click Add/Remove Windows Components.
3. In the Windows Components Wizard, in the Components box, select the Certificate Services check box.
4. In the Microsoft Certificate Services message box, click Yes.
5. On the Windows Components page, click Next.
6. On the CA Type page, click Enterprise Subordinate CA , select the Use Custom Settings To Generate The Key Pair And CA Certificate check box, and then click Next.

7. On the Public And Private Key Pair page, select the following options:
   a. In the CSP box, verify that Microsoft Strong Cryptographic Provider is selected.
   b. In the Hash Algorithm box, verify that SHA-1 is selected.
   c. From the Key Length drop-down list, select 2048.

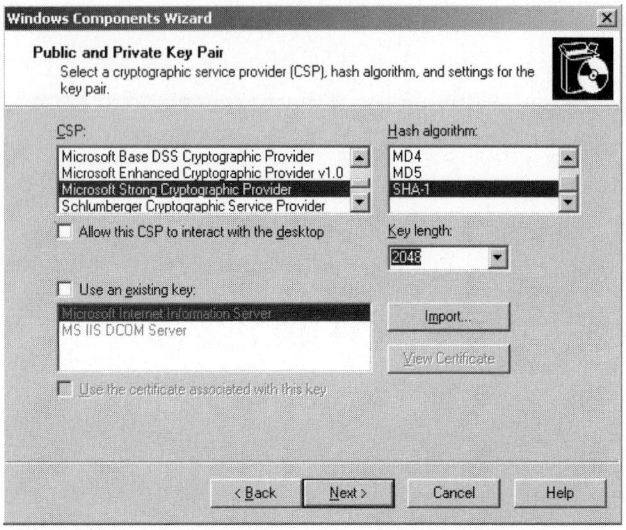

In the next step, you will configure the CN for the CA.

8. Click Next.
9. On the CA Identifying Information page, type **Contoso*dd*IssuingCA** (where *dd* is the two-digit number for your domain) in the Common Name text box, verify that DC=contoso*dd*,DC=msft appears in the Distinguished Name Suffix box, and then click Next.

> **QUESTION** What is the validity period for this CA?

10. On the Certificate Database Settings page, click Next to accept the default settings.

11. On the CA Certificate Request page, click Save The Request To A File, type **C:\certreq.req** in the Request File text box, and then click Next.

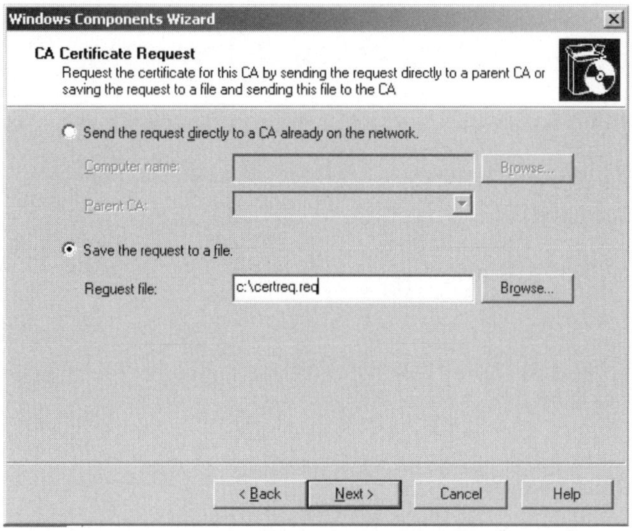

12. In the Microsoft Certificate Services message box stating that the installation must temporarily stop IIS, click Yes to continue.

13. The Configuring Components page appears and Certificate Services is installed.

    If prompted, insert the Windows Server 2003 Enterprise Edition CD, and on the Welcome To Microsoft Windows Server 2003 screen, click Exit.

14. In the Microsoft Certificate Services message box, click OK to acknowledge that you still have several steps to perform to complete the installation.

15. On the Completing The Windows Components Wizard page, click Finish, and then close the Add Or Remove Programs dialog box.

    In the next steps, you will process the request for a certificate on the stand-alone root CA by using the Certreq.req file. In these steps, you will transfer the file over the network, which is not a recommended practice for this kind of transaction. Normally, you would copy the request file to a secure medium, and then manually transfer it under strict security conditions to the vault containing the offline stand-alone root CA. A select group of highly trusted individuals might be involved in this process. Different individuals might perform different parts of the task to ensure security through role separation. Other individuals might be on hand to audit the process and to provide verification and documentation of the steps being performed.

Steps 16 through 31 should be performed by the student at Computer*yy*. The student at Computer*xx* should observe the steps.

16. On Computer*yy*, click Start, select Run, type **\\computer*xx*\c$** in the Open text box, and then click OK.
17. In the displayed folder, right-click the Certreq.req file, and select Copy.
18. Open Windows Explorer and navigate to the local C: drive. Paste the file to the root of the C: drive.
19. Click Start, point to Administrative Tools, and select Certification Authority.
20. In the console tree, right-click Contoso*dd*RootCA, point to All Tasks, and select Submit New Request.

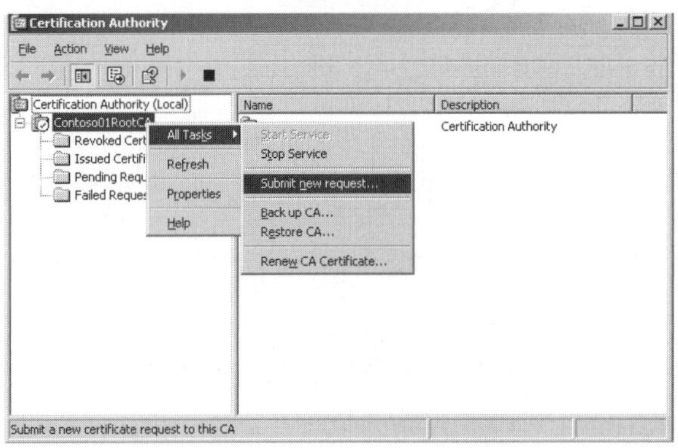

21. In the Open Request File dialog box, in the Look In drop-down list, select Local Disk (C:), select the Certreq.req file, and then click Open.
22. In the console tree, expand Contoso*dd*RootCA and select Pending Requests. In the details pane, right-click the certificate request, point to All Tasks, and then select Issue.

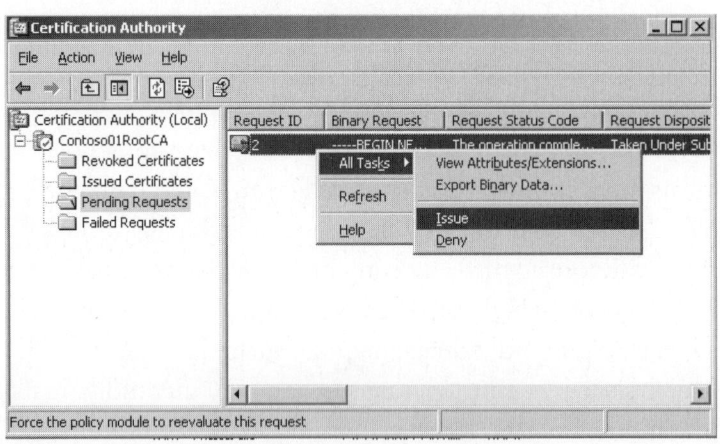

23. In the console tree, select Issued Certificates.
24. In the details pane, double-click the issued certificate, and click the Details tab in the Certificate dialog box.

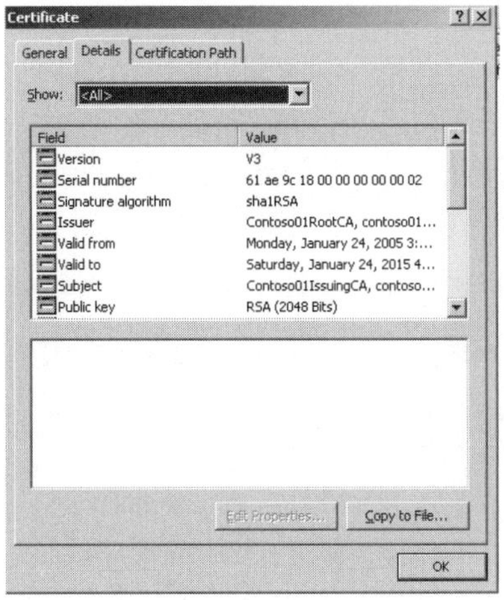

25. In the Certificate dialog box, click Copy To File. The Certificate Export Wizard appears.

26. On the Welcome To The Certificate Export Wizard page, click Next.

27. On the Export File Format page, select the Cryptographic Message Syntax Standard – PKCS # 7 Certificates (.P7B) option, select the Include All Certificates In The Certification Path If Possible check box, and then click Next.

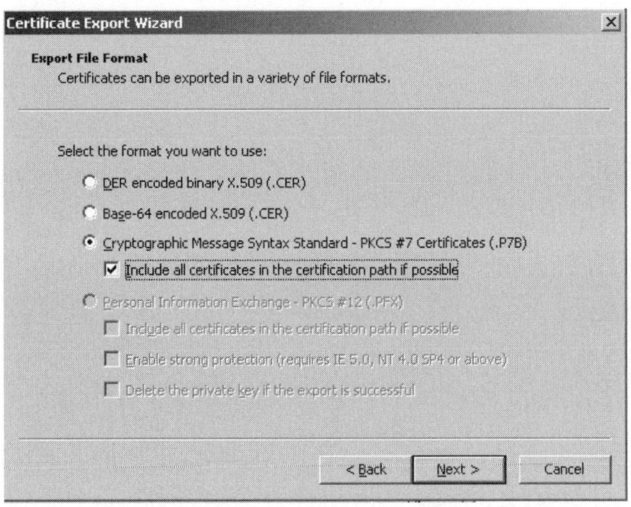

28. On the File To Export page, type **c:\subca.p7b**, and then click Next.

29. On the Completing The Certificate Export Wizard page, click Finish, and then click OK.

30. In the Certificate dialog box, click OK.

31. Close the Certification Authority console, and close all open windows.

    The student at Computer*xx* will now perform steps 32 through 42 to complete the installation of the CA.

32. On Computer*xx*, click Start, select Run, type **\\computer*yy*\c$** in the Open text box, and then click OK.
33. In the displayed folder, right-click the Subca.p7b file, and select Copy.
34. In Windows Explorer, navigate to the local hard drive, and copy the file to the root of the C: drive.
35. Click Start, point to Administrative Tools, and select Certification Authority.
36. In the console tree, right-click Contoso*dd*IssuingCA, and point to All Tasks, and then select Install CA Certificate.
37. In the Select File To Complete CA Installation, in the File Name box, type **c:\subca.p7b**, and then click Open.
38. In the Certification Authority console tree, right-click Contoso*dd*IssuingCA, point to All Tasks, and select Start Service.

    You will now modify the validity period for certificates that are issued by the subordinate CA.

39. In Windows Explorer, navigate to C:\Lab Manual\Lab 09, right-click the SetValidityPeriodSubCA.cmd file, and select Edit.
40. Review the commands in the file and then close it without saving.
41. Double-click the SetValidityPeriodSubCA.cmd file to execute it.
42. Close all open windows.

Verifying CA Installation and CDP and AIA Extensions

In this section, you will verify the installation of the subordinate CA and confirm that it is working properly. Both students should perform the following steps:

1. Open a command prompt window, type **gpupdate /force**, and then press ENTER.
2. At the command prompt, type **certutil –dump**, and press ENTER. Note that Computer*yy* displays two entries, one for the Contoso*dd*RootCA and another for the Contoso*dd*IssuingCA.

3. At the command prompt, type **certutil –store -enterprise Root**, and press ENTER. Information on the certificate used for the root CA is displayed.
4. At the command prompt, type **certutil –store -enterprise NTAuth**, and press ENTER. Information from the NTAuth store in Active Directory is displayed. NTAuth CAs are trusted throughout the forest to issue a wide variety of certificates. In this case, the trusted server is the subordinate CA.
5. Close the command prompt window.

   In the next steps, you will use the Windows Server 2003 Resource Kit PKI Health Tool to validate all the CDP and AIA extensions. You first have to register the dynamic linked library (DLL) by using the regsvr32 command.

6. Click Start, select Run, type **regsvr32 "c:\lab manual\lab 09\pkiview.dll"** (including the quotation marks) in the Open text box, and click OK.
7. Click OK to acknowledge the RegSvr32 message box.
8. Click Start, select Run, type **mmc "c:\lab manual\lab 09\pkiview.msc"** (including the quotation marks) in the Open text box, and then click OK.
9. In the console tree, expand Contoso*dd*RootCA.
10. Select Contoso*dd*RootCA. The status column in the details pane should list "OK" for all certificates. This indicates that the locations that AIA and CDP locations specified in the certificate were contacted and that the certificates were downloaded.
11. Spend a few moments, double-clicking and examining the entries in the details pane of the ContosoddRootCA and the ContosoddIssuingCA node.
12. Close the PKI Health Tool, and close all open windows.

Backing Up Certificate Services Database

An essential part of the maintenance of a CA is ensuring that you can restore the CA from a backup. Although you can back up the CA as part of a System State backup, you can also back up the CA separately from a System State backup. In this section, you will back up your CA.

1. Click Start, point to Administrative Tools, and select Certification Authority.

2. In the console tree, right-click your CA, point to All Tasks, and select Back Up CA. The Certification Authority Backup Wizard appears.
3. On the Welcome To The Certification Authority Backup Wizard page, click Next.
4. On the Items To Back Up page, select the Private Key And CA Certificate and the Certificate Database And Certificate Database Log check boxes.
5. In the Backup To This Location box, type **C:\CABackup**, and then click Next.
6. In the Certification Authority Backup Wizard message box, click OK.
7. On the Select A Password page, type **P@ssw0rd** in the Password and Confirm Password text boxes, and then click Next.
8. On the Completing The Certification Authority Backup Wizard page, click Finish.
9. Close the Certification Authority console.

Removing Certificate Services on the Even-Numbered Computer

Now that you have created a subordinate enterprise CA, there is no need for the Root CA to be online, except to create additional CAs, to publish CRLs, and to perform other tasks. You will now remove the root CA from the network by uninstalling certificate services on the even-numbered computer.

> **IMPORTANT** *Perform the following steps only on the even-numbered computer (Computeryy).*

1. Click Start, point to Control Panel, and select Add Or Remove Programs.
2. In the Add Or Remove Programs dialog box, click Add/Remove Windows Components.
3. In the Windows Components Wizard, in the Components box, clear the Certificate Services check box, and click Next.
4. On the Completing The Windows Components Wizard page, click Finish. Close the Add Or Remove Programs dialog box.

EXERCISE 9.4: MANAGING COMPUTER AND USER CERTIFICATES

Estimated completion time: 40 minutes

In this exercise, you will use several tools to manage computer and user certificates. You will request a computer certificate manually by using the Certificates snap-in. You will also configure version 2 certificate templates and Group Policy to support the autoenrollment of user certificates.

Viewing and Requesting Computer Certificates by Using the Certificates Snap-In

In this section, you will use the Certificates snap-in to examine and request computer certificates.

1. Click Start, select Run, type **mmc** in the Open box, and then click OK.
2. From the File menu of Console1, select Add/Remove Snap-In.
3. In the Add/Remove Snap-In dialog box, click Add.
4. In the Add Stand-Alone Snap-In dialog box, select Certificates, and click Add.
5. In the Certificates Snap-In dialog box, select the Computer Account option, and then click Next.
6. In the Select Computer dialog box, click Finish.
7. In the Add Stand-Alone Snap-In dialog box, click Close.
8. In the Add/Remove Snap-In dialog box, click OK.
9. From the File menu of Console1, select Save As.
10. In the Save As dialog box, select Desktop from the Look In drop-down list, type **Certificates.msc** in the File Name text box, and click Save. The name of the console changes to Certificates.
11. In the Certificates console tree, expand Certificates (Local Computer), expand Personal, and select Certificates. The details pane is populated with two certificates if you are sitting at the domain controller or no certificates if you are sitting at the member server.

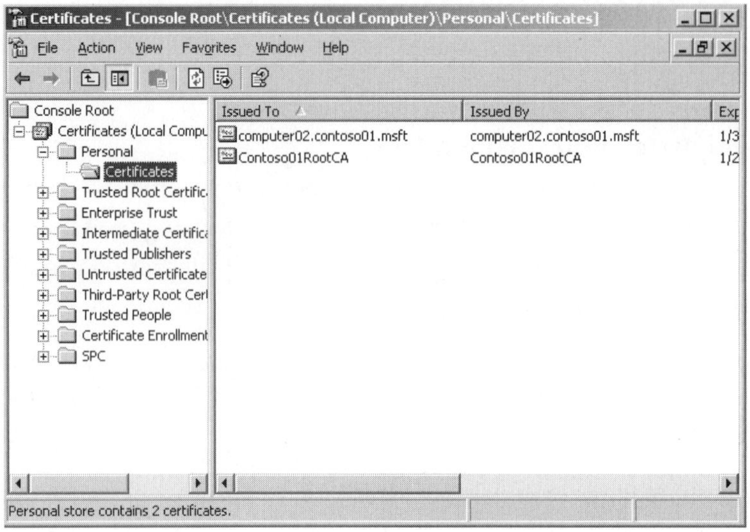

NOTE When you have an enterprise CA, domain controllers are automatically issued a computer certificate through a certificate autoenrollment process. If you do not see two certificates on the domain controller, the reason is likely that autoenrollment process for the computer certificate has not occurred. You might have to issue a gpupdate /force command to cause the certificate to appear on the domain controller sooner. Also, you might have to refresh the display in the Certificate console tree.

12. On the odd-numbered computer, in the details pane, right-click the certificate that displays Computer*zz*.contoso*dd*.msft in the Issued To column and select Properties.

QUESTION What is listed for the intended purpose for your certificate and for your partner's certificate? What entity issued the certificate to your computer and your partner's computer?

Computer*yy* needs a similar certificate that can be used for both server and client authentication. In steps 13 through 20, the student assigned to Computer*yy* will request a Computer Certificate from the enterprise subordinate CA.

13. On Computer*yy*, right-click Certificates, point to All Tasks, and select Request New Certificate. The Certificate Request Wizard appears.

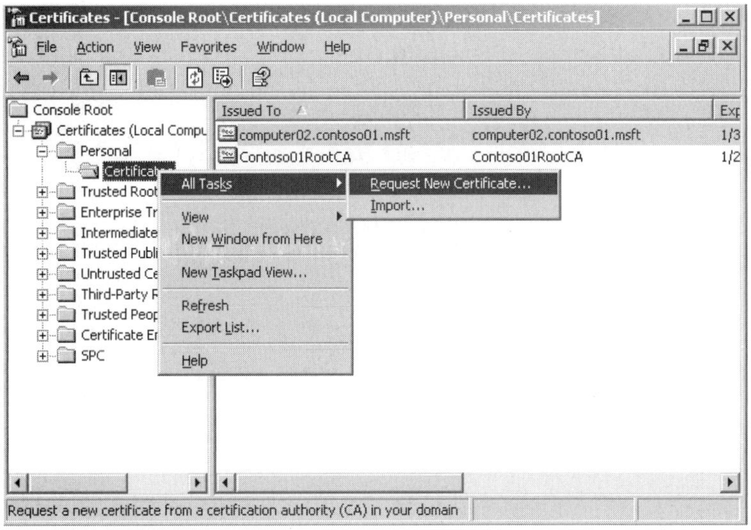

14. On the Welcome To The Certificate Request Wizard page, click Next.
15. On the Certificate Types page, click Next to accept the default certificate type of Computer.
16. On the Certificate Friendly Name And Description page, in the Friendly Name text box, type **Client-Server Authentication**, and then click Next.
17. On the Completing The Certificate Request Wizard page, click Finish.
18. In the Certificate Request Wizard message box, click OK.
19. In the details pane of the Certificates console, verify that the certificate was issued by Contoso*dd*IssuingCA in the Issued By column
20. Right-click the certificate, select Properties, verify that the intended purpose is client and server authentication, and then click Cancel.

Examining Role-Based Permissions

On Windows Server 2003, Enterprise and Datacenter Editions, it is possible to use role-based permissions to enforce the separation of roles for managing a PKI. In this section, you will spend a few moments examining this feature and considering its implications without making any configuration changes to your PKI.

1. On both computers, click Start, point to Administrative Tools, and select Certification Authority.
2. On Computer*yy*, in the Certification Authority console tree, right-click Certification Authority (Local), and select Retarget Certification Authority.

3. On Computer*yy*, in the Certification Authority dialog box, select the Another Computer option, type **Computer*xx*** in the text box, and then click Finish.
4. In the Certification Authority console tree, right-click Contoso*dd* IssuingCA, and select Properties.
5. In the Contoso*dd*IssuingCA Properties dialog box, click the Security tab, and examine the permission types.

   QUESTION What four roles are listed in the Permissions box?

6. Leave the Contoso*dd*IssuingCA Properties dialog box open.
7. Click Start, select Run, type **c:\windows\help\cs.chm** in the Open text box, and then click OK.
8. In the Certificate Services Help console, click the Search tab, and type **"role-based administration"** (including the quotation marks) in the Type The Word(s) To Search For Box, and click List Topics.
9. Double-click Role-Based Administration in the Select Topic box, read the help file, and answer the following questions.

   QUESTION Some of the roles described in the article are CA-based roles, and some are operating system–based roles. List the roles according to their category.

   QUESTION Why does role-based administration of a CA enhance its security?

10. Using the help file, find the command you would use to enforce separation of roles.

    QUESTION What is the command you would use to enforce separation of roles?

11. Close the Certificate Services Help console.

Managing Certificate Templates for Autoenrollment

Autoenrollment allows for easy distribution of certificates to end entities such as users, computers, smart cards, and so on. Autoenrollment is a function of version 2 certificate templates, Group Policy settings, and, in some cases, the client operating system. For example, only Microsoft Windows XP and later clients can automatically enroll user certificates. Version 2 certificate templates are available only on CAs installed on servers running the Microsoft Windows Server 2003 Enterprise and Datacenter Editions.

In this section, you will create a version 2 certificate template based on the User version 1 template and then configure a Group Policy for autoenrollment.

> **NOTE** Autoenrollment is especially useful in facilitating the deployment of smart card certificates. It is also useful for situations in which you need to deploy computer certificates or user certificates, or both, to support 802.1X authentication for wireless networks. However, as with any technology, you should evaluate the potential risks before you deploy it.

1. In the Certification Authority console that you opened in the previous section, in the console tree, right-click Certificate Templates, and select Manage. The Certificate Templates console opens.
2. In the Certificate Templates console, scroll down the details pane to locate the User certificate, right-click the User Certificate, and select Duplicate Template.

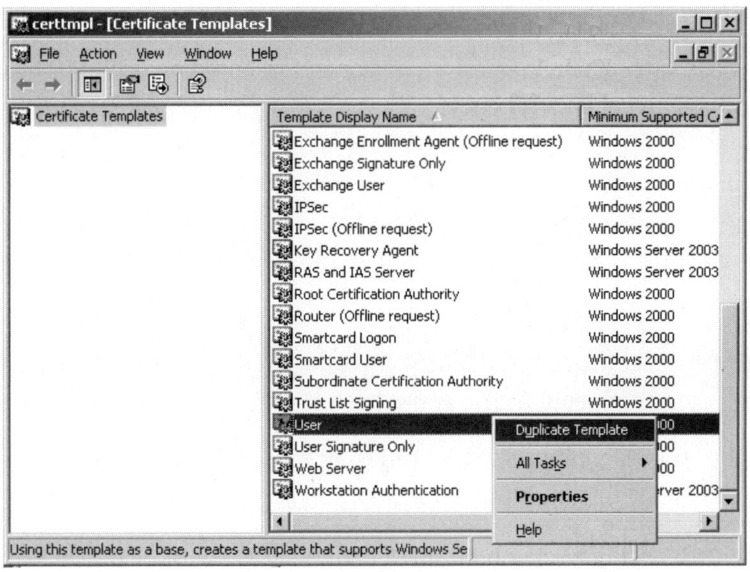

The Properties Of New Template dialog box appears.

3. In the Properties Of New Template dialog box, in the Template Display Name text box, type **Auto Enroll User** *zz*, ensure that the Publish Certificate In Active Directory check box is selected, and ensure that the Do Not Automatically Reenroll If A Duplicate Certificate Exists In Active Directory check box is *not* selected (enabling this setting overrides other settings that allow autoenrollment of the certificate).

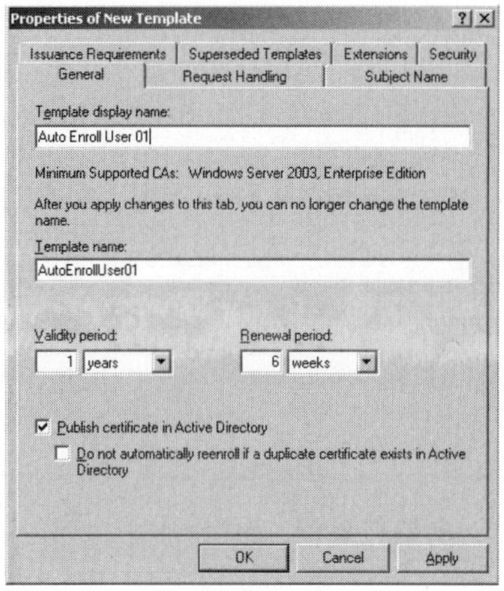

4. Click the Security tab.

   In the next step, you will configure permissions on the template to allow autoenrollment of the certificate. Normally, you would assign these permissions to a group. However, for this demonstration, you will assign permissions to a user account. Both the Enroll and Autoenroll allow permissions are required. Domain Users has the Enroll allow permission by default.

5. On the Security tab, click Add.
6. In the Enter The Object Names To Select box, type **sburk*zz***, and then click OK.
7. On the Security tab, in the Permissions For SBurk*zz* box, in the Allow column, select the Autoenroll check box, and then click OK.
8. Close the Certificates Template console.
9. Switch to the Certification Authority console. Verify that Certificate Templates is still selected in the console tree.
10. On the Action menu, point to New, and then select Certificate Template To Issue.
11. In the Enable Certificates Template dialog box, select the Auto Enroll User *zz* template, and click OK.

    QUESTION What are the intended purposes of the certificate?

    You will now configure a GPO to configure automatic enrollment of the certificate.

12. Click Start, point to Administrative Tools, and select Group Policy Management.
13. In the Group Policy Management console tree, if necessary, expand the Forest node, expand the Domains node, expand the Contoso*dd*.msft node, expand the Location*zz* node, and select the R and D OU.
14. Right-click the R and D OU, and select Create And Link A GPO Here.
15. In the New GPO dialog box, in the Name text box, type **Auto Enroll User Policy** ***zz***, and click OK.
16. In the details pane, right-click Auto Enroll User Policy *zz*, and select Edit.
17. In the Group Policy Object Editor, navigate to User Configuration\Windows Settings\Security Settings, and select Public Key Policies.
18. In the details pane, double-click Autoenrollment Settings.
19. In the Autoenrollment Settings dialog box, select the Renew Expired Certificates, Update Pending Certificates, And Revoked Certificates check box. Select the Update Certificates That Use Certificate Templates check box, and then click OK. These settings will enable certificate cleanup, automatic renewal, and publication in Active Directory.
20. Close the Group Policy Object Editor, and close the Group Policy Management console.
21. Open a command prompt window, and at the command prompt, type **gpupdate /force**, and then press ENTER.
22. Close the command prompt window.
23. Close the Certificates console, and click No when prompted to save the console settings.

    The accounts that are used in these labs were set up by using batch scripts. During the account creation, none of the user accounts was configured with an e-mail address. Without an e-mail address in the properties of the user account, the automatic enrollment of the user certificate will fail. Before proceeding to test the autoenrollment, you must add an e-mail address to SBurk*zz* account object.

24. Click Start, select Run, type **dsa.msc** in the Open box, and click OK.
25. In the Active Directory Users And Computers console, navigate to the Location*zz*\R and D OU, and in the details pane, double-click the SBurk*zz* account object.

26. In the SBurkzz Properties dialog box, in the E-mail text box, type **sburk*zz*@contoso*dd*.msft**, and click OK.

27. Close the Active Directory Users And Computers console, close any remaining open windows, and log off.

28. Log on as Contoso*dd*\SBurk*zz* using P@ssw0rd as the password.

    In steps 29 through 32, you will examine the details of the certificate issued through the autoenrollment process to the SBurk*zz* account. The certificate could take several minutes to appear. If the certificate does not appear immediately, proceed to the review questions and then return to these steps to complete this exercise.

29. Click Start, select Run, type **certmgr.msc** in the Open text box, and click OK.

30. In the console tree of the Certificates – Current User console, expand Personal, and click Certificates.

31. In the details pane, double-click the certificate issued to SBurk*zz*, click the Details tab, and spend a few moments examining the details of the certificate, and then click OK to close the Certificates dialog box.

32. Close the Certificates – Current User console.

33. Click Start, select Run, **type runas /user:Contoso*dd*\admin*zz* "mmc c:\windows\system32\certsrv.msc"** (including the quotation marks) in the Open box, click OK, enter your password in the command prompt, and press ENTER. The Certification Authority console opens.

34. On Computer*yy*, right-click Certification Authority (local), and select Retarget Certification Authority.

35. On Computer*yy*, in the Certification Authority dialog box, select the Another Computer option, type **computer*xx***, and then click Finish.

36. On both computers, in the console tree, expand ContosoddIssuingCA, and click Issued Certificates. The details pane shows a number of certificates.

37. Double-click the sburk*xx* and sburk*yy* certificates, and briefly examine the details of each.

38. Close all open windows and log off.

LAB REVIEW QUESTIONS

Estimated completion time: 15 minutes

1. You do not have sufficient hardware to dedicate a computer to be an offline stand-alone CA. Also, the only "secure vault" to which you have access is a safety deposit box at a financial institution. What could you do to create an offline stand-alone root CA?
2. Why do you specify an empty CDP and AIA in the Capolicy.inf file for the stand-alone root CA?
3. You want to limit the length of a certificate chain, that is, the number of CAs below the root CA in the CA hierarchy. When and where do you define this?
4. You use Outlook Web Access (OWA) to allow users access to their Exchange mailboxes by using a Web browser. Users access the OWA Web site by connecting to the external IP address of your corporate firewall. You are using an SSL certificate issued by your internal Enterprise CA to encrypt the Web traffic. Users are complaining about the length of time that it takes to connect to the OWA Web site. You suspect that the client computers cannot download the CRL and that this is causing the delay. What should you do to ensure that the CRL is available to external clients?
5. You have enforced separation of roles on your CA. To how many roles can a user account belong?

LAB CHALLENGE 9.1: DESIGNING A PUBLIC KEY INFRASTRUCTURE

Estimated completion time: 45 minutes

Contoso Pharmaceuticals makes very limited use of digital certificates. For some time, Contoso has been using a digital certificate that it purchased from a third-party Certification Authority. This certificate is used to encrypt HTTP traffic for Outlook Web Access and for a Microsoft SharePoint Portal Server that is available to external customers and partners. This solution has been adequate for some time. However, Contoso's network and its security requirements have grown. Moreover, Contoso has planned several projects that make it desirable for Contoso to implement its own PKI.

Currently, the Contoso network consists of a single forest with three domains. These domains are located at each of Contoso's locations in Toronto, Boston, and Seattle. The forest root domain is named contoso.com and is located at corporate headquarters in Boston. The two child domains are named Toronto.contoso.com and Seattle.contoso.com.

Contoso Pharmaceuticals uses a distributed administration model. All aspects of network administration in the three locations are performed locally. Further, within each domain, separate teams of administrators are delegated the authority to manage user and computer accounts. The Boston office is also responsible for the management of all centralized network services. This includes the proposed PKI.

You are a member of the PKI team that has been assembled to design the PKI. The team leader begins the project by stating the following:

"As you know, we have a number of proposed projects that require the implementation of PKI. The Research and Development department based in Seattle wants to use Internet Protocol Security (IPSec) with certificate-based authentication to secure transmission of data over the network. We have an issue in a satellite office in Mississauga, Canada, where they have a need to implement a wireless network in the shipping department. Ideally, they would like to use 802.1X to ensure the secure distribution of keys that are used to encrypt the wireless traffic. We would like to start issuing smart cards to users who require remote access. Eventually, all VPN access will require certificate-based authentication, and beyond that we will start making extensive use of smart cards once we upgrade more internal client desktop operating systems to Windows XP. Potentially, that is a lot of certificates to distribute.

"Currently, only about 50 percent of the users are running Windows XP. A number of users who are running down-level clients will require user certificates. All the computers in the Research and Development department will be upgraded to Windows XP, and all users who require VPN access will be issued new laptops with Windows XP installed.

"We have recently revised our security policy and Service Level Agreements in anticipation of the PKI implementation. The security policy states that we take the necessary and prudent measures to prevent against the theft of any encryption keys. This means, among other things, that we protect the servers hosting the CAs as much as possible.

"We have a number of other requirements. First, because of our delegated administration model, the OU computer and user admins must be able to manage and issue certificates to computers and users. That is, the CA hierarchy should support the separate management of computer and user accounts. Second, we want to keep the task of auditing of these servers separate from the network administrators. Third, we want to prevent any CA admins in the regional offices from creating additional subordinate CAs. Finally, our partner, Northwind Traders, has its own PKI and we need a mechanism whereby we trust each other's internal certificates, but we need to ensure that by creating this trust, we don't create an unintended trust with another organization. I know that in Windows 2000 you can do this with certificate trust lists, but I understand there is a new feature in Windows Server 2003 that replaces this functionality."

For this lab challenge, working with your partner or in small groups assigned by your instructor, consider this scenario and answer the following questions. When you have finished, your instructor will review your results in a class discussion.

1. What is the minimum number of CAs you need to meet the requirements of the scenario?
2. Where will these CAs be located?
3. What is the number of CAs you would place in the Toronto and the Seattle offices?
4. What is the minimum version of Windows Server 2003 that you require for each CA?
5. Given your answer to question 3, what implicit or explicit requirements in the scenario will cause you to choose one version of Windows Server 2003 over another?
6. What file do you have to prepare before you install the first CA in the hierarchy?
7. One of the requirements is that you be able to limit the ability of domain administrators to create additional subordinate CAs. How would you accomplish this?
8. One of the requirements of the scenario is that you establish a trust relationship with Northwind Traders and you further establish the trust in such a way as to prevent the creation of an unintended trust. How can you accomplish this?

9. If your design calls for an offline stand-alone root CA, what do you need to do to ensure the availability of the Certificate Revocation Distribution Point (CDP) and the Authority Information Access (AIA) locations?
10. Does your design call for the separation of roles? If so, what are the separate roles?
11. Will your CA hierarchy be based on geography, certificate use, departments, or some combination of these?
12. You need to provide an extremely high degree of protection for the root CA. What measures should you take to provide this protection?
13. What can you do during the installation of the first CA in the hierarchy to provide a high degree of assurance?

LAB 10

PROTECTING INTRANET COMMUNICATIONS

This lab contains the following exercises and activities:

- Exercise 10.1: Auditing Firewall Logs
- Exercise 10.2: Configuring Local IPSec Policies
- Exercise 10.3: Examining Wireless Settings for 802.1x Authentication
- Lab Review Questions
- Lab Challenge 10.1: Designing Security for Data Transmission

SCENARIO

As a network administrator at Contoso Pharmaceuticals, you have wide-ranging responsibilities. For example, you are responsible for auditing the firewall logs on the computer running Microsoft Internet Security and Acceleration (ISA) Server that is installed at a small branch office and assisting the network administrator at the branch office as needed. You are also responsible for ensuring the security of servers in the screened subnet, in particular the DNS server that hosts an authoritative zone for public DNS records. Finally, you have been asked to help design security for a proposed wireless network.

After completing this lab, you will be able to:

- **Interpret and analyze Web Proxy firewall logs to detect possible compromises.**
- **Configure and implement IPSec policies.**
- **Use Network Monitor to view IPSec-encrypted traffic.**
- **Use the IP Security Monitor tool to verify IPSec communications.**
- **Use the Netsh command-line tool to view static and dynamic IPSec settings.**
- **Configure RADIUS settings for 802.1x using EAP-TLS authentication.**
- **Configure Group Policy settings for wireless clients.**

Estimated lesson time: 135 minutes

BEFORE YOU BEGIN

To complete this lab, you will need to have done the following:

- Created a Member Servers organizational unit (OU) and moved the Computer*yy* member server object to the OU, as instructed in steps 3 through 7 of Lab Exercise 3.4, "Using Group Policy to Configure Automatic Update Clients," in Lab 3, "Reducing the Risk of Software Vulnerabilities."
- Performed the steps in the "Before You Begin" section of Lab 4, "Designing a Management Infrastructure," to create user accounts and to grant the Domain Users the right to log on locally to the domain controller.

NOTE In this lab, you will see the characters *dd*, *pp*, xx, yy, and zz. These directions assume that you are working on computers that are configured in pairs and that each computer has a number.

When you see *dd*, substitute the number used for your domain. When you see *pp*, substitute the number of your partner's computer. When you see xx, substitute the unique number assigned to the lower-numbered (odd-numbered) computer of the pair. When you see yy, substitute the unique number assigned to the higher-numbered (even-numbered) computer of the pair. When you see zz, substitute the number assigned to the computer you are using. The following example assumes that the partner pair of computers has been assigned the names Computer05 and Computer06 and that you have been assigned Computer05.

Computer*pp* = Computer06 = your partner's computer

Computerxx = Computer05 = lower-numbered computer

Computeryy = Computer06 = higher-numbered computer

Computerzz = Computer05 = computer you are using

Contoso*dd*.msft = Contoso03.msft = Active Directory directory service domain you are using

Additionally, in Exercise 10.2, you will work with a student who has been assigned a computer in another domain. Your lab partner should be a member of the domain with which you established a forest trust in Exercise 5.3 of Lab 5, "Designing Active Directory Security." Before Exercise 10.2, your instructor will assign you a partner for this lab. In Lab Exercise 10.2, this partner is referred to as your DNS partner. When you see the characters *n* or *nn*, these refer to the number assigned to your DNS partner; for example, 10.1.1.*n* refers to the Internet Protocol (IP) address of your DNS partner.

EXERCISE 10.1: AUDITING FIREWALL LOGS

Estimated completion time: 25 minutes

You are the remote administrator of an ISA Server computer used in a branch office of Contoso Pharmaceuticals. There is a single overworked branch-office network administrator who spends most of his time dealing with helping users and has been neglectful of patch-management procedures. The ISA Server computer logs traffic to and from the Internet in log files. The Web Proxy log records all the traffic handled by the Web Proxy Service of the ISA 2000 Server computer. Every Monday morning, you examine the ISA Server logs that were generated over the weekend. Normally, no one is in the office over the weekend. Before reviewing the logs, you verify that only one employee was in the office during the weekend to complete work on a special project, and the employee did not open Microsoft Internet Explorer or access the Internet from his computer. However, several computers in the office were left on during the weekend.

In this exercise, you will examine a sample Internet Security and Acceleration (ISA) Server Web Proxy log to determine if it has recorded any events that should cause concern. Your instructor will provide specific instructions about completing the exercise, including whether the exercise will be completed individually, in groups, or as an instructor-led discussion.

1. Log on as Contoso*dd*\Admin*zz*.
2. Click Start, select Run, type **explorer** in the Open box, and then click OK.
3. In Windows Explorer, browse to C:\Lab Manual\Lab 10, and then double-click IsaWebPrx040306.log.

   The sample ISA Web Proxy log file opens in Notepad.

> **NOTE** This log file is based on events recorded in an actual ISA Server log file. However, the domain names and IP addresses have been changed. The internal network is represented by the address range 192.168.100.1 to 192.168.100.255. All other IP addresses, including those that use the private address ranges of 10.x.y.z and 172.16.x.y, represent external hosts. The external IP address of the ISA Server computer is represented by the IP address 172.16.25.239. All domain names that use examplex.com represent external domains.
>
> To help you read the log files, note the meaning of the various prefixes used to describe the fields in the log file: "c" indicates client actions, "s" indicates server actions, "cs" indicates client-to-server actions, "sc" indicates server-to-client actions, and "r" indicates remote.

4. In the log file, toward the top, locate the entry that represents a GET request for a file named Default.ida from the ISA Server computer, and answer the following questions.

   Throughout this exercise, you might find it helpful to use the Find feature of Notepad from the Edit menu to quickly locate the entries of interest.

   QUESTION Does this entry look like a legitimate request? If not, why not? Hint: Look at the length of the request.

   QUESTION Why would an attacker send an excessively long Uniform Resource Locator (URL) to a Web server?

   QUESTION Was the request successful? Hint: Look at the Hypertext Transfer Protocol (HTTP) status code in the sc-status column (the last entry on the line); an HTTP status code of 200 would indicate a successful request.

5. In the log file, locate the group of entries that display the IP address of 10.12.209.34 in the C-IP field (the left-most entry on each of the lines), and answer the following questions.

   QUESTION What kinds of files do the requests attempt to invoke?

   QUESTION What features of these requests lead you to believe that they represent an attempt to compromise a Web server?

   QUESTION A directory traversal attack attempts to invoke executable files that are found on the local hard drive outside of the virtual directories used by the Web site. Does this group of requests represent an attempted directory traversal attack?

   QUESTION Was the attempt to compromise the server successful? Hint: An HTTP status code of 200 indicates a successful request.

6. In the log file, locate the group of entries that displays the internal IP address of 192.168.100.222 in the C-IP field (the left-most entry on each of the lines), and answer the following questions.

   QUESTION Based on the scenario that begins this lab exercise, what features of these requests might cause you to believe that an internal computer might have been compromised? Hint: Look at the times the requests are made.

   QUESTION Were the requests from the internal computer to the Example2.net Web site successful?

QUESTION What information in the log file can you use to do research on the Internet to determine whether the internal computer has been compromised?

QUESTION If the internal computer has been compromised, what protection does the firewall offer?

QUESTION Firewall administrators are generally conscientious when configuring firewall rules to limit inbound traffic. Why is it also important to restrict and inspect (where possible) outbound traffic? Hint: Consider how stateful filtering works.

QUESTION Assuming that the user of the computer did nothing malicious, was using the computer in accordance with a thorough Acceptable Internet Use Policy, and the exploit was well known, speculate as to how the computer might have become infected and what general vulnerability led to the compromise.

7. Close Notepad and all open windows.

EXERCISE 10.2: CONFIGURING LOCAL IPSEC POLICIES

Estimated completion time: 60 minutes

One of your responsibilities is to manage security on a DNS server that is located in the screened subnet of your company. To provide fault tolerance and availability, the primary standard zone is replicated to standard secondary zones at your Internet service provider (ISP) by using standard-zone transfer mechanisms. You want to ensure the confidentiality of the DNS records when they are replicated from the primary to the standard DNS zones. You and the ISP decide to implement Internet Protocol Security (IPSec) to ensure the confidentiality of the zone transfer.

To implement this IPSec configuration, you have to take into account several considerations. In particular, the DNS server is a member of a domain within the screened subnet and you must ensure that the IPSec configuration does not interfere with domain communications.

To complete this exercise, you will configure a Microsoft Management Console (MMC) that you will use to manage IPSec. If you are working at an even-numbered computer, you will install the DNS service. You will then use a batch file to create and configure a standard primary zone for this exercise. You will then configure an IPSec policy that contains the rules, filters, and filter actions to create a working configuration that meets the requirements of the scenario. Finally, you will use Microsoft Network Monitor and the IP Security Monitor console to verify the IPSec negotiation with your partner computer.

IMPORTANT In this lab exercise, in addition to your regular lab partner, you will partner with a student in another domain. This additional partner should be one who is assigned to a computer in the domain with which you established a forest trust in Lab 5. Throughout this exercise, your partner in the other domain is referred to as the "DNS partner." Also, when referring to your DNS partner's assigned number, the characters *nn* are used in the lab steps. Before proceeding with this lab, ensure that you have been assigned a DNS partner and that you record your partner's assigned number and IP address. This lab exercise works best with an even number of student domains. If there is an odd number of domains in the classroom, your instructor might assign two DNS partners to one student pair. If this is the case, please pay attention to the information in the following steps that are specific to this situation. Alternatively, your instructor might ask some students to double up on computers for this exercise.

Configuring an MMC to Manage IPSec

In this section, you will create a custom MMC that collects two important tools for managing IPSec, IP Security Management and IP Security Monitor, into a single location.

1. Click Start, select Run, type **mmc** in the Open dialog box, and then click OK.
2. From the File menu, select Add/Remove Snap-In.
3. In the Add/Remove Snap-In dialog box, click Add.
4. In the Add Standalone Snap-In dialog box, select the IP Security Policy Management snap-in, and then click Add.
5. In the Select Which Computer Or Domain dialog box, ensure that the Local Computer option is selected, and then click Finish.
6. In the Add Standalone Snap-In dialog box, select the IP Security Monitor snap-in, click Add, and then click Close.
7. In the Add/Remove Snap-In dialog box, click OK.
8. From the File menu, select Save As.
9. Select the Save In drop-down list, select Desktop, type **IP Sec Tools** in the File Name box, and then click Save.
10. Minimize the IP Sec Tools console.

Installing DNS on Even-Numbered Computers

To complete this lab exercise, it is necessary to install the DNS service on the even-numbered computers in the lab. You will need to have your Microsoft Windows Server 2003 Enterprise Edition CD available to install the DNS service. Perform these steps on only the even-numbered computers (Computeryy).

1. Click Start, point to Control Panel, and select Add Or Remove Programs.
2. In the Add Or Remove Programs dialog box, click Add/Remove Windows Components to open the Windows Components Wizard.
3. On the Windows Components page, in the Components box, select Networking Services, and then click Details.
4. In the Networking Services Dialog box, select the Domain Name System (DNS) check box, and click OK.
5. On the Windows Components page, click Next. The Configuring Components page appears.
    a. If the Insert Disk dialog box appears, insert the Windows Server 2003 CD in the CD-ROM, and click OK if necessary.
    b. If the Welcome to Microsoft Windows Server 2003 screen appears, click Exit.
6. On the Completing The Windows Components Wizard page, click Finish.
7. Close the Add Or Remove Programs dialog box.

Creating and Configuring a DNS Standard Primary Zone

In this section, you will create a standard primary DNS zone for use in the IPSec lab exercise. You create the zone by editing and then running a batch file. Perform this excercise on both the odd- and even-numbered computers.

> **NOTE** *To help avoid confusion, the batch file creates a DNS zone for the Fabrikamzz.com domain, rather than the Contosozz.com domain.*

1. Open Windows Explorer, navigate to the C:\Lab Manual\Lab 10 folder, right-click DNSzoneCreate.bat, and select Edit.
2. In Notepad, select the Edit menu, and select Replace.
3. In the Replace dialog box, type **zz** in the Find What text box, type your two-digit assigned number (01, 02, 03, and so on) in the Replace With box, and click Replace All.

4. Click Cancel to close the Replace dialog box.
5. Save the file and close Notepad.
6. Double-click DNSzoneCreate.bat. The batch file creates a standard primary zone for Fabrikam*zz*.com, configures the zone to allow zone transfers, and then adds DNS records to the zone.

Verifying Zone Transfer Settings

In this section, you will verify that you can transfer zone information from your DNS partner server. Before proceeding, make sure you know your DNS partner's IP address and assigned computer number.

1. Open a command prompt window, type **nslookup**, and then press ENTER.
2. At the Nslookup prompt, type **server 10.1.1.*n*** (where *n* is the last octet of your DNS partner's IP address).
3. At the Nslookup prompt, type **fabrikam*nn*.com** (where *nn* is the two-digit number assigned to your DNS partner), and then press ENTER.
4. Type **ls -d fabrikam*nn*.com**, and press ENTER. The zone records for the zone should be displayed in the output.

   If you have two DNS partners, repeat steps 2 through 4 using the numbers assigned to your second DNS partner.

5. At the Nslookup prompt, type **exit**, and then press ENTER. Leave the command prompt window open and proceed to the next section.

Creating an IPSec Policy to Secure Zone Transfer Traffic

In this section, you will create an IPSec policy that will allow normal communications within your domain, but restrict traffic outside of your domain. The IPSec interface can initially be a little confusing. So, before proceeding, you should consider the elements of an IPSec policy. They are as follows:

- **IPSec Policy** An IPSec policy is a collection of one or more policy rules. Only one IPSec policy can be assigned (active) at a time.
- **Policy Rule** A policy rule is a correlation of a single filter list with a filter action.
- **Filter List** A filter list contains packet filters that define the types of traffic to which a filter action may be applied. A filter list includes IP address, protocols, ports, and directions. Note that the IPSec driver orders rules according to filter-list specificity. For example, the IPSec

driver will process a rule containing a filter that specifies individual IP addresses before processing a rule containing more general subnet addresses.

- **Filter Action** A filter action defines the types of action and the methods by which security is established. The three basic filter actions are permit, block, or negotiate. Permit means that no security negotiation will be performed for the matching traffic. Block means that the traffic will be dropped. Negotiate means that one or more security methods will be attempted (in order of preference). Each security method determines the security protocol, hashing algorithms, and so on.
- **Authentication Methods** Authentication methods define (in order of preference) the authentication used for IPsec peers during IPSec negotiations. The three authentication methods are Kerberos version 5 protocol, certificate, and shared-key.

When you are ready to continue, perform the following steps:

1. Open the IPSec tools console you created earlier, right-click IP Security Policies On Local Computer and select Create IP Security Policy.

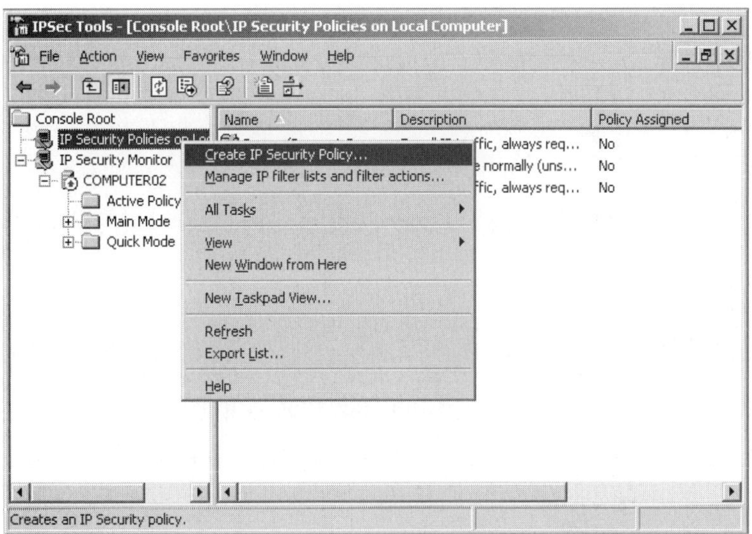

   The IP Security Policy Wizard appears.

2. On the Welcome To The IP Security Policy Wizard page, click Next.
3. On the IP Security Policy Name, type **Secure DNS Zone Transfers** in the Name box, and then click Next.

4. On the Requests For Secure Communication page, verify that the Activate The Default Response Rule check box is selected, and then click Next.

5. On the Default Response Rule Authentication Method page, select the Use This String To Protect The Key Exchange (Preshared Key) option, type **123456** in the box, and then click Next.

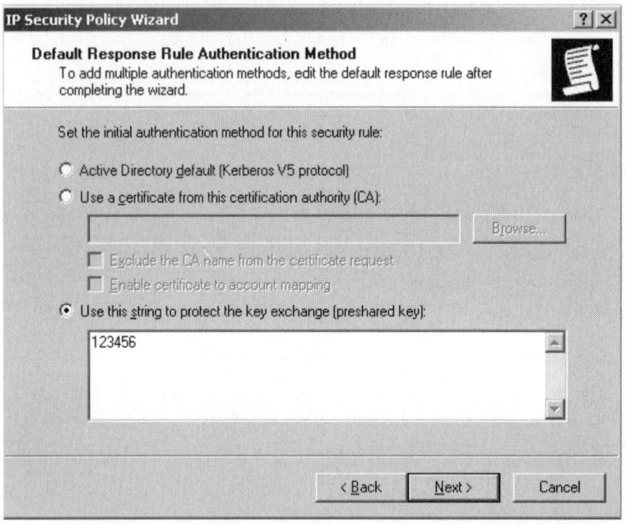

NOTE Using a pre-shared key is not a recommended authentication method. You are only choosing it as a demonstration of IPSec configuration. You should use Kerberos or certificate-based authentication, if possible, in a production environment. Because the scenario calls for IPSec negotiation with an entity outside your forest, you can use either certificate-based authentication or a pre-shared key. To simplify the lab instructions and to minimize dependencies on previous labs, you use a pre-shared key for the IPSec negotiation.

6. On the Completing The IP Security Policy Wizard page, click Finish. The Secure DNS Zone Transfers Properties page appears.

   In the next step, you will add the Kerberos authentication protocol to the Default Response rule.

7. In the Secure DNS Zone Transfers Properties dialog box, verify that the Default Response rule is highlighted, and then click Edit.

8. In the Edit Rule Properties dialog box, click the Authentication Methods tab, click Add, verify that the Active Directory default (Kerberos V5 Protocol) option is selected, and then click OK. The Edit Rule Properties dialog box appears.

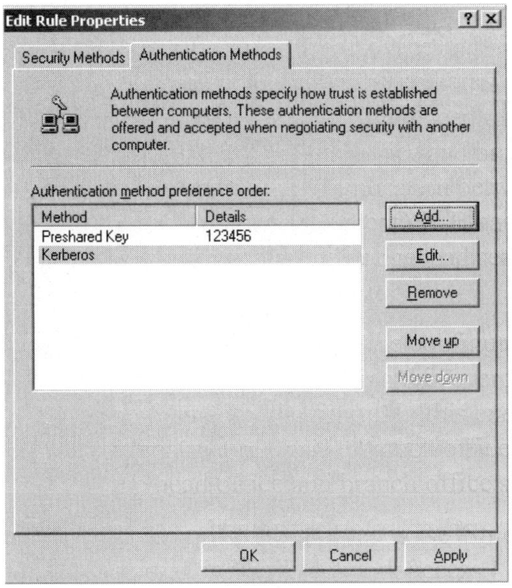

9. Click OK to close the Edit Rule Properties dialog box.
10. In the Secure DNS Zone Transfers Properties dialog box, clear the Use Add Wizard check box.

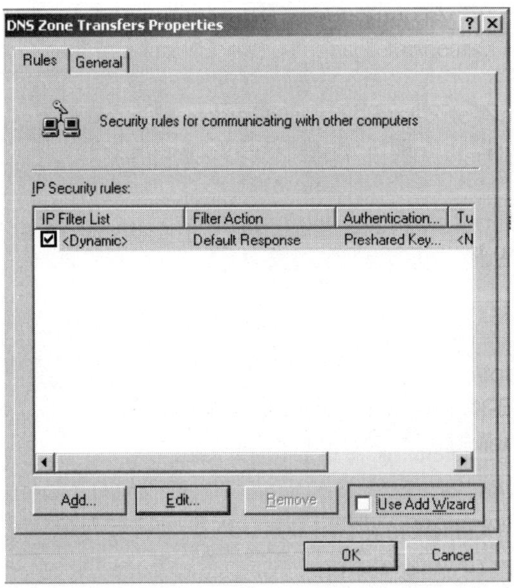

To gain a better understanding of IPSec policies, you will configure them without using wizards. Throughout this exercise, you must verify that you clear the Add Wizard check box to follow the steps as written.

In the remaining steps, you will create a rule to add to the DNS Zone Transfer policy. You will then create a filter list to be used with the rule and then create a filter action. Finally, you will correlate the filter list with the filter action in the rule.

11. Click Add. The New Rule Properties dialog box appears.

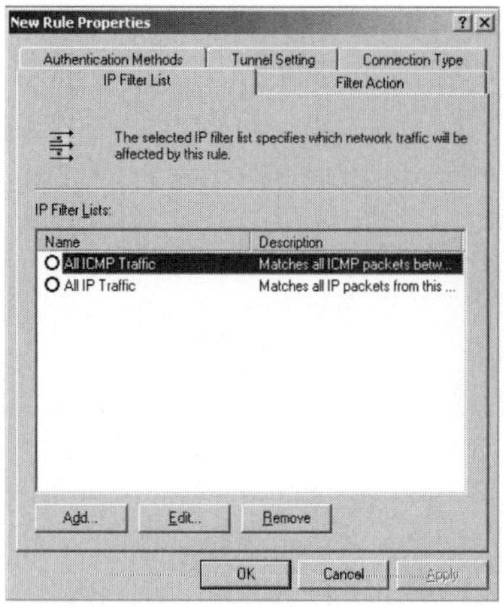

12. On the IP Filter List tab, click Add. The IP Filter List dialog box appears.

13. In the IP Filter List dialog box, type **DNS Zone Transfer** in the Name box, clear the Use Add Wizard check box, and then click Add.

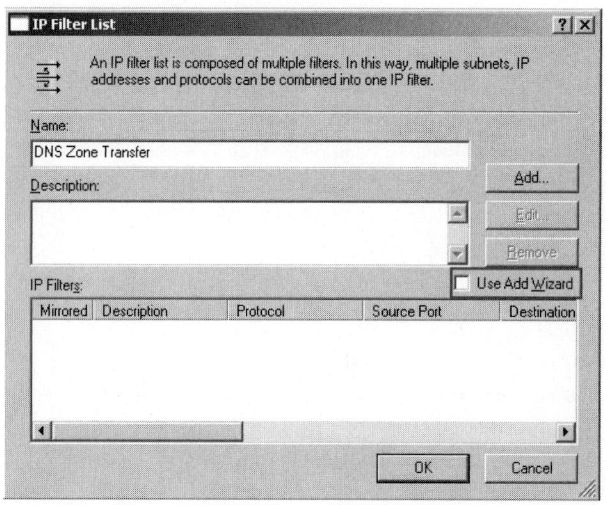

The IP Filter Properties dialog box appears.

14. In the Source Address drop-down list, select A Specific IP Address and type **10.1.1.*n*** (where *n* is the last octet of your DNS partner's IP address).

15. In the Destination Address drop-down list, select My IP Address.

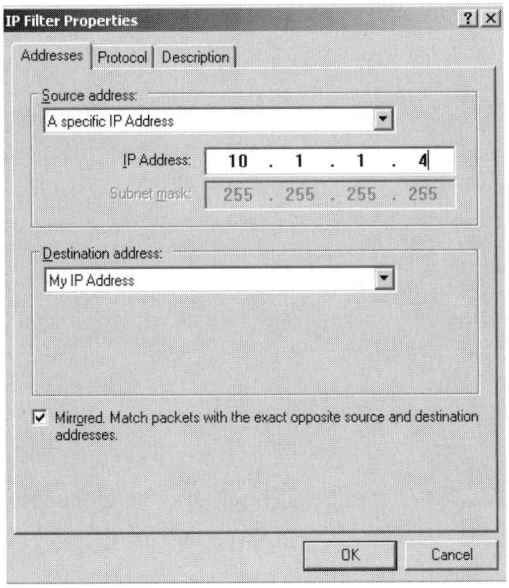

16. In the IP Filter Properties dialog box, click the Protocol tab.
17. In the Select A Protocol Type drop-down list, select TCP.
18. In the Set The IP Protocol Port area, select the To This Port option, and type **53**.

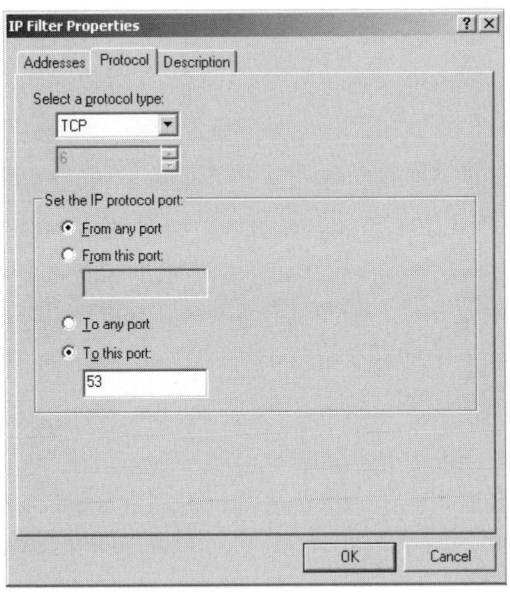

19. Click the Addresses tab, verify that the Mirrored check box is selected, and then click OK.

    The Mirrored setting makes it possible for the computer to reply to the traffic specified in the rule, without having to create another rule.

NOTE If you have two DNS partners, you will need to add your second DNS partner's address, protocol, port, and direction to the IP Filter List. To do this, perform the steps that follow. Otherwise, proceed to step 20.

- In the IP Filter List dialog box, click Add. The IP Filter Properties dialog box appears.
- Repeat steps 14 through 19, using your second DNS partner's address in step 14.

20. In the IP Filter List dialog box, click OK.
21. In the New Rule Properties dialog box, on the IP Filter List tab, select the DNS Zone Transfer option.

    An IPSec policy rule is a correlation of a single filter list with a filter action. Consequently, it is necessary to specify both a filter list and a filter action in the rule. In steps 22 through 26, you will specify a preconfigured filter action, Require Security, for the rule to use and then specify an Authentication Method for the IPSec negotiation.

22. In the New Rule Properties dialog box, click the Filter Action tab.
23. On the Filter Action tab, select the Require Security option, and then click the Authentication Methods tab.

    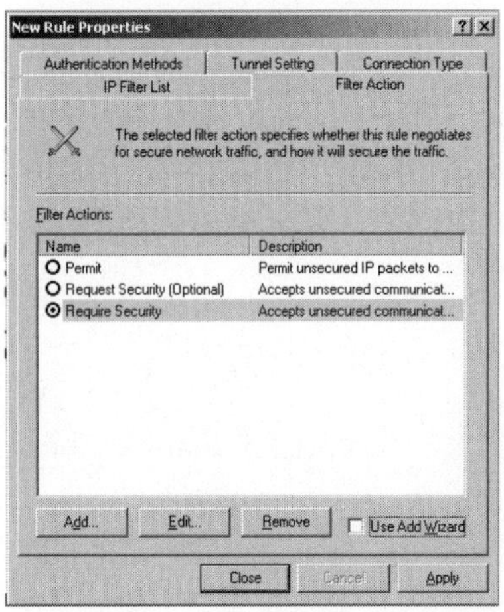

    The Require Security filter action requires clients (IPSec peers) to establish trust and security methods. When this filter action is used, clients cannot communicate unless they successfully authenticate and negotiate security protocols.

24. On the Authentication Methods tab, click Add.
25. In the New Authentication Method Properties dialog box, select the Use This String (Preshared key), type **123456** in the text box, and then click OK.
26. On the Authentication Methods tab, verify that the Preshared Key entry is selected in the Authentication Preference Order box, and click Move Up so that the interface is similar to the screen shot shown on the next page.

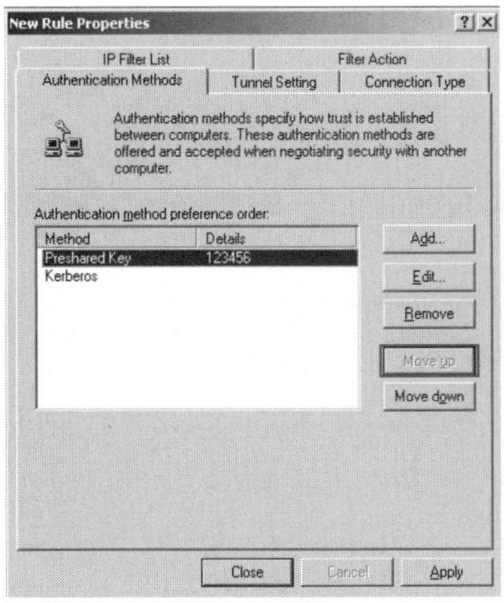

27. Click the Tunnel Setting tab and verify that the This Rule Does Not Specify A Tunnel option is selected, and then click the Connection Type tab.

28. On the Connection Type tab, verify that the All Network Connections option is selected, and then click Close.

At this point, the IPSec Policy consists of two rules: the Default Response rule and the DNS Zone Transfer rule. You need to add a few more rules to complete the creation of the IPSec Policy. Specifically, you need additional rules in the policy for the following:

- A rule that permits all traffic between the domain controller and the member server
- A rule that permits traffic sent to UDP Port 53 from any computer
- A rule that blocks all traffic from all computers
- A rule that permits traffic sent from UDP Port 53 to any computer

In the next section, you will create these additional rules

Adding Rules to an IPSec Policy

In this section you will add the additional rules described previously to complete the IPSec policy.

1. In the Secure DNS Zone Transfers Properties dialog box, verify that the Use Add Wizard check box is cleared, and then click Add.

In steps 2 through 7, you will create a rule that will permit all traffic between your computer and the other computer in your domain.

2. In the New Rule Properties dialog box, on the IP Filter List tab, click Add.

3. In the IP Filter List dialog box, in the Name box, type **Allow Domain Computers**, verify that the Use Add Wizard check box is cleared, and then click Add. The IP Filter Properties dialog box appears.
4. In the IP Filter Properties dialog box, in the Source Address drop-down box, select A Specific IP Address, type **10.1.1.*p*** (where *p* is the last octet of the IP address of your regular lab partner's computer), and in the Destination Address drop-down list, select My IP Address.

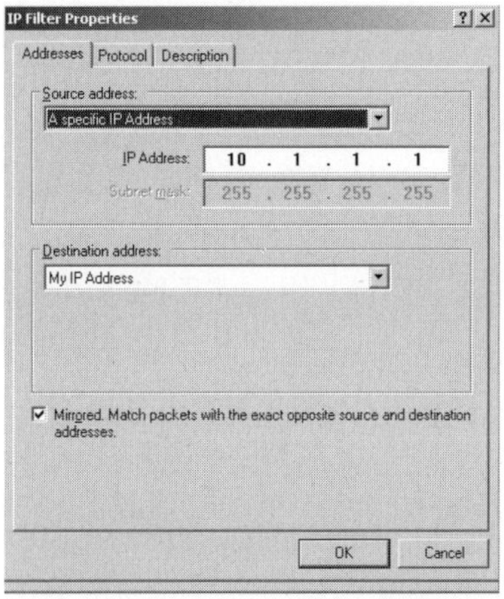

5. Click OK to close the IP Filter Properties dialog box, and click OK to close the IP Filter List dialog box.
6. On the IP Filter List tab, select the Allow Domain Computers option, and click the Filter Action tab.
7. On the Filter Action tab, select the Permit option, as shown below, and then click Close.

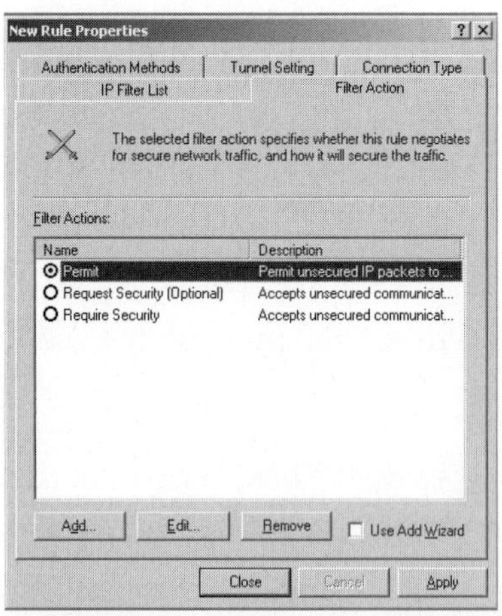

Because you are hardening a DNS server, depending on the DNS server roles, you need to allow the DNS server to receive and send DNS queries. In steps 8 through 25, you will create two rules that will permit inbound traffic and outbound traffic sent to UDP Port 53 (the protocol and port used for DNS queries).

NOTE In cases where the response to the DNS query exceeds 512 bytes, Transmission Control Protocol (TCP) will be used as the transport protocol for the response to the DNS query. However, this is not a common occurrence and usually happens when there is a large number of name server records in the zone, as might be the case with a large deployment of Active Directory directory service.

8. In the Secure DNS Zone Transfers Properties dialog box, verify that the Use Add Wizard check box is cleared, and then click Add.
9. On the IP Filter List tab, click Add.
10. In the IP Filter List dialog box, in the Name box, type **Allow UDP 53 Outbound**, verify that the Use Add Wizard check box is cleared, and then click Add. The IP Filter Properties dialog box appears.
11. In the IP Filter Properties dialog box, verify that My IP Address is selected from the Source Address drop-down list, verify that Any IP Address is selected from the Destination Address drop-down list, and click the Protocol tab.
12. On the Protocol tab, select UDP in the Select A Protocol Type drop-down list.
13. On the Protocol tab, select the To This Port option, type **53** in the text box, and then click OK.

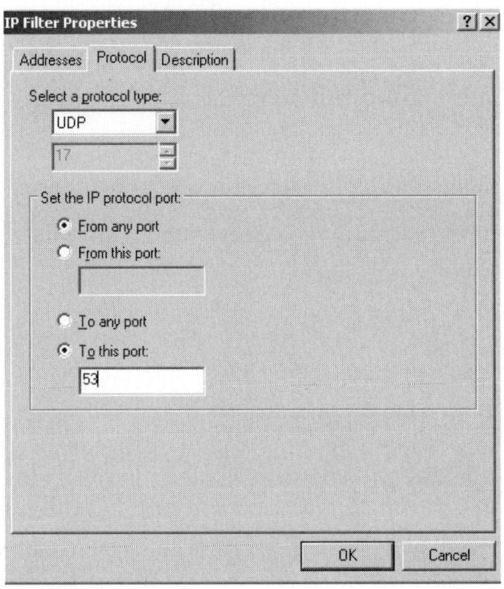

14. Click OK to close the IP Filter List dialog box.
15. In the New Rule Properties, on the IP Filter List tab, select the Allow UDP 53 Outbound option, and then click the Filter Action tab.

16. On the Filter Action tab, select the Permit option, and then click Close.
17. In the Secure DNS Zone Transfers Properties dialog box, verify that the Use Add Wizard check box is cleared, and then click Add.
18. On the IP Filter List tab, click Add.
19. In the IP Filter List dialog box, in the Name box, type **Allow UDP 53 Inbound**, verify that the Use Add Wizard check box is cleared, and then click Add. The IP Filter Properties dialog box appears.
20. In the IP Filter Properties dialog box, select Any IP Address in the Source Address drop-down list, select My IP Address from the Destination Address drop-down list, and then click the Protocol tab.
21. On the Protocol tab, select UDP in the Select A Protocol Type drop-down list.
22. On the Protocol tab, select the To This Port option, type **53** in the text box, and then click OK.
23. Click OK to close the IP Filter List dialog box.
24. In the New Rule Properties dialog box, on the IP Filter List tab, select the Allow UDP 53 Inbound option, and then click the Filter Action tab.
25. On the Filter Action tab, select the Permit option, and then click Close.
26. In the Secure DNS Zone Transfers Properties dialog box, verify that the Use Add Wizard check box is cleared, and then click Add.
27. In the New Rule Properties dialog box, on the IP Filter List tab, click Add.

    In steps 28 through 40, you will create a rule that blocks all inbound traffic. These steps provide a demonstration of configuring a filter action that blocks inbound traffic and is not mirrored.

28. In the IP Filter List dialog box, in the Name box, type **Block All Other Inbound**, verify that the Use Add Wizard check box is cleared, and click Add. The IP Filter Properties dialog box appears.
29. In the IP Filter Properties dialog box, on the Address tab, clear the Mirrored Match Packets With The Exact Opposite Source And Destination Address option.
30. On the Addresses tab, in the Source Address drop-down list, select Any IP Address.

31. On the Addresses tab, in the Destination Address drop-down list, select My IP Address.

    You could also create a much more comprehensive rule that blocks traffic from Any IP Address to Any IP Address at this point. Here, the steps demonstrate how to block all inbound traffic except that permitted by other rules.

32. Click OK to close the IP Filter Properties dialog box.
33. Click OK to close the IP Filter List dialog box.
34. In the New Rule Properties dialog box, on the IP Filter List tab, select the Block All Other Inbound option, and click the Filter Action tab.
35. On the Filter Action tab, clear the Use Add Wizard check box, and then click Add.
36. In the New Filter Action Properties dialog box, on the Security Methods tab, select the Block option, and then click the General tab.
37. On the General tab, in the Name box, type **Block**, and then click OK.
38. On the Filter Action tab, select the Block option, and then click Close.
39. In the Secure DNS Zone Transfers Properties dialog box, click OK.
40. In the IPsec Tools console, in the details pane, right-click Secure DNS Zone Transfers, and select Assign.

    In the next step, you will open a command prompt to stop and start the IPSec Policy Agent service. Although this step is probably not necessary, performing it will ensure that your IPSec policy is in place to test it.

41. Open a command prompt, type **net stop policyagent & net start policyagent**, and then press ENTER.

Verifying IPSec Policy Settings

In this section, you will verify the IPSec policy settings by using Microsoft Network Monitor and the IP Security Monitor console. Before proceeding with these steps, ensure that your DNS partner has completed the lab exercise to this point.

1. At the command prompt, type **ping computer*pp*** (where *pp* is the two-digit number assigned to your lab partner's computer), and then press ENTER.

> **QUESTION** Are you able to ping your lab partner's computer? Why or why not?

2. At the command prompt, type **ping computer*nn*** (where *nn* is the two-digit number assigned to your DNS partner's computer), and then press ENTER.

   QUESTION Are you able to ping your DNS partner's computer? Why or why not?

3. At the command prompt, type **nslookup**, and then press ENTER.
4. At the Nslookup prompt, type **server 10.1.1.*n*** (where *n* is the last octet of your DNS partner's IP address).

   Before proceeding, you will view data in the IP Security Monitor console, and you will prepare Microsoft Network Monitor to capture network traffic.

5. Switch to the IPSec Tools console.
6. In the console tree of the IPSec Tools console, expand IP Security Monitor, expand Computer*zz*, expand Main Mode, and expand Quick Mode.
7. In the IPSec Tools console tree, under both Main Mode and Quick Mode, select Security Associations to verify that there are no items shown in the details pane.
8. Click Start, point to Administrative Tools, and select Network Monitor.
   a. If the Microsoft Network Monitor message box appears, prompting you to specify a network, click OK.
   b. In the Select A Network dialog box, expand Local Computer, select Local Area Connection, and click OK.
9. From the Capture menu of Microsoft Network Monitor, select Start. Microsoft Network Monitor starts to capture data.

   If you have two DNS partners, perform steps 10 through 12 a single time for only one of your DNS partners.

10. Switch to the Nslookup prompt you left open earlier, type **server 10.1.1.*n*** (where *n* is the last octet of your DNS partner's IP address), and then press ENTER.
11. At the Nslookup prompt, type **ls –d fabrikam*nn*.com** (where *nn* is the two-digit number assigned to your DNS partner's computer), and then press ENTER.

12. Switch to Microsoft Network Monitor, and, from the Capture menu, select Stop.
13. Switch to the IPSec Tools console.
14. In the Main Mode portion of the console tree, select Security Associations. If you do not see any security associations in the details pane, right-click on the Security Associations folder in the console tree and select Refresh.
15. In the details pane, double-click the security association entry, and answer the following questions.

QUESTION What algorithm is being used for encryption?

QUESTION What algorithm is being used for integrity?

You can use the Netsh command to create, modify, view, and delete IPSec policy settings. Some IPSec policy settings, such as the configuration of persistent policies and computer startup security, can be configured only by using the Netsh command. In the next few steps, you will execute some Netsh commands to view static and dynamic IPSec policy information.

16. Switch to the Nslookup command prompt, type **exit**, and then press ENTER.
17. At the command prompt, type **netsh ipsec static show all > c:\ipsecstatic.txt**, and then press ENTER.
18. When the command has finished executing, type **notepad c:\ipsecstatic.txt** and press ENTER. Notepad opens, showing the static IPSec configuration.
19. Scroll through the text file, briefly reviewing the contents, and then close Notepad.
20. At the command prompt, type **netsh ipsec dynamic show qmfilter all type=specific > c:\ipsecqms.txt**, and then press ENTER.
21. When the command has finished executing, type **notepad c:\ipsecqms.txt** and press ENTER. Notepad opens, showing the dynamic Quick Mode Specific Filters.
22. Scroll through the text file, paying particular attention to the weight values that are displayed in the output, and then close Notepad.

QUESTION What do the weight values indicate for the specific filters?

23. Switch to Network Monitor.
24. From the Capture menu, select Display Captured Data, and review the data in the summary screen, paying particular attention to the data in the Protocol column.

> **QUESTION** What two protocols indicate the presence of an IPSec policy that requires negotiation?

25. Double-click one of the frames that indicates IPSec negotiation, and spend a few moments reviewing the details of that and other frames.
26. Close Microsoft Network Monitor without saving the captured data or addresses.

    To provide maximum security in an environment that uses IPSec, it is necessary to make use of persistent policies and computer startup security policies. In the next few steps, you will use the Windows Server 2003 help files to answer questions about persistent policy and computer startup security policies.

27. Click Start, select Run, type **c:\windows\help\ipsecsnp.chm** in the Open text box, and then click OK.
28. Using the Search feature of Help, find information about persistent policies and computer startup security policies, and answer the following questions.

> **QUESTION** What is a persistent policy, where is it stored, and what are the benefits of using it?

> **QUESTION** What is a computer startup security policy, and what are the benefits of using it?

29. Close the help file.

Unassigning an IPSec Policy

Because the IPSec policy you created might interfere with future lab exercises, you will unassign the policy in this section.

1. In the IPsec Tools console, in the IP Security Policies On Local Computer portion of the console tree, right-click Secure DNS Zone Transfers, and select Unassign.

2. Switch to the command prompt, type **net stop policyagent & net start policyagent**, and then press ENTER.
3. Close the command prompt window and any open windows, but remain logged on for the next exercise.

EXERCISE 10.3: EXAMINING WIRELESS SETTINGS FOR 802.1X AUTHENTICATION

Estimated completion time: 30 minutes

Your branch office needs to implement a wireless network to enhance productivity. You have been asked to make detailed recommendations regarding the configuration of a wireless network to ensure a high degree of security. As preparation for writing your recommendations, and even though you have not decided the wireless access point (WAP) to purchase, you choose to explore in a test lab the configuration changes you would have to make to implement a wireless network that uses 802.1x authentication.

Installing Internet Authentication Service (IAS)

In this section, you will install Internet Authentication Service (IAS). You will need your 180-day evaluation Windows Server 2003 Enterprise Edition *CD*.

1. Click Start, select Control Panel, and then click Add Or Remove Programs.
2. In the Add Or Remove Programs dialog box, click Add/Remove Windows Components to open the Windows Components Wizard.
3. On the Windows Components page, select Networking Services to highlight it, and then click Details.
4. In the Networking Services dialog box, select the Internet Authentication Services check box, click OK, and then click Next.
5. After IAS has finished installing, click Finish in the Completing The Windows Components Wizard dialog box.
6. Close Add Or Remove Programs.

Configuring RADIUS for 802.1x Authentication

In this section, you will configure a remote access policy for 802.1x authentication.

1. Click Start, point to Administrative Tools, and select Internet Authentication Service.

2. In the Internet Authentication Service console, right-click Radius Clients, and then click New Radius Client.
3. In the New Radius Client dialog box, type **802.1x - capable wireless access point** in the Friendly Name text box.
4. In the Client address (IP or DNS) text box, type **172.16.0.1**, and then click Next.

> **NOTE** The IP address that you enter is the one used by the WAP. That is, the WAP is a RADIUS client and must be capable of supporting 802.1x authentication. WAPs that are sold in the general consumer retail market generally cannot support 802.1x authentication.

5. On the Additional Information page, ensure that RADIUS Standard is selected in the Client-Vendor drop-down list, type **R@d1u$** in the Shared Secret and Confirm Shared Secret boxes, select the Request Must Contain The Message Authenticator Attribute check box, and then click Finish.

> **NOTE** For the shared secret RADIUS password, it is considered a good practice to use a long password (more than 20 characters in length) and to use password-generating software to ensure the use of random characters. Also, you should change this password frequently.

6. Right-click Remote Access Policies, and select New Remote Access Policy.

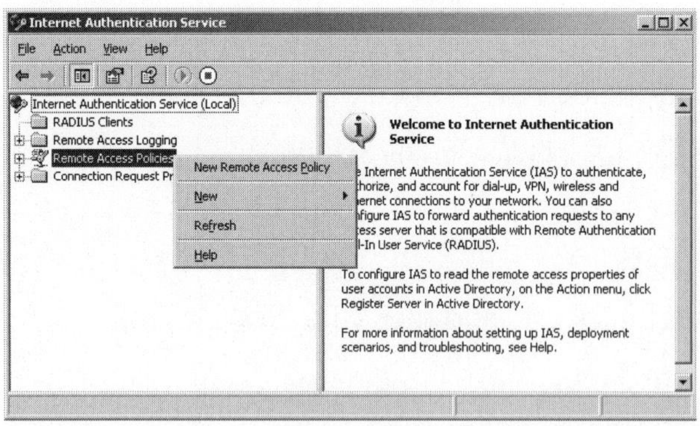

7. In the Welcome To The Remote Access Policy Wizard page, click Next.

   Although it is possible to set up a wireless policy by using the wizard, you will use a custom method to set up the policy.

8. On the Policy Configuration Method page, select the Set Up A Custom Policy option, type **802.1x Wireless Policy** in the Policy Name box, and then click Next.

9. On the Policy Conditions page, click Add.
10. In the Select Attribute dialog box, select NAS-Port-Type, and then click Add.
11. In the NAS-Port-Type dialog box, select Wireless – IEEE 802.11 in the Available Types box, and then click Add to move it to the Selected Types box.
12. Repeat step 11 for Wireless – Other, and then click OK.

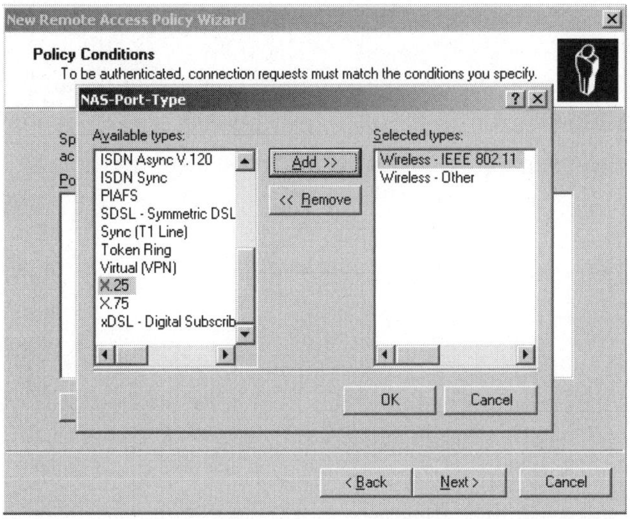

NOTE This sample remote access policy does not control access by Windows groups. In a production environment, it is better to specify individual user accounts or groups that are allowed access.

13. On the Policy Conditions page, click Next.
14. On the Permissions page, select the Grant Remote Access Permission option, and then click Next.
15. On the Profile page, click Edit Profile.
16. On the Edit Dial-In Profile page, click the Authentication tab.
17. Clear the check boxes for Microsoft Encrypted Authentication Version 2 (MS-CHAP v2) and Microsoft Encrypted Authentication (MS-CHAP), and then click EAP Methods.

NOTE "CHAP" stands for "Challenge Handshake Authentication Protocol."

18. In the Select EAP Providers dialog box, click Add.
19. In the Add EAP dialog box, select Smart Card Or Other Certificate in the Authentication Methods box and click OK. Click OK again to close the Select EAP Providers dialog box.

NOTE You could also select Protected Extensible Authentication Protocol (PEAP). This method is somewhat easier to implement because it is password-based and does not require a public key infrastructure (PKI) and the use of both user and computer digital certificates on the wireless client workstation, as does Extensible Authentication Protocol-Transport Layer Security (EAP-TLS), the method used when you select the Smart Card Or Other Certificate option. However, because authentication with EAP-TLS is certificate-based rather than password-based, EAP-TLS provides a stronger authentication method.

20. In the Edit Dial-in Profile dialog box, click the Advanced tab, and in the Attributes box, select Framed Protocol, select Remove, click OK, and then click No to close the Dial-In Setting message box that prompts you to consult the help files regarding multiple authentication methods.
21. On the Profile page, click Next.
22. On the Completing The New Remote Access Policy Wizard page, click Finish.

QUESTION If the classroom had an 802.1x-capable WAP, what would you do next to complete the RADIUS configuration?

23. Minimize the Internet Authentication Service.

Examining Wireless Group Policy Settings

In this section, you will examine wireless Group Policy settings that you can apply to client computers with the appropriate wireless network adapters installed.

NOTE Normally, you would implement the wireless Group Policy before deploying the WAP and configuring the RADIUS server. The reason for this is to ensure that the wireless client computers are configured with a standard policy once you implement the wireless network.

1. Click Start, select Run, type **gpmc.msc** in the Open text box, and then click OK.
2. In the tree pane of the Group Policy Management console, right-click the Location*zz* OU, and select Create And Link A GPO Here.
3. In the New GPO dialog box, type **Wireless Policy** *zz*, and then click OK.
4. In the console tree, expand Group Policy Objects. Right-click Wireless Policy *zz*, and then select Edit.
5. In the Group Policy Object Editor, under Computer Configuration, expand Windows Settings, and then expand Security Settings.

6. Select and then right-click Wireless Network (IEEE 802.11) Policies. Select Create Wireless Network Policy.

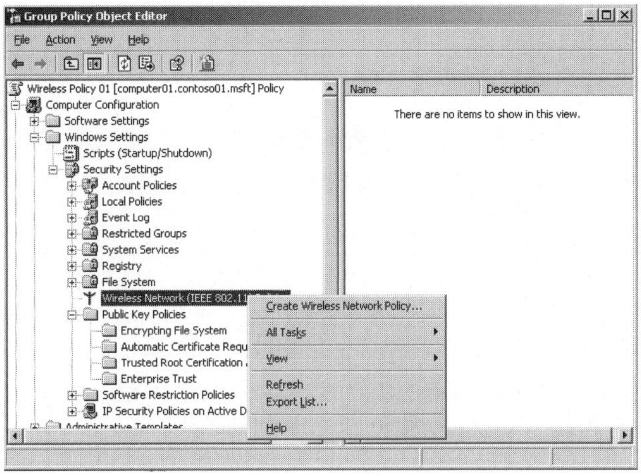

7. On the Welcome To The Wireless Network Policy Wizard page, click Next.

8. On the Wireless Network Policy Name page, type **802.1xWireless Policy** in the Name box, and then click Next.

9. On the Completing The Wireless Network Policy Wizard dialog box, ensure that the Edit Properties check box is selected, and then click Finish.

10. On the 802.1x Wireless Policy Properties dialog box, select the Networks To Access drop-down list, select Access Point (Infrastructure) Networks Only, and then click the Preferred Networks tab.

11. In the Preferred Networks tab, click Add.

12. In the New Preferred Settings dialog box, type **WAP-01** in the Network Name (SSID) box, ensure that the Data Encryption (WEP Enabled) and The Key Is Provided Automatically check boxes are selected, and then select the IEEE 802.1x tab.

NOTE The service set identifier (SSID) is analogous to a network name. Generally, a WAP should be configured not to broadcast this name. When a WAP is configured not to broadcast the SSID, the wireless-enabled computers must be configured in advance with the SSID. The 802.1x protocol provides a delivery mechanism for WEP keys, so the check box that indicates the key is provided automatically must be selected.

QUESTION What does WEP stand for?

13. In the 802.1x tab, ensure that the Enable Network Access Control Using IEEE 802.1x check box is selected and that Smart Card Or Other Certificate option appears in the EAP Type drop-down list, and then click Settings.
14. In the Smart Card Or Other Certificate Properties dialog box, ensure that the Use A Certificate On This Computer, Use Simple Certificate Selection (Recommended), and Validate Server Certificate check boxes are selected.

    NOTE Using these settings, Windows automatically tries to select the appropriate certificate for authentication and will verify that the certificate presented to the client is within a valid date range. Other settings on this dialog box enhance security somewhat, but at the cost of usability. For example, if you specify the name of a server in the Connect To These Servers text box, users will be prompted to verify the name when connecting to the wireless network.

15. In the Trusted Root Certificate Authorities frame, select Contoso-RootCA. (If you see two certificates, you can select either one.)
16. Click OK three times to close the 802.1x Wireless Policy Property dialog box.
17. Close the Group Policy Object Editor, and then close the Group Policy Management console.

Authorizing a RADIUS Server

Before a RADIUS server can process authentication and accounting requests, it must be able to access user account dial-in properties of Active Directory. This access requires that the computer on which IAS is installed be a member of the RAS and IAS Servers domain local group. You can assign the computer to this group by using the Active Directory Users And Computers console, the IAS console, or by using the Netsh Ras Add Registeredserver command. In the following steps, you will create this assignment by using the IAS console:

1. Switch to the Internet Authentication Service console.
2. In the console tree, right-click Internet Authentication Service (Local), and select Register Server In Active Directory.
3. In the Register Internet Authentication Server In Active Directory message box, click OK.
4. In the Server Registered message box, click OK.
5. Close the Internet Authentication Service console.
6. Close all open windows and log off.

LAB REVIEW QUESTIONS

Estimated completion time: 20 minutes

1. Although firewalls are integral components for protecting your network, explain why they need to be complemented with other measures to provide defense-in-depth. Give a few examples of those defense-in-depth measures you would take.
2. You want to both encrypt and sign network traffic by using IPSec. Do you need to implement both Authenticated Headers (AH) and Encapsulating Security Payload (ESP)?
3. What determines the order in which IPSec policy rules will be processed?
4. What determines the order that authenticating methods are attempted during IPSec negotiation?
5. You have two IPSec policy rules. One policy rule contains a filter and a filter action that blocks all IP traffic from a particular subnet. The other policy rule contains a filter and a filter action that permits traffic from a specific host on the blocked subnet. Will the host on the remote subnet be able to communicate with the computer where the IPSec policy is implemented? Briefly explain your answer.
6. List two advanced IPSec features you might implement in a high-security environment to protect computers.
7. What are the minimum requirements for implementing 802.1x authentication using EAP-TLS?

LAB CHALLENGE 10.1: DESIGNING SECURITY FOR DATA TRANSMISSION

Estimated completion time: 30 minutes

You are helping Contoso Pharmaceuticals to design the security for its network infrastructure. Your manager asks you to a meeting to discuss enhancing the security of internal data transmissions within the company. At the meeting your manager states the following:

"A couple of issues have come up recently that require our attention.

"First, the CIO has been meeting with the department heads to discuss their security needs. I guess the departmental admins have got department heads excited about using IPSec to secure network transmission of data. The department heads for Sales, Human Resources, Legal, and R and D are clamoring for IPSec. I am not sure about the feasibility of some of these requests. First, all the departments still have some Microsoft Windows NT 4.0 clients and Windows 98 clients. Second, I am not sure the need for IPSec is really there for all departments. All departments deal with confidential and proprietary data as a matter of course. But the risk to the company if the confidentiality or integrity of the data is compromised varies, based on the department. For example, the risk to the company is far greater if the R-and-D data is compromised than if the Sales data is compromised. So, I would rank risk by department as follows, in descending order, R and D, Legal, Human Resources, Sales. However, our cabling infrastructure is fairly secure, so I am not sure how much value would be added using IPSec. At the very least, where possible and if we can justify the cost of countermeasure based on the risk, we want to mitigate man-in-the-middle attacks for all data transmissions. For some high-risk data we want to mitigate spoofing, replay attacks, and, in some cases, encrypt the data on the wire.

"The second issue concerns the proposal for a wireless network. As you know, there has been a request to implement a wireless network in the Sales department. The need is justified, but I am very concerned about the security of wireless networks. For any wireless network, I want to ensure that the strongest measures are in place to ensure the confidentiality of data transmissions. Furthermore, I want to deny any casual war drivers or motivated attackers the ability to connect to the wireless network and acquire an IP address. The algorithm for WEP encryption is compromised, and we know that there are a number of utilities out there that make it possible for attackers to acquire WEP keys. If we implement a wireless network, I want to make sure we are practicing defense-in-depth.

"Please let me know your general thoughts on this issue."

To complete this lab challenge, work with your lab partner or in small groups assigned by your instructor to answer the following questions. When you are finished, your instructor will review your responses as a class discussion.

1. Would you need to make any hardware upgrades to support IPSec?
2. At a minimum, your manager wants to mitigate man-in-the-middle attacks. Is there a way to do this without implementing IPSec? If so, what is it?

3. If there is an alternative method to IPSec for mitigating man-in-middle attacks, which method is easier to implement?
4. In what departments would you implement IPSec Authenticated Header (AH)? In what departments would you implement Encapsulating Security Payload (ESP)?
5. For the wireless network in the Sales department, what would you do to reduce the threat of WEP keys being compromised?
6. Do you need to implement a PKI to secure the wireless network? Briefly explain your answer.
7. Would you use DHCP for the wireless clients?
8. What should you do to limit the number of IP addresses that are available for use by wireless clients?
9. One of the stated requirements is that you practice defense-in-depth to protect wireless communications. What other recommendations would you make to ensure the security of wireless communications?

LAB 11

PROTECTING EXTRANET COMMUNICATIONS

This lab contains the following exercises and activities:

- Exercise 11.1: Configuring RRAS for Remote Communications
- Exercise 11.2: Using the Connection Manager Administration Kit (CMAK) to Create Service Profiles
- Exercise 11.3: Comparing PPTP and L2TP/IPSec Traffic
- Exercise 11.4: Using RADIUS Authentication
- Lab Review Questions
- Lab Challenge 11.1: Designing Remote Access Policies

SCENARIO

As a network administrator for Contoso Pharmaceuticals, you have been asked by your manager to improve the security for remote-access clients who connect to the corporate network through a virtual private network (VPN). Your manager wants to ensure the use of strongest authentication methods and encryption that can be reasonably justified. There is a proposal to implement smart cards for remote access, but this is still under consideration as a result of budgetary constraints. Contoso has just implemented a public key infrastructure (PKI), so your manager is interested in leveraging the enterprise certification authority (CA) for VPNs connected by the Layer 2 Tunneling Protocol over Internet Protocol Security (L2TP/IPSec). However, she wonders whether L2TP/IPSec is actually more secure than Microsoft Challenge Handshake Authentication Protocol version 2 (MS-CHAPv2), and whether the extra effort is justified.

Your manager is also concerned about the risk that having to create policies and monitor logs on separate Remote Access Service (RAS) servers creates. The administrative burden of ensuring consistent remote access policies and collecting the various logs into a central location for auditing and analysis is difficult and leads to error.

Finally, your manager wants to find a way to reduce the administrative burden of configuring company-issued laptops with VPN connection objects. Further, she does not want users to be able to save their account credentials on the VPN connection objects, and she would like you to provide a solution.

After completing this lab, you will be able to:

- Configure a remote access server for VPN access.
- Configure remote access policies.
- Understand how remote access policies are processed.
- Configure VPN connection objects to use Point-to-Point Tunneling Protocol (PPTP) or L2TP/IPSec.
- Use the Connection Manager Administration Kit (CMAK) to create service profiles that can be distributed to clients.
- Use CMAK to enhance the security of VPN connection objects.
- Analyze PPTP and L2TP/IPSec traffic by using Microsoft Network Monitor.
- Compare the strengths and weaknesses of PPTP and L2TP/IPSec.
- Configure a remote-access server to use a Remote Authentication Dial-In User Service (RADIUS) server for authentication and accounting.
- Analyze Internet Authentication Service (IAS) log files by using the Windows Support Tools utility, Iasparse.exe.

Estimated lesson time: 130 minutes

BEFORE YOU BEGIN

To complete this lab, you will need to have done the following:

- Created a Member Servers organizational unit (OU) and moved the Computer*yy* member server object to the OU, as instructed in steps 3 through 7 of Lab Exercise 3.4, "Using Group Policy To Configure Automatic Update Clients," in Lab 3, "Reducing the Risk of Software Vulnerabilities."
- Performed the steps in the Before You Begin section of Lab 4, "Designing a Management Infrastructure," to create user accounts and to grant the Domain Users group the right to log on locally to the domain controller.
- Have installed an enterprise subordinate certification authority (CA), as instructed in Lab 9, "Designing a Public Key Infrastructure," to allow L2TP-over-IPSec VPN connections to work properly.
- Have installed Internet Authentication Services (IAS) as instructed in Lab 10, "Protecting Intranet Communications."

NOTE In this lab, you will see the characters *dd*, *pp*, xx, yy, and zz. These directions assume that you are working on computers configured in pairs and that each computer has a number.

When you see *dd*, substitute the number used for your domain. When you see *pp*, substitute the number of your partner's computer. When you see xx, substitute the unique number assigned to the lower-numbered (odd-numbered) computer of the pair. When you see yy, substitute the unique number assigned to the higher-numbered (even-numbered) computer of the pair. When you see zz, substitute the number assigned to the computer you are using. The following example assumes that the partner pair of computers has been assigned the names Computer05 and Computer06 and that you have been assigned Computer05.

Computer*pp* = Computer06 = your partner's computer

Computerxx = Computer05 = lower-numbered computer

Computeryy = Computer06 = higher-numbered computer

Computerzz = Computer05 = computer you are using

Contoso*dd*.msft = Contoso03.msft = Active Directory domain you are using

EXERCISE 11.1: CONFIGURING RRAS FOR REMOTE COMMUNICATIONS

Estimated completion time: 35 minutes

In this exercise, you will install and configure the Routing and Remote Access Service (RRAS) on your computer. You will then create a remote access policy that will grant dial-in permissions to a Microsoft Windows group that you create at the beginning of this exercise. You will also configure a VPN client-connection object that will force the establishment of a PPTP connection with the RRAS server.

Verifying Server Permissions for Enabling RRAS on a Member Server

In this section, you will verify that your computer has the appropriate level of permissions to read user account properties in the Active Directory directory service. In Lab 10, you registered the IAS server in Active Directory. In the steps that follow, you will verify that your computer has been added to the RAS and IAS Servers group when you performed those steps.

NOTE By default, member servers configured as RRAS servers cannot access the dial-in properties of user accounts and cannot authenticate domain accounts. If the member server provides dial-in access to domain accounts rather than local accounts, it must be able to read Active Directory information.

1. Log on as Contoso*dd*\Admin*zz* using **P@ssw0rd** as the password.
2. Click Start, select Administrative Tools, and then select Active Directory Users And Computers.
3. In Active Directory Users And Computers, expand Contoso*dd*.msft, select Users, and then double-click the RAS And IAS Servers security group.
4. In the RAS And IAS Servers Properties page, click the Members tab.

   You should see your assigned computer listed as a member of this group. By default, the IAS And RAS Servers group is empty. In Lab 10, when you registered the IAS server in Active Directory, you added your server to this group.

   QUESTION Why is it a good security practice to limit members of this group?

5. In the RAS And IAS Servers Properties dialog box, click Cancel.

   Leave Active Directory Users And Computers open for the next section.

Configuring User and Group Objects to Test VPN Access

In this section, you will create a group object that will be used to test RRAS and VPN configurations.

1. In Active Directory Users And Computers, expand the Location*zz* OU, right-click the R and D OU, select New, and then select Group.
2. In the New Object – Group dialog box, type **Vpn Access Group*zz*** and then click OK.

   Normally, you might want to follow the A-G-DL-P model for managing access to resources. However, to simplify the steps, you will use the default global group scope.

3. Double-click the VPN Access Group*zz* you created in the previous step, click the Members tab, and then click Add.
4. In the Select Users, Contacts, Computers, Or Groups dialog box, in the Enter The Object Names To Select text box, type **Jgeist*zz*** and then click OK.

5. Click OK to close the VPN Access Group*zz* Properties dialog box.
6. Minimize Active Directory Users And Computers, and leave it open.

Configuring RRAS for Inbound VPN Connections

In this section, you will configure RRAS on your computer to accept VPN connections.

1. Click Start, select Administrative Tools, and then select Routing And Remote Access.

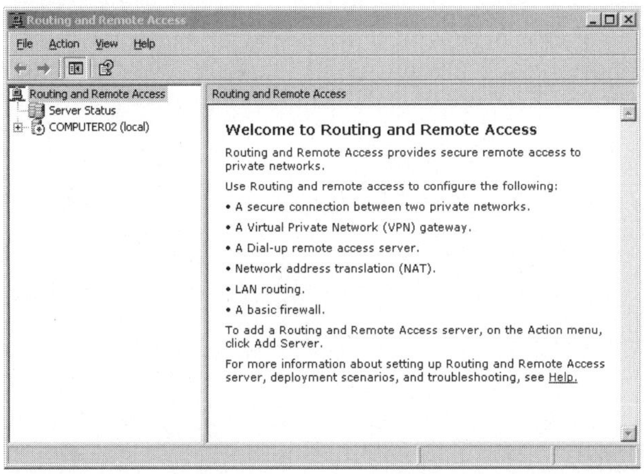

2. In the Routing And Remote Access console, right-click Computer*zz* (Local), and then select Configure And Enable Routing And Remote Access.
3. In the Welcome To The Routing And Remote Access Server Setup Wizard page, click Next.
4. On the Configuration page, select the Custom Configuration option, and then click Next.

> **NOTE** Normally, an RRAS VPN server has two network adapters, one for the internal network, and another for the external network. On a computer that has two adapters, you can select the Remote Access (Dial-Up Or VPN) option. However, the computers used in this classroom have only one adapter. So, although it appears that you can select the Remote Access (Dial-Up Or VPN) option, you will encounter an error message later in the process, informing you that you need two network adapters. For a computer with only one network adapter, you must select the Custom Configuration option.

5. On the Custom Configuration page, select the VPN Access box, and then click Next.
6. On the Completing The Routing And Remote Access Server Setup Wizard page, click Finish.
7. In the Routing And Remote Access dialog box, click Yes to start the service.

   After a few moments, the service starts, and a green up-arrow appears on the computer icon in the Routing And Remote Access console.

8. In the Routing And Remote Access console, right-click Computer*zz* (Local), and then select Properties.
9. On the Computer*zz* (local) Properties page, click the Security tab.
10. In the Authentication Provider drop-down list, ensure that Windows Authentication is selected, and then click Authentication Methods.
11. In the Authentication Methods page, ensure that the Microsoft Encrypted Authentication Version 2 (MS-CHAP v2) check box is selected, and then immediately below it, clear the Microsoft Encrypted Authentication (MS-CHAP) check box.

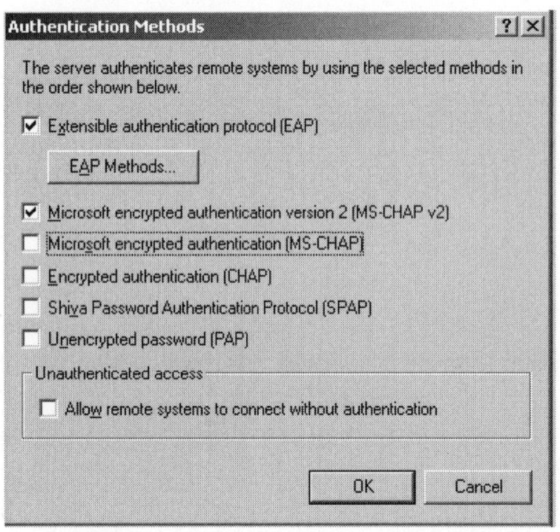

NOTE "CHAP" stands for "Challenge Handshake Authentification Protocol."

Click OK.

12. Click the IP tab.
13. In the IP Address Assignment area, select the Static Address Pool option, and then click Add.

14. In the New Address Range dialog box, enter the following IP addresses:
    - In the Start IP Address box, type **192.168.*z*.10** (where *z* is your student number).
    - In the End IP Address box, type **192.168.*z*.20**.
15. Click OK to close the New Address Range dialog box, and then click OK to close the Computer*zz* (Local) Properties dialog box.
16. Minimize the RRAS console.

Configuring a VPN Client-Connection Object

In this section, you will configure a VPN connection object in the Network Connections folder to connect to your partner's computer. You will then connect to your partner's computer to test the RRAS server and VPN client settings.

1. Click Start, select Control Panel, select Network Connections, and then select New Connection Wizard.
2. In the Welcome To The New Connection Wizard page, click Next.
3. In the Network Connection Type page, select the Connect To The Network At My Workplace option, and then click Next.
4. In the Network Connection page, select the Virtual Private Connection option, and then click Next.
5. In the Connection Name dialog box, type **computer*pp*** (where *pp* is the two-digit version of your partner's student number) in the Company Name box, and then click Next.
6. On the VPN Server Selection page, type **computer*pp*** in the Host Name Or IP Address box, and then click Next.
7. In the Connection Availability dialog box, accept the default selection (My Use Only), and then click Next.
8. On the Completing The New Connection Wizard page, click Finish.

   The Connect Computer*pp* dialog box appears, prompting you to establish a VPN connection with the remote computer. Before testing the connection, you will explore and change some of the default properties of the VPN connection object.

9. In the Connect Computer*pp* dialog box, click Properties.
10. On the Connection Computer*pp* Properties page, click the Security tab.

QUESTION *What are the default security settings for the VPN connection object?*

11. On the Security tab, select the Advanced (Custom Settings) option, and then click Settings.
12. In the Advanced Security Settings dialog box, select the Data Encryption drop-down list and examine the choices, but do not change any of the settings.

QUESTION *What is the most secure setting for data encryption?*

13. In the Logon Security area, clear the check box for Microsoft CHAP (MS-CHAP), ensure that the Microsoft CHAP Version 2 (MS-CHAP v2) check box is selected, and then click OK.
14. Click the Networking tab.
15. From the Type Of VPN drop-down list, select PPTP VPN, and then click OK.

NOTE *Given the current configuration of the classroom computers, they should connect to the remote server using PPTP. However, step 15 ensures that the VPN connection that occurs actually uses PPTP.*

16. In the Connect To Computer01 dialog box, type **Jgeist*zz*** in the User Name box, type **P@ssw0rd** in the Password box, and then click Connect.

    The connection attempt fails.

QUESTION *What error message did you receive?*

NOTE *Wait until your partner has attempted to connect to your RRAS server before proceeding with the next steps.*

17. In the Error Connecting To Computer*pp* dialog box, click Close.
18. Click Start, select Run, type **eventvwr** in the Open box, and then click OK.
19. In Event Viewer, select the System log, and then double-click the system event that displays 20189 in the Event ID column. This error documents your partner's failed connection attempt to your RRAS server.

QUESTION *What configuration changes do you need to make to enable remote-access permissions for the user account?*

20. Click Cancel to close the Event Properties dialog box. Close Event Viewer.

Examining Remote Access Permissions and Configuring Remote Access Policies

In this section, you will explore settings related to remote access permissions for user accounts.

1. Switch to Active Directory Users And Computers, and then navigate to the Location*zz*\R and D OU.
2. Right-click Jgeist*zz*, and then click Properties.
3. On the JGeist*zz* Properties page, click the Dial-In tab.

QUESTION *Without changing the default settings of the dial-in user account, how would you grant the user remote access permissions?*

QUESTION *The dial-in properties include a setting for assigning a static IP address. Why would it be useful to assign a static IP address to a remote user?*

QUESTION *In what circumstances will the option Control Access Through Remote Access Policy be dimmed?*

4. Click Cancel to close the JGeist*zz* Properties dialog box.
5. Minimize Active Directory Users and Computers.
6. Switch to the Routing And Remote Access console.
7. In the Routing And Remote Access tree pane, select Remote Access Policies.
8. In the details pane, double-click the Connections To Microsoft Routing And Remote Access Server policy.

QUESTION *What is the action if the connection request matches the policy conditions?*

9. Click Cancel.

10. In the details pane, double-click the Connections To Other Access Servers policy.

    QUESTION *What are the policy conditions for denying remote access?*

11. Click Cancel.
12. Right-click Remote Access Policies, and then click New Remote Access Policy.
13. In the Welcome To The New Remote Access Policy Wizard page, click Next.
14. On the Policy Configuration Method page, accept the default settings, type **Access By Windows Group** in the Policy Name box, and then click Next.
15. On the Access Method page, ensure that VPN is selected, and then click Next.
16. In the User Or Group Access dialog box, ensure that the Group option is selected, and then click Add.
17. On the even-numbered computer (Computer*yy*), in the Select Groups dialog box, select Locations, select Contoso*dd*.msft, and then click OK.
18. In the Enter The Object Names To Select box, type **vpn access group*pp*** (where *pp* is your partner's student number), click OK, and then click Next.

    If the Multiple Names Found dialog box appears, select your lab partner's VPN Access Group*pp* account from the Matching Names box, click OK, and then click Next.

19. On the Authentication Methods page, ensure that Microsoft Encrypted Authentication Version 2 (MS-CHAPv2) is selected, and then click Next.
20. On the Policy Encryption Level page, accept the defaults, and then click Next.
21. In the Completing The New Remote Access Policy Wizard dialog box, click Finish.

    NOTE *Note the order in which the Remote Access Policies are listed, and wait until your partner has completed step 21 before proceeding.*

22. Click Start, select Connect To, select Computer*pp*, type **jgeist*zz*** in the User Name box, type **P@ssw0rd** in the Password box, and then click Connect.

> **QUESTION** What can you infer about how remote access policies are processed?

23. Click Start, select Run, type **cmd** in the Open text box, and then click OK.

24. At the command prompt, type **ipconfig /all** and then press ENTER.

> **QUESTION** How many IP addresses are on your computer? What are they?

25. At the command prompt, type **route print** and then press ENTER.

26. At the bottom of the output of the Route.exe command, identify the IP address that is listed as the default gateway.

> **QUESTION** What IP address is listed as the default gateway?

27. Close the command prompt window.

28. In the notification area (system tray), right-click the connection icon for the VPN connection, and then select Status.

29. On the Computer*pp* Status dialog box, click the Details tab, and then review the information.

> **QUESTION** What authentication method is being used? What is the encryption strength?

30. Click the General tab, and then click Disconnect.

EXERCISE 11.2: USING THE CONNECTION MANAGER ADMINISTRATION KIT (CMAK) TO CREATE SERVICE PROFILES

Estimated completion time: 30 minutes

Although Contoso Pharmaceuticals is very security-conscious and provides regular security awareness training to users, your manager is concerned about VPN connection objects on laptops that employees use for VPN access. One of her concerns is that it takes too much time for administrators to configure the VPN objects on the laptops and she doesn't want the users to do it. The other concern she has relates to users who use the Save Password settings on the VPN connection objects. Recently, a laptop went missing and its loss wasn't noticed for days. Fortunately, the user had not used the Save Password settings on the VPN connection object, but the possibility was present for him to have done so. Your manager would like to mitigate the particular vulnerability that this presents.

In this exercise, you will install the CMAK, create a CMAK service profile to distribute to users, and verify the CMAK service profile.

1. Click Start, point to Control Panel, and select Add Or Remove Programs. Click Add/Remove Windows Components. The Windows Components Wizard appears.
2. On the Windows Components page, in the Components box, select to highlight Management And Monitoring Tools, and then click Details.
3. In the Management And Monitoring Tools dialog box, select the Connection Manager Administration Kit check box, and click OK.
4. On the Windows Components page, click Next. The Configuring Components page appears. If prompted, insert the Microsoft Windows Server 2003 installation CD-ROM and click Retry to copy the necessary files.
5. On the Completing the Windows Components Wizard page, click Finish. Close Add Or Remove Programs.
6. Click Start, point to Administrative Tools, and select Connection Manager Administration Kit. The Connection Manager Administration Kit Wizard appears.
7. On the Welcome To The Connection Manager Administration Kit Wizard page, click Next.
8. On the Service Profile Selection page, ensure that the New Profile option is selected and click Next.
9. On the Service And File Names page, type **Contoso VPN** in the Service Name text box, type **L2TPVPN** in the File Name text box, and then click Next.
10. On the Realm Name page, click Next.
11. On the Merging Profile Information page, click Next.

12. On the VPN Support page, select the Phone Book From This Profile check box, type **10.1.1.*p*** (where *p* is the last octet of your partner's IP address), and click Next.

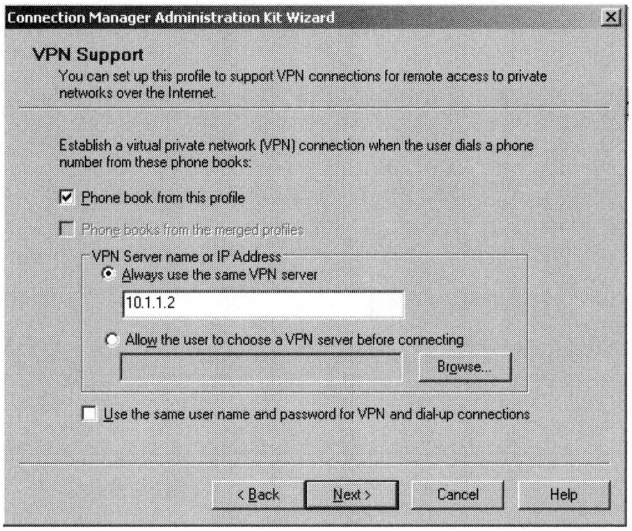

13. On the VPN Entries page, click Edit. The Edit Virtual Private Networking Entry dialog box appears.

14. Click the Security tab.

15. On the Security tab, in the Security Settings drop-down list, select Use Advanced Security Settings.

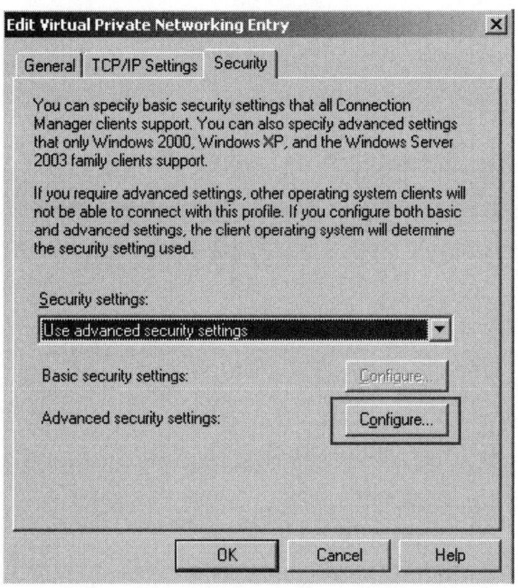

16. On the Security tab, to the right of Advanced Security Settings, click Configure.

17. In the Advanced Security Settings dialog box, clear the Microsoft CHAP (MS-CHAP) check box, verify that the Microsoft CHAP Version 2 (MS-CHAPv2) check box is selected, and select Only Use Layer 2 Tunneling Protocol (L2TP) in the VPN Strategy drop-down list, and click OK.

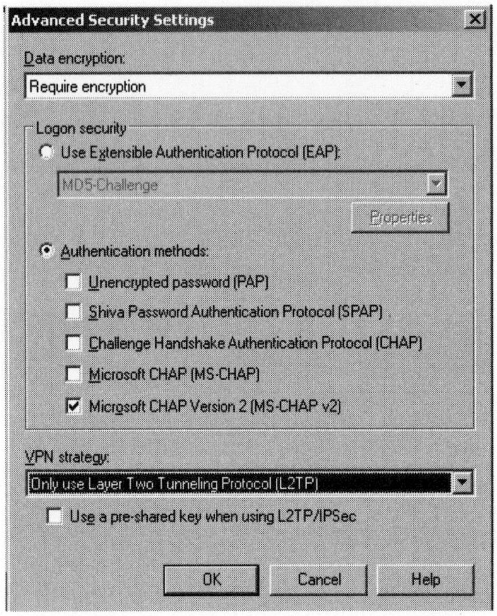

18. In the Advanced Security Settings dialog box, click OK. In the Edit Virtual Private Networking Entry dialog box, click OK.
19. On the VPN Entries page, click Next.
20. On the Phone Book Entries page, clear the Automatically Download Phone Book Updates check box, and click Next.

    You now see the Dial-Up Networking Entries page. Note that this page is where you configure dial-up entries, not VPN entries, and is different from the page you encountered in step 14 and step 19.

21. On the Dial-up Networking Entries page, click Next.
22. On the Routing Table Update page, click Next.
23. On the Automatic Proxy Configuration page, click Next.
24. On the Custom Actions page, click Next.

    As a point of information, the Custom Actions page is one place where you would configure VPN quarantine settings.

25. On the Logon Bitmap page, click Next.
26. On the Phone Book Bitmap page, click Next.

27. On the Icons page, click Next.
28. On the Notification Area Shortcut Menu page, click Next.
29. On the Help file page, click Next.
30. On the Support Information page, click Next.
31. On the Connection Manager Software page, click Next.
32. On the License Agreement page, click Next.
33. On the Additional Files page, click Next.
34. On the Ready To Build Service Profile page, select the Advanced Customization check box, and then click Next.

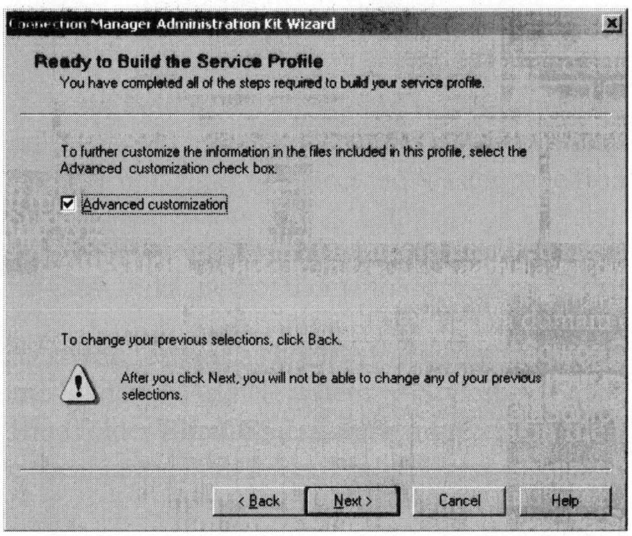

35. In the Connection Manager Administration Kit dialog box, click Yes.

In steps 36 through 39, you will create a CMAK service profile that mitigates a serious vulnerability associated with VPN and dial-up connection objects: the use of the remember password settings. If a user configures the remember password setting and his or her computer is stolen, the attacker potentially has access to the corporate network through the VPN settings.

> **NOTE** The Advanced Customization page contains some important settings. Ensure that you edit the values on this page carefully and that you click Apply when you have entered the settings.

36. On the Advanced Customization page, in the Section Name drop-down list, select Connection Manager.

37. In the Key Name text box, type **HideRememberPassword**.

38. In the Value text box, type **1**.

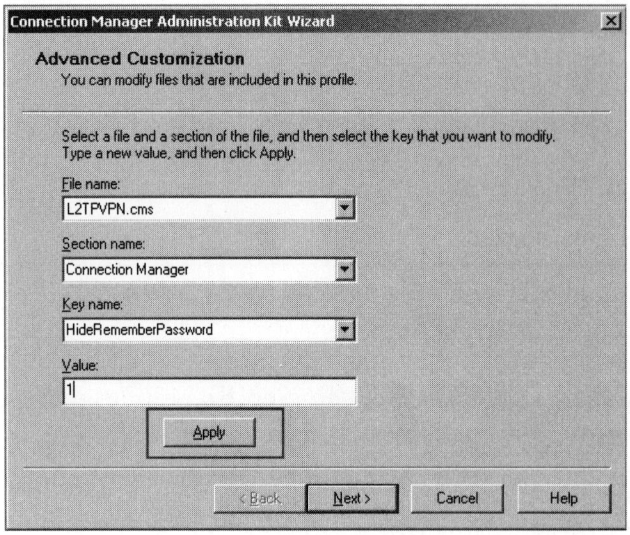

NOTE Make sure you perform the next step before proceeding.

39. On the Advanced Customization page, click Apply to save your changes.

40. On the Advanced Customization page, click Next. The CMAK Service profile is built.

41. On the Completing The Connection Manager Administration Kit Wizard page, click Finish.

42. Open Windows Explorer, navigate to C:\Program Files\CMAK\Profiles\L2TPVPN, and copy the L2TPVPN.exe file to the C:\Lab Manual\Lab 11 folder.

43. Close all open windows and log off.

Verifying CMAK Service Profile Settings

In this section, you will verify the CMAK service profile settings that you configured in the previous section.

1. Log on as Contoso*dd*\JGeist*zz*.

2. Click Start, select Run, type **c:\lab manual\lab 11\lt2pvpn.exe**, and click OK.

3. In the Contoso VPN message box, click Yes.
4. In the Contoso VPN dialog box, select the Add A Shortcut To The Desktop check box, and click OK. The CMAK service profile is installed, the Network Connections folder opens, and the CMAK service profile opens and initializes. Note that even though the JGeist*zz* account does not have administrative privileges, it is still able to install the service profile.

> **QUESTION** *Do you see any place where you can save the user name or password? Why or why not?*

5. In the Contoso VPN dialog box, click Properties to open the Contoso VPN Properties dialog box. Spend a few moments exploring the settings on the various tabs. Note the limited number of settings that are available to this user to configure.
6. Click Cancel.
7. In the Contoso VPN service profile, log on as Contoso*dd*\jgeist*zz*.
8. In the notification area (system tray), right-click the connection icon for the VPN connection, and then select Status.
9. On the Contoso VPN Status dialog box, click the Details tab, and then review the information.

> **QUESTION** *What authentication method is being used? What encryption is being used?*

10. Click the General tab, and then click Disconnect.
11. Log off and then log on as Contoso*dd*\Admin*zz* for the next exercise.

EXERCISE 11.3: COMPARING PPTP AND L2TP/IPSEC TRAFFIC

Estimated completion time: 25 minutes

In this section, you will compare the PPTP and L2TP/IPSec traffic by using saved Microsoft Network Monitor capture files. The files are named Pptp.cap and L2tp.cap and are located in the C:\Lab Manual\Lab 11 folder.

You will first examine PPTP traffic and then examine L2TP/IPSec traffic.

1. Open Network Monitor.

2. From the File menu, select Open, select C:\Lab Manual\Lab 11 in the Look-in drop-down list, select Pptp.cap, and then click Open.

3. In the Microsoft Network Monitor capture summary window, locate and double-click the first row (Ethernet frame) that displays PPTP in the Protocol column (frame 10).

   QUESTION What transport protocol and what destination port number are used for PPTP?

4. Locate and select the first frame that displays LCP in the Protocol column (frame 16), and then highlight IP Protocol in the middle pane.

   QUESTION What IP protocol type is used in this frame? Hint: Look at the description immediately to the right of "IP: Protocol =".

5. Locate and select the first frame that displays PPPCHAP in the Protocol column; then in the middle pane, expand the PPPCHAP header. Select the PPPCHAP: Data row.

   In the bottom pane, note the information that is highlighted.

   QUESTION What information is sent in clear text in this frame?

6. Locate and examine other instances of frames that display PPPCHAP in the Protocol column.

   QUESTION What other information is sent in clear text in these frames?

7. Locate and examine the frames that display PPP in the Protocol column and MPPE/MMPC in the Description column.

   QUESTION What do these frames represent?

8. From the Microsoft Network Monitor File menu, select Open.
9. In the Open dialog box, select L2tp.cap, and then click Open.
10. In the Microsoft Network Monitor capture summary window, locate and double-click the first frame that displays ISAKMP in the Protocol column.

QUESTION What transport protocol and destination and source port number are used for ISAKMP?

11. In the same frame that you selected in step 10, in the middle pane, expand the ISAKMP header, and scroll to the bottom of the middle pane.

QUESTION What are the ISAKMP payload types listed in this frame?

12. Examine other frames that display ISAKMP in the Protocol column.

QUESTION Name at least four other ISAKMP payload types.

13. Locate and click the first frame that displays ESP in the Protocol column.

QUESTION What does ESP stand for, as indicated in the IP datagram?

QUESTION What is contained within the ESP payload?

14. Scan the remaining frames in the capture of L2TP data.

QUESTION Do you see any frames indicating the use of the Challenge Handshake Authentication Protocol (CHAP) or the Point-to-Point Protocol (PPP)?

15. Close the capture summary windows, and then close Network Monitor. If you are prompted to save entries in your address database, click No.

EXERCISE 11.4: USING RADIUS AUTHENTICATION

Estimated completion time: 25 minutes

One of the disadvantages of using remote access policies is that each RAS server becomes a kind of authentication island unto itself. Managing authentication and performing audits on authentication requests is difficult when an administrator has to view the logs on each individual RAS server. Furthermore, the administrator has to configure policies on each RAS server. RADIUS solves these difficulties by centralizing authentication and remote access policy management.

In this exercise, you will configure your RAS servers to use the Internet Authentication Server you installed in Lab 10.

Configuring the RADIUS Server

1. Click Start, select Administrative Tools, and then select Internet Authentication Service.
2. Right-click Internet Authentication Service (Local), and then select Properties.

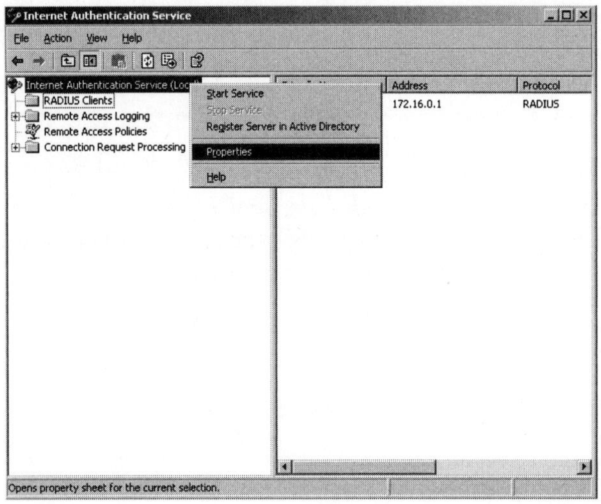

3. On the Internet Authentication Service (Local) Properties page, note the settings on the General tab, and then click the Ports tab.

> **QUESTION** *What ports are used for RADIUS authentication and accounting?*

4. Click OK.
5. Select Remote Access Logging, right-click Local File in the details pane, and then select Properties.
6. In the Local File Properties dialog box, review the selections, and then, on the Settings tab, select all the check boxes.

   For more information about these settings, consult the article, "Logging User and Authentication Requests," in Windows Help.
7. Click the Log File tab, select the Database-Compatible option, select the Daily option, and then click OK.
8. Right-click RADIUS Clients, and then select New RADIUS Client to open the New RADIUS Client wizard.

9. On the Name And Address page, type **Computer*pp*** (where *pp* is the two-digit version of your lab partner's student number) in the Friendly Name text box and in the Client Address (IP Or DNS) text box, and then click Next.

10. On the Additional Information page, ensure that RADIUS Standard is selected from the Client-Vendor drop-down list, type **R@d1u$** in the Shared Secret and Confirm Shared Secret text boxes, select the Request Must Contain Message Authenticator Attribute check box, and then click Finish.

> **NOTE** In a production environment, you should use a long and complex shared secret password. An ideal password for RADIUS is 22 or more characters long and is created by a random password-generation program. Also, you should change this password frequently.

11. Select Remote Access Policies, right-click Access By Windows Group, and then select Properties.

12. In the Access By Windows Group Properties dialog box, select the entry Windows-Groups Matches "CONTOSOdd\VPN Access Group*yy*" (where *yy* is your lab partner's student number) in the Policy Conditions box, and then click Edit.

13. In the Groups dialog box, click Add.

14. In the Select Groups dialog box, select Locations, select Contoso*dd*.msft, and then click OK.

15. In the Enter Object Names To Select box, type **VPN Access Group*zz*** (where *zz* is your student number), and then click OK.

    The reason for this step is that, although you will establish a VPN connection with your partner's server, your server will provide the authorization through the RADIUS policy. Note that members of either of the VPN access groups will be allowed to establish a connection as a result of this policy.

16. In the Access By Windows Group Properties dialog box, click OK.

17. Minimize the Internet Authentication Service console.

Configuring a RADIUS Client

In this section, you will configure your RRAS server to be a RADIUS client to your lab partner's RADIUS server.

IMPORTANT *Wait until your partner has completed the previous section before proceeding.*

1. Click Start, point to Administrative Tools, and select Routing And Remote Access.
2. Right-click Computer*zz* (Local), and then click Properties.
3. In the Computer*zz* (Local) Properties dialog box, click the Security tab.
4. Select the Authentication Provider drop-down list, select RADIUS Authentication, and then click Configure.
5. In the RADIUS Authentication dialog box, click Add.
6. In the Add RADIUS Server dialog box, type **Computer*pp*** (where *pp* is the two-digit version of your lab partner's student number) in the Server Name text box.
7. Click Change, type **R@d1u$** in the New Secret and Confirm New Secret text boxes, and then click OK.
8. Select the Always Use Message Authenticator check box, click OK, and then click OK to close the RADIUS Authentication dialog box.
9. Select the Accounting Provider drop-down list, select RADIUS Accounting, and then click Configure.
10. In the RADIUS Accounting dialog box, click Add.
11. In the Add RADIUS Server dialog box, type **Computer*pp*** in the Server Name text box.
12. Select Change, type **R@d1u$** in the New Secret and Confirm New Secret text boxes, click OK to close the Change Secret dialog box, click OK to close the Add RADIUS Server dialog box, and then click OK to close the RADIUS Accounting dialog box.
13. Click OK to close the Computer*zz* (Local) Properties dialog box, click OK when prompted to restart RRAS to configure a new authentication provider, and then click OK when prompted to restart RRAS to configure a new accounting provider.
14. In the tree pane of the RRAS console, note that the Remote Access Policies and Remote Access Logging nodes are removed upon restart of the RRAS service.

QUESTION *Why are the Remote Access Policies and Remote Access Logging nodes removed?*

15. Minimize the Routing And Remote Access console.

Testing RADIUS Authentication

In this section, you will establish a VPN connection to your lab partner's server and then view the IAS log files to verify that authentication is working properly.

> **IMPORTANT** Wait until your lab partner has completed the previous section before proceeding.

1. Click Start, select Connect To, click Computer*pp* (where *pp* is the two-digit version of your partner's student number), and connect as jgeist*zz*.
2. After you have established the VPN connection, select Start, select Run, type **%windir%\system32\logfiles** in the Open text box, and then click OK.
3. Double-click the file In*yymmdd*.log (where *yy* is the year, *mm* is the month, and *dd* is the day) to open it in Notepad.

   If you do not see the log file in the directory, open the C:\ Lab Manual\Lab 11\ IN050129.log sample file, and proceed to step 4.
4. Examine the entries in the log file and then close Notepad.

> **QUESTION** In general, what information is recorded in the log file?

IAS log files can be difficult to read and interpret. To facilitate reading of these log files, Microsoft Windows Server 2003 ships with a tool called Iasparse.exe, which can be found in the \Support\Tools folder of the Windows Server 2003 Enterprise Edition CD. These tools have been installed on your computer as part of the classroom setup. In the remaining steps, you will use the Iasparse.exe utility to examine the log files.

5. Open a command prompt window, type **cd\windows\system32\logfiles**, and press ENTER.
6. At the command prompt, type **dir IN***, and press ENTER. Record the name of the IAS log file in the output of the dir command.
7. At the command prompt, type **iasparse –f:[name-of-IAS-log-file] > output.txt & notepad output.txt**, and press ENTER.

   For example, to open the sample log file in the Lab 11 folder, you would type **iasparse -f:in050129.log > output.txt & notepad output.txt**.
8. Review the output in Notepad.
9. Close Notepad, and close all open windows and log off.

LAB REVIEW QUESTIONS

Estimated completion time: 15 minutes

1. Which protocol, PPTP or L2TP, provides greater security? Explain your answer.
2. Which protocol, PPTP or L2TP, is more efficient for transmitting data? Provide reasons for your answer.
3. Why is it important to use strong passwords if you are using PPTP?
4. What are some of the advantages of using RADIUS authentication for VPN or dial-in access?
5. How can you protect the traffic between a dial-in server and a RADIUS server?
6. You want to implement L2TP/IPsec for VPN connections. For maximum security, what needs to be installed on the RAS servers and the VPN clients?

LAB CHALLENGE 11.1: DESIGNING REMOTE-ACCESS POLICIES

Estimated completion time: 25 minutes

You are an administrator responsible for configuring remote access polices for employees of your company.

A number of employees are sales personnel who often work out of the office. When the sales personnel come into the office, they sit at any available cubicle in a designated area. Because this area does not have enough network ports for the maximum number of sales personnel who can be there at any one time, your company implemented a wireless network that uses 802.1x authentication. All sales personnel have laptop computers that they bring to the office and take to sales meetings outside the office.

Your company wireless access policy stipulates that only members of the SalesStaff group can access the wireless network. Access to the wireless network is allowed only between the hours of 7:00 A.M. and 6:00 P.M. on weekdays. A group called SalesManager is a member of the SalesStaff group. Members of the SalesManager group have assigned offices and should not have access to the wireless network.

Your company's remote access policy stipulates that PPTP VPN access is allowed at all times, but only to members of the SalesStaff group. The VPN connection must use the strongest authentication method possible and no less than 128-bit encryption. If the VPN connection is idle for more than five minutes, it must be disconnected by the server. A group named SalesTrainees is a member of the SalesStaff group. Members of this group should not have remote access permissions, either to establish a VPN connection or to use the wireless network.

For this lab challenge, in the Location*zz*\Sales OU, create the appropriate groups and configure remote-access policies on the RADIUS server that you configured in Exercise 11.4, "Using RADIUS Authentication," and Exercise 10.4, "Examining Wireless Settings for 802.1x Authentication." The remote-access policies should implement the requirements described in this scenario.

> **TIP** You can use the remote access policies you created in earlier exercises.

POSTLAB CLEANUP

Estimated completion time: 5 minutes

Perform the following steps before proceeding to the next lab.

1. Log on as Contoso*dd*\Admin*zz*.
2. Click Start, point to Administrative Tools, and select Routing and Remote Access.
3. In the Routing And Remote Access console tree, right-click Computer*zz* (local), and select Disable Routing And Remote Access. Click Yes to confirm that you want to disable the Routing And Remote Access services.
4. Log off.

LAB 12

HARDENING WEB SERVERS

This lab contains the following exercises and activities:

- Exercise 12.1: Comparing Basic with Integrated Windows Authentication
- Exercise 12.2: Using Certificates for Web Server Security
- Exercise 12.3: Implementing Application Pools to Enhance Reliability, Performance, and Security of Web Sites
- Exercise 12.4: Securing Web Services
- Lab Review Questions
- Lab Challenge 12.1: Implementing Certificate-Based Authentication for Web Sites

SCENARIO

As a network administrator for Contoso Pharmaceuticals, you are responsible for ensuring that a number of Contoso's Web servers are configured to provide an appropriate level of security. This means ensuring that the Web servers use appropriate authentication methods and that applications are configured so that an error in a particular application will not affect the entire Web server. You must also ensure that Secure Sockets Layer (SSL) is implemented appropriately on only selected virtual directories. Finally, you must ensure that the Web servers have been hardened by removing unnecessary services.

After completing this lab, you will be able to:

- Configure Basic and Integrated Windows authentication.
- Analyze Basic authentication traffic by using Microsoft Network Monitor.
- Analyze Integrated Windows authentication traffic by using Microsoft Network Monitor.
- Request a certificate for a Web server by using the Web-based certificate enrollment tools.
- Install a certificate to enable SSL encryption.
- Configure Web application pools to provide additional fault tolerance and availability for a Web server and Web applications.
- Examine services that should potentially disabled on a Web server to reduce its attack surface.

Estimated lesson time: 115 minutes

BEFORE YOU BEGIN

To complete this lab, you will need to have done the following:

- Created a Member Servers organizational unit (OU) and moved the Computer*yy* member server object to the OU as instructed in steps 3 through 7 of Lab Exercise 3.4, "Using Group Policy to Configure Automatic Update Clients," in Lab 3, "Reducing the Risk of Software Vulnerabilities."
- Performed the steps in the "Before You Begin" section of Lab 4, "Designing a Management Infrastructure," to create user accounts and to grant the Domain Users the right to log on locally to the domain controller.
- Implemented an enterprise subordinate certification authority (CA), as per the instructions in Lab 9, "Designing a Public Key Infrastructure."
- Disabled Internet Explorer Enhanced Security Settings as described in steps 1 through 7 of the section titled "Examining Internet Explorer Security Settings" of Lab Exercise 8.2, "Configuring Internet Explorer Security Settings" in Lab 8, "Hardening Client Computers."

NOTE In this lab, you will see the characters *dd*, *pp*, *xx*, *yy*, and *zz*. These directions assume that you are working on computers configured in pairs and that each computer has a number.

When you see *dd*, substitute the number used for your domain. When you see *pp*, substitute the number of your partner's computer. When you see *xx*, substitute the unique number assigned to the lower-numbered (odd-numbered) computer of the pair. When you see *yy*, substitute the unique number assigned to the higher-numbered (even-numbered) computer of the pair. When you see *zz*, substitute the number assigned to the computer at which you are using. The following example assumes that the partner pair of computers has been assigned the names Computer05 and Computer06 and that you have been assigned Computer05.

Computer*pp* = Computer06 = your partner's computer

Computer*xx* = Computer05 = lower-numbered computer

Computer*yy* = Computer06 = higher-numbered computer

Computer*zz* = Computer05 = computer you are using

Contoso*dd*.msft = Contoso03.msft = Active Directory domain you are using

EXERCISE 12.1: COMPARING BASIC WITH INTEGRATED WINDOWS AUTHENTICATION

Estimated completion time: 30 minutes

In this exercise, you will use Network Monitor to compare the difference between Basic authentication and Integrated Windows authentication when connecting to Web virtual directories that require authentication. You will first create two Web virtual directories, and then configure each of the virtual directories to require that users authenticate using either Basic or Integrated Windows authentication before they can gain access to it. You will then use Network Monitor to analyze the authentication traffic when you connect to the virtual directories on your lab partner's computer.

Creating Virtual Directories for Basic and Integrated Windows Authentication

1. Click Start, point to Administrative Tools, and then select Internet Information Services (IIS) Manager.
2. In the Internet Information Services (IIS) Manager console, expand Web Sites, right-click Default Web Site, select New, and then select Virtual Directory.

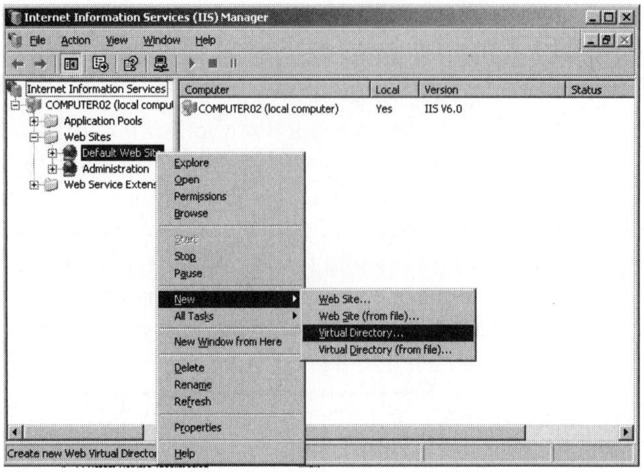

3. On the Welcome To The Virtual Directory Creation Wizard page, click Next.
4. On the Virtual Directory Alias page, type **Basic** in the Alias text box, and then click Next.
5. On the Web Site Content Directory page, click Browse.
6. In the Browse For Folder dialog box, expand Local Disk (C:), expand Inetpub, select Wwwroot, and then click Make New Folder.
7. In the folder name box, type **Basic** for the folder name, and then click OK.

   If you are not automatically given the opportunity to enter a new folder name for the folder you just created, right-click New Folder, select Rename, type **Basic** for the folder name, and then click OK.

8. On the Web Site Content Directory page, ensure that the Path box contains C:\Inetpub\Wwwroot\Basic, and then click Next.
9. On the Virtual Directory Access Permissions page, accept the default settings, and then click Next.
10. On the You Have Successfully Completed The Virtual Directory Creation Wizard page, click Finish.
11. In the Internet Information Services (IIS) Manager console, expand Web Sites, right-click Default Web Site, select New, and then select Virtual Directory.
12. On the Welcome To The Virtual Directory Creation Wizard page, click Next.

13. On the Virtual Directory Alias dialog box, type **Integrated** in the Alias text box, and then click Next.
14. On the Web Site Content Directory dialog box, click Browse.
15. In the Browse For Folder dialog box, expand Local Disk (C:), expand Inetpub, select Wwwroot, and then click Make New Folder.
16. In the Folder Name box, type **Integrated** for the folder name, and then click OK.

    If you are not automatically given the opportunity to enter a new folder name for the folder you just created, right-click New Folder, select Rename, type **Integrated** for the folder name, and then click OK.

17. In the Web Site Content Directory dialog box, ensure that the Path box contains C:\Inetpub\Wwwroot\Integrated, and then click Next.
18. In the Virtual Directory Access Permissions dialog box, accept the default settings, and then click Next.
19. In the You Have Successfully Completed The Virtual Directory Creation Wizard page, click Finish.
20. Leave open the Internet Information Services (IIS) Manager console.

Configuring Virtual Directories for Basic and Integrated Windows Authentication

In this section, you will create Hypertext Markup Language (HTML) files for use in the virtual directories you have just created. You will then configure the directories to require either basic or integrated authentication.

1. Click Start, select Run, type **notepad** in the Open text box, and then click OK.
2. In Notepad, type the following HTML code (where *zz* is the two-digit version of your student number):

    <html>

    <title>

    Basic Authentication Virtual Directory for Computer*zz*

    </title>

    <body>

Virtual directory on Computer*zz* to examine Basic Authentication.

</body>

</html>

3. From the File menu, select Save As; from the Save In drop-down list, navigate to C:\Inetpub\Wwwroot\Basic, type "**default.htm**" (including the quotation marks to ensure that the file is not saved with a .txt extension) in the File Name box; and then click Save.
4. With Notepad still open, replace all instances of the word "**Basic**" with the word "**Integrated**."
5. From the File menu, select Save As; from the Save In drop-down list box, navigate to C:\Inetpub\Wwwroot\Integrated; type "**default.htm**" (including the quotation marks) in the File Name box; and then click Save.
6. Close Notepad.
7. In the Internet Information Services (IIS) Manager console, right-click the Basic virtual directory and then select Properties.

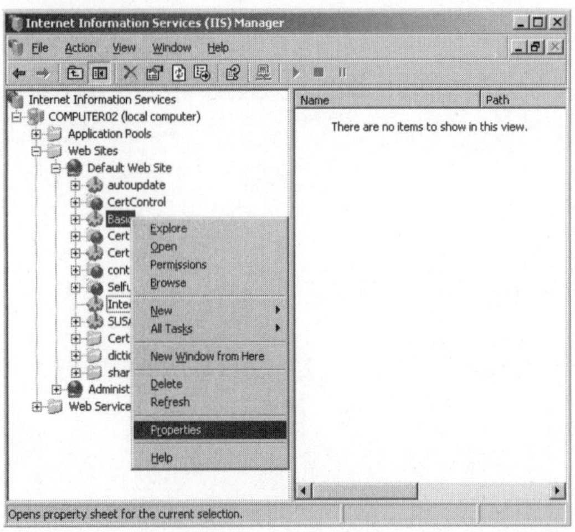

8. In the Basic Properties dialog box, click the Directory Security tab.
9. In the Authentication And Access Control area, select Edit.
10. In the Authentication Methods dialog box, clear the Enable Anonymous Access check box, clear the Integrated Windows Authentication check box, and then select the Basic Authentication (Password Is Sent In Clear Text) check box.

11. Read the warning that appears in the IIS Manager message box, and then click Yes to continue.

> **QUESTION** *Why does the warning not apply to Hypertext Transfer Protocol Secure (HTTPS) connections?*

12. In the Authenticated Access area, in the Default Domain text box, type **contoso*dd*.msft**, click OK, and then click OK again to close the Basic Properties dialog box.

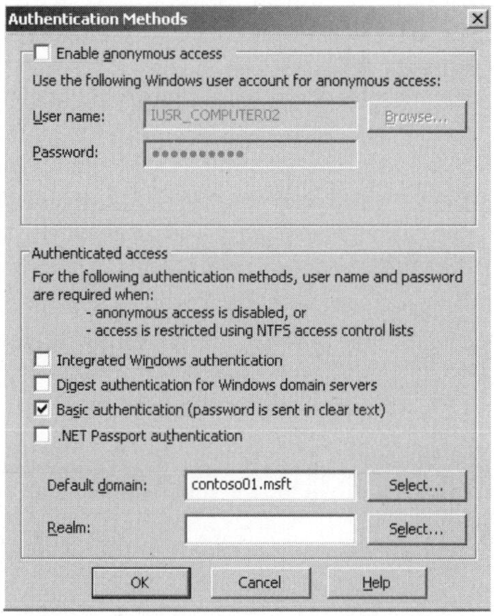

13. Right-click the Integrated virtual directory, and then click Properties.
14. In the Integrated Properties dialog box, click the Directory Security tab.
15. In the Authentication And Access Control area, click Edit.
16. In the Authentication Methods page, clear the Enable Anonymous Access check box, click OK, and then click OK again to close the Integrated Properties dialog box.

> **QUESTION** *What authentication methods are selected by default when you create a virtual directory?*

17. Open Windows Explorer, navigate to the C:\Inetpub\wwwroot folder, right-click the Basic folder, and select Properties.

18. In the Basic Properties dialog box, click the Security tab, and examine the default inherited permissions and then answer the question below.

> **QUESTION** In the preceding steps, you used Web permissions to remove anonymous access. What other method can and should you use to remove anonymous access?

19. Close the Basic Properties dialog box, close Windows Explorer, and then close the Internet Information Services (IIS) Manager console.

Capturing and Analyzing Basic and Integrated Windows Authentication by Using Network Monitor

> **IMPORTANT** Wait until your lab partner has completed the previous section before proceeding. To make it easier to interpret the resulting network capture traffic, only one student at a time should perform steps 1 through 7. As an alternative to creating a capture of actual basic and integrated authentication traffic, you can use the Network Monitor capture file named Webauthentication.cap, which is found in the C:\Lab Manual\Lab 12 folder. To use this file, open it from the File menu of Network Monitor. If you choose to use the capture file, proceed to step 8.

1. Click Start, point to Administrative Tools, and then select Network Monitor.
2. Open Microsoft Internet Explorer.
3. Switch to Network Monitor, and then, from the Capture menu, select Start.
4. Switch to Internet Explorer, type **computer*pp*/basic** (where *pp* is the two-digit version of your partner's student number) in the Address box, and then press Enter.
5. In the Connect To Computer*yy* dialog box, type **admin*zz*** in the User Name text box, type your password in the Password text box, and then click OK.
6. In the Address box, type **computeryy/integrated** (where *yy* is the two-digit version of your partner's student number), and then press ENTER.

If you are prompted for credentials, type **adminzz** in the User Name text box, type your password in the Password text box, and then click OK.

If you are prompted for credentials, the most likely reason is that you did not disable the Internet Explorer Enhanced Security Settings in steps 1 through 7 of the section titled "Examining Internet Explorer Security Settings" of Exercise 8.2. Note that you are not prompted for authentication credentials when you connect to a virtual directory that requires integrated authentication when this setting is disabled. The reason for this is the relaxed Internet Explorer security settings allow the browser to use the current user name and password of the logged-on user when connecting to Intranet (Local) sites for the Adminzz account. There are two ways to "correct" this: explicitly add your partner's computer to the Intranet (Local) security zone in Internet Explorer or relax the Internet Explorer Enhanced Security settings.

You should take either of the two actions cited above. Otherwise, the steps for the next exercise will not work as written.

7. Switch to Network Monitor, and, from the Capture menu, select Stop And View.

> **IMPORTANT** The second lab partner can now proceed with steps 1 through 7. After that, proceed to the next steps listed here.

8. From the Display menu, select Filter.
9. In the Display Filter dialog box, double-click Protocol == Any.
10. In the Expression page, on the Protocol tab, click Disable All.
11. In the Disabled Protocols window on the right side, select HTTP, and then click Enable so that HTTP is listed as the only protocol in the Enabled Protocols window. Click OK to close the Expression dialog box, and then click OK to close the Display Filter dialog box.

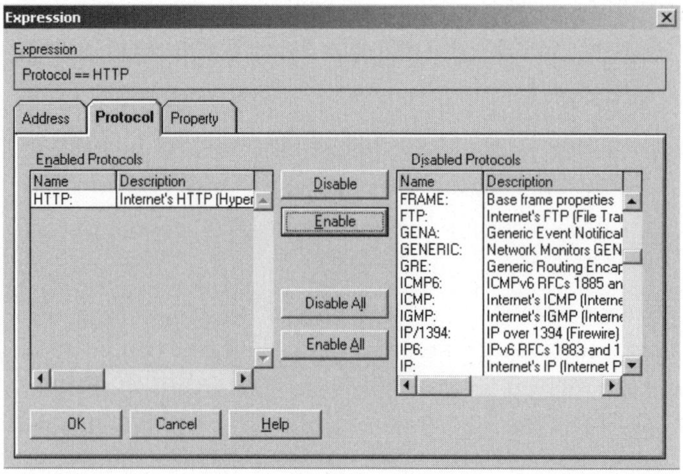

12. In the Microsoft Network Monitor capture summary screen, double-click the first frame that displays Status Code – 401 in the Description column (you may have to extend the Description column to see this), expand HTTP in the middle pane, and then examine the details of the HTTP payload.

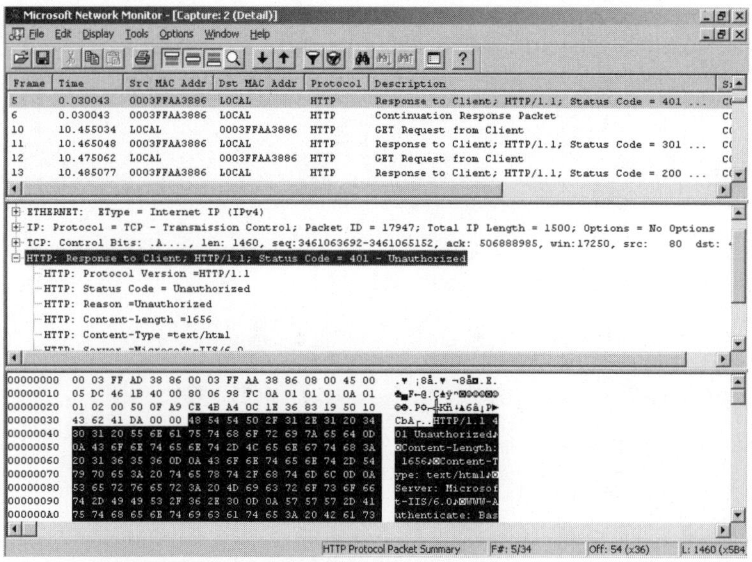

QUESTION *What is listed as the authentication method?*

13. In the top pane, immediately below the frame you examined in step 12, select the first frame that displays GET Request From Client in the Description column.

14. With HTTP: GET Request From Client expanded in the middle pane, locate the header field labeled HTTP: Authorization and examine the contents of the field.

> **QUESTION** What does this field contain?

> **TIP** If the classroom has a connection to the Internet, go to *http://www.wc.cc.va.us/dtod/base64/* and decode the content of this field by copying and pasting the alphanumeric string following the word "Basic." (You can copy the fields from captured frames by selecting the field and pressing CTRL+C. Paste it into the Web-Based Base64 Converter text box by pressing CTRL+V.)

15. In the top pane, immediately below the frame you examined in step 14, select the first frame that displays Status Code = 200.

> **QUESTION** What does a status code of 200 indicate?

16. In the top pane, immediately below the frame you examined in step 15, select the frame that displays Status Code – 401 in the Description column; in the middle pane, ensure that HTTP: Response To Client is expanded; and then locate the two fields that are labeled HTTP: WWW-Authenticate.

> **QUESTION** What authentication methods are listed in the HTTP payload?

17. In the top pane, below the frame you examined in step 16, select the frame that displays Status Code – 301 in the Description column; in the middle pane, ensure that HTTP: Response To Client is expanded; and then locate the HTTP: WWW-Authenticate header field.

    This field represents a Type 2 NTLM response. It contains the challenge that the Web server sends to the client browser as well as the agreed-upon options in response to previous NTLM authentication traffic from the client.

18. Toward the bottom of the captured frames in the top pane, locate the frame that displays Status Code = 200 in the Description column.

19. Immediately above the preceding frame, examine the details of the frames that display GET Request From Client and Continuation Response Packet in the Details column.

> **NOTE** These frames contain the response to the NTLM challenge to prove to the Web server that the client browser knows the password. To respond to the challenge, the client browser performs operations on the entered password to generate keys, which are used to encrypt the challenge. The encrypted challenge is concatenated with other information, encoded, and sent back to the server. The server decrypts the challenge and allows access if the correct credentials have been entered on the Web browser client.

20. Close Network Monitor, and if prompted, do not save the capture or unsaved entries in the address database.
21. Close all open windows and remain logged on for the next exercise.

EXERCISE 12.2: USING CERTIFICATES FOR WEB SERVER SECURITY

Estimated completion time: 30 minutes

In this exercise, you will install a Web server certificate on your computer. You will then establish a secure Web session with your computer. In this exercise, you will use the Web certificate enrollment tools to request and install the certificate.

Generating a Certificate Signing Request (CSR)

1. Click Start, point to Administrative Tools menu, and select Internet Information Services (IIS) Manager.
2. In the Internet Information Services (IIS) Manager console, expand Computer*zz*, expand Web Sites, and then select Default Web Site.
3. Right-click Default Web Site, and then select Properties.
4. In the Default Web Site Properties dialog box, on the Directory Security tab, click Server Certificate to open the Welcome To The Web Server Certificate Wizard.

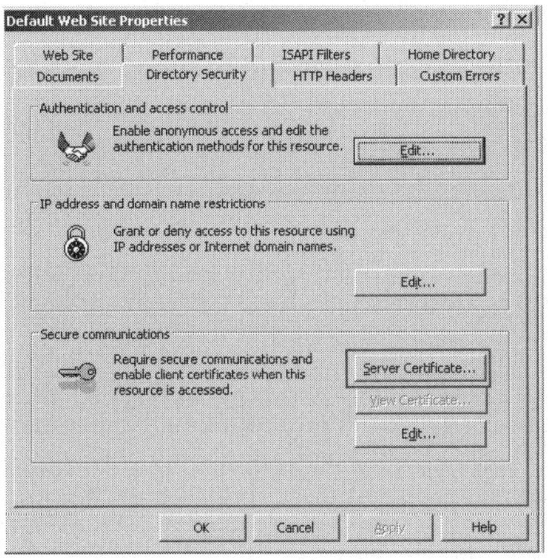

5. On the Welcome To The Web Server Certificate Wizard page, click Next.
6. On the Server Certificate page, ensure that Create A New Certificate is selected, and then click Next.
7. On the Delayed Or Immediate Request page, ensure that Prepare The Request Now, But Send It Later is selected, and then click Next.

> **QUESTION** What must be in place before you can select the Send The Request Immediately To An Online Certification Authority option?

8. On the Name And Security Settings page, type **Computer*zz* Web Certificate** in the Name text box; from the Bit Length drop-down list, select 2048; and then click Next.
9. On the Organization Information page, type **Contoso** in the Organization box, type **IT Group** in the Organizational Unit box, and then click Next.
10. On the Your Site's Common Name page, ensure that the name of your computer appears in the Common Name text box, and then click Next.

> **NOTE** The Common Name (CN) is an important value. When a client connects to a Web site by using a particular Uniform Resource Locator (URL), the name in the URL must match the CN. Otherwise, the client will see a warning message. Although the message might appear harmless, consider that one of the main purposes of Web certificates is to provide assurances about the identity of the Web server itself. Also, problems with the CN of the certificate can sometimes cause problems with applications and the client might encounter a Server 500 error, rather than just a warning message, and not be able to access the Web site at all.

11. On the Geographical Information page, type the appropriate information for your location (do not use abbreviations for the State/Province and City/Locality fields), and then click Next.
12. On the Certificate Request File Name page, ensure that the File Name box contains C:\Certreq.txt, and then click Next.
13. On the Request File Summary page, review the information, and then click Next.
14. On the Completing The Web Server Certificate Wizard page, click Finish.
15. In the Default Web Site Properties dialog box, click OK to close it.
16. Minimize Internet Information Services (IIS) Manager, and leave it open to complete steps in the next procedure.

Enabling Session State on an Enterprise CA

For the Web enrollment components to work properly on the CA, it is necessary to ensure that session state has been enabled for the Web certificate enrollment applications. It is generally not a good idea to enable session state for an entire Web site, and session state should be enabled only when it is necessary. Sessions remain in memory and consume resources. These resources are not freed until the user terminates the session, such as by closing the browser or when the session times out. If many concurrent users are accessing a Web site, a server with session state enabled can become depleted of resources.

In this section, the student assigned to the domain controller will verify that session state is enabled for the virtual directory that is used for Web enrollment.

1. On the odd-numbered computer, Computer*xx*, in the Internet Information Services (IIS) Manager console, expand Web Sites, expand the Default Web Site, right-click the CertSrv virtual directory, and select Properties.
2. In the CertSrv Properties dialog box, in the Application Settings area, click Configuration.
3. In the Application Configuration dialog box, click the Options tab.
4. On the Options tab, in the Application Configuration area, select the Enable Session State check-box, and click OK.

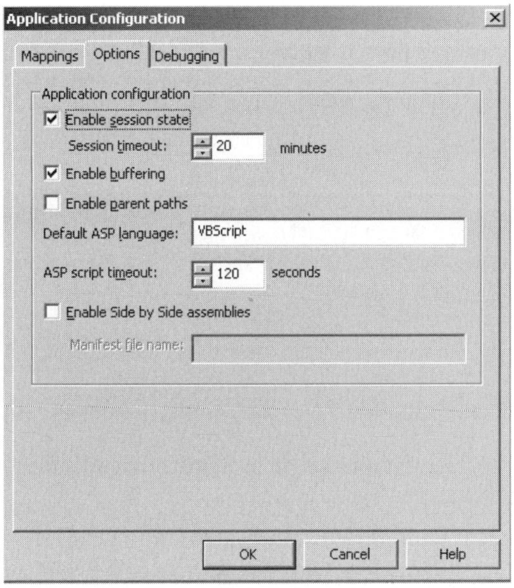

5. In the CertSrv Properties dialog box, click OK.
6. Leave open the Internet Information Services (IIS) Manager console.

Using Web-Based Enrollment to Request a Web Certificate

In this section, you will use Web-based enrollment to request the certificate for your web server. Because the Web-based enrollment site uses a number of Active Server Page (ASP) scripts, you must configure the security settings of Internet Explorer appropriately. Before proceeding with these steps, ensure that the odd-numbered computer is listed in either the Local Intranet or the Trusted Sites security zones of Internet Explorer. Alternatively, you can disable Internet Explorer Enhanced Security Configuration through the Add/Remove Windows Components icon in Control Panel.

1. Click Start, select Run, type **notepad c:\certreq.txt** in the Open box, and then click OK.
2. In Notepad, press CRTL+A to select all the text, and then press CTRL+C to copy the text to the clipboard.

> **NOTE** Ensure that all the text in the Certreq.txt file is selected, including the lines that indicate the beginning and the end of the certificate request.

3. Close Notepad.

4. Restore Internet Explorer and connect to *http://computerxx/certsrv* (where *xx* is the number assigned to the domain controller).
5. On the Welcome page, under Select A Task, click Request a Certificate.

> **NOTE** Make sure that you submit the request (steps 6 through 12) only once. If you request a second certificate, you will not be able to install the second certificate on the Web server, and you will have to delete the pending request and start the exercise over from the beginning.

6. On the Request A Certificate page, click Advanced Certificate Request.
7. On the Advanced Certificate Request page, select Submit A Certificate Request By Using A Base64-Encoded CMC Or PKCS #10 File, Or Submit A Renewal Request By Using A Base 64-Encoded PKCS #7 File.
8. On the Submit A Certificate Request Or Renewal Request page, place the cursor in the Saved Request box and press CTRL+V to paste the certificate request from the clipboard.
9. From the Certificate Template drop-down list, select Web Server, and then click Submit.

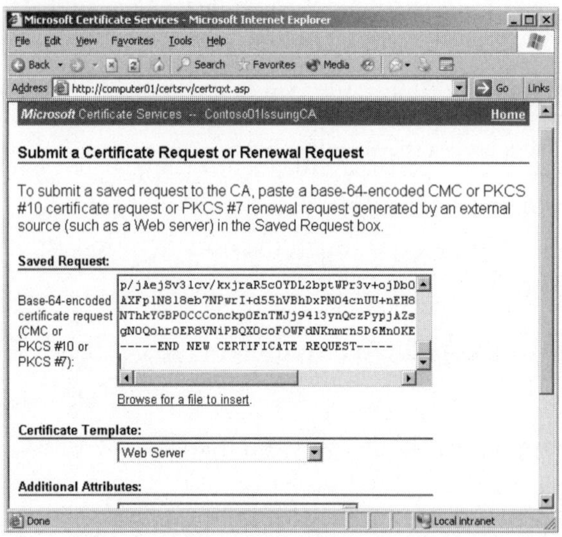

> **NOTE** It is possible that several of the other certificate templates would work as well. However, with certificates, as with so much else, it is important to follow the principle of least privilege. You should create and use certificate templates that are configured with only the minimum required intended purposes.

10. On the Certificate Issued page, ensure that DER Encoded is selected, and then click Download Certificate.
11. In the File Download dialog box, click Save.
12. In the Save As dialog box, ensure that Local Disk (C:) appears in the Save In drop-down list and that Certnew.cer appears in the File Name box, and then click Save.
13. In the Download Complete dialog box, click Close.

Installing a Web Server Certificate

1. Minimize Internet Explorer.
2. Maximize Internet Information Services (IIS) Manager, right-click the Default Web Site, and then select Properties.
3. In the Default Web Site Properties dialog box, on the Directory Security tab, click Server Certificate.
4. On the Welcome To The Web Server Certificate Wizard page, click Next.
5. On the Pending Certificate Request page, ensure that Process The Pending Request And Install The Certificate is selected, and then click Next.
6. On the Process A Pending Request page, in the Path And File Name box, ensure that C:\Certnew.cer appears, and then click Next.
7. On the SSL Port page, ensure that 443 appears, and then click Next.
8. On the Certificate Summary page, review the details of the certificate, and then click Next.
9. On the Completing The Web Server Certificate Wizard page, click Finish.
10. In the Default Web Site Properties dialog box, click OK.

Configuring a Virtual Directory to Require HTTPS

1. In the Internet Information Services (IIS) Manager console, right-click Default Web Site, select New, and then select Virtual Directory.
2. On the Welcome To The Virtual Directory Creation Wizard page, click Next.

3. In the Alias box, type **CertSecure** and then click Next.
4. On the Web Site Content Directory page, click Browse.
5. In the Browse For Folder dialog box, select Local Disk (C:), click Make New Folder, type **CertSecure** for the folder name, and then click OK.
6. On the Web Site Content Directory page, click Next.
7. On the Virtual Directory Access Permissions page, accept the defaults, and then click Next.
8. On the You Have Successfully Completed The Virtual Directory Creation Wizard page, click Finish.
9. In the Internet Information Services (IIS) Manager console, right-click the CertSecure virtual directory, and then select Properties.
10. In the CertSecure Properties dialog box, click the Directory Security tab.
11. In the Secure Communications area, click Edit.
12. In the Secure Communications dialog box, select the Require Secure Channel (SSL) check box, and then click OK.
13. Click OK to close the CertSecure Properties dialog box.

QUESTION *What is the effect of the configuration in step 12?*

14. Minimize Internet Information Services (IIS) Manager.
15. Click Start, select Run, and in the Open box, type **notepad c:\certsecure\default.htm**; then click OK.
16. In the Notepad dialog box, click Yes to create a file.
17. In Notepad, type the following HTML code:

```
<html>

<head>

<title>Computerzz SSL Virtual Directory</title>

</head>

<body>
```

This virtual directory requires SSL encryption.

</body>

</html>

18. When you have finished typing the HTML code, save the file and close Notepad.

    Wait for your partner to complete the previous step before proceeding.

19. Restore Internet Explorer, and then connect to *https://computer*pp*/certsecure* (where *pp* is the two-digit version of your student number). The Security Alert message box appears.

20. In the Security Alert dialog box, click OK. The CertSecure virtual directory appears. Note the lock icon on the bottom of the screen.

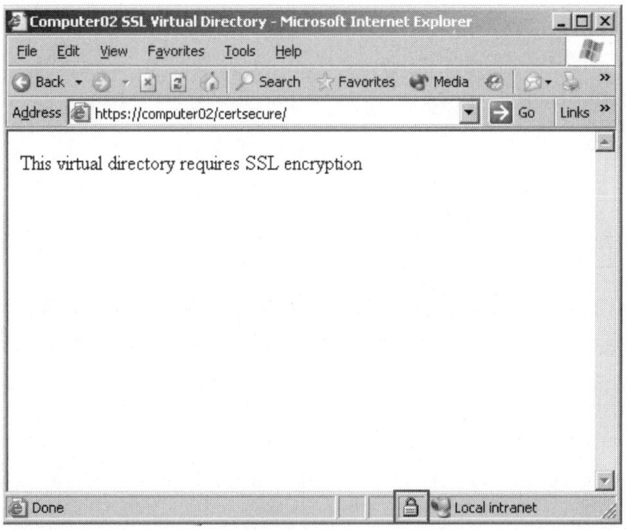

21. Double-click the lock icon.

22. In the Certificate dialog box, spend a few moments viewing the details of the certificate.

23. Close the Certificate dialog box, and then close Internet Explorer.

EXERCISE 12.3: IMPLEMENTING APPLICATION POOLS TO ENHANCE RELIABILITY, PERFORMANCE, AND SECURITY OF WEB SITES

Estimated completion time: 20 minutes

In this exercise, you will configure an application pool that will be used to isolate the processes used for a Web application from the process used by other Web applications that reside in other virtual Web sites or virtual directories. After creating an application pool, you will create an additional Web site that coexists with the default Web site on your computer. You will configure the new Web site to use the newly created application pool.

As you go through these steps, click the question mark on the application pool dialog boxes and drag it to the various settings to better understand the purpose of the settings you are configuring.

1. In the Internet Information Services (IIS) Manager console, right-click Application Pools, select New, and then select Application Pool.
2. In the Add New Application Pool dialog box, type **Web Service AppPool** in the Application Pool ID box, and then click OK.
3. Right-click the Web Service AppPool object, and then click Properties.
4. In the Web Service AppPool Properties dialog box, select the Recycle Worker Process (Number Of Requests) check box, and then set the value to **60,000** requests.
5. In the Web Service AppPool Properties dialog box, select the Recycle Worker Processes At The Following Times check box, and then click Add.
6. In the Select Time dialog box, select 6:00, and then click OK.

   Note that this dialog box presents a 24-hour clock so that 6:00 A.M. is represented as 6:00 and 6:00 P.M. is represented as 18:00.

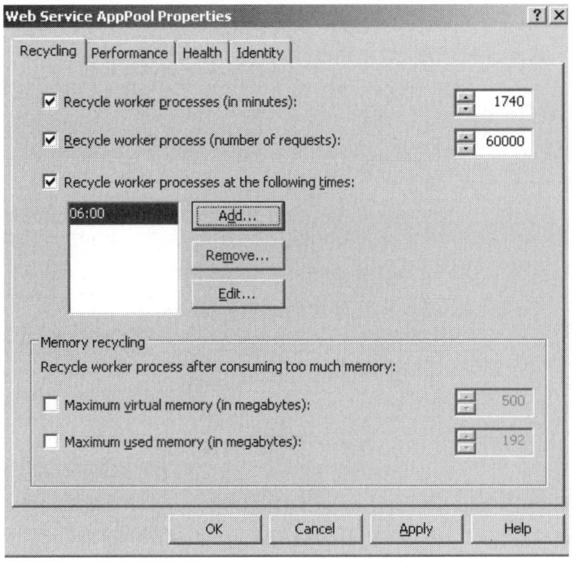

7. Select the Performance tab, and then, in the Web Garden area, select **3** in the Maximum Number Of Worker Processes box.

   QUESTION What is a Web garden?

8. Select the Health tab, and then review the default settings.

   QUESTION What is a primary purpose of the settings on this tab?

9. Select the Identity tab, and then select the Predefined drop-down list.

   QUESTION What are the three predefined accounts?

10. Verify that Network Service is selected in the Predefined drop-down list, and then click OK.

    The Network Service account is a special account that has the fewest user rights required to run a Web application.

11. In the Internet Information Services (IIS) Manager console, right-click Web Sites, select New, and then click Web Site.

12. In the Welcome To The Web Site Creation Wizard page, click Next.

13. On the Web Site page, type **Web Service** in the Description text box and then click Next.

14. On the IP Address And Port Settings page, type **8000** in the TCP Port This Web Site Should Use (Default: 80) text box, and then click Next.

> **NOTE** *Changing the default port will allow this new Web site to coexist with the default Web site on the same server. To allow multiple Web sites to coexist on the same server, you could also add additional IP addresses to the server for use by individual Web sites or use host headers to distinguish between Web sites that share the same IP address.*

15. In the Web Site Home Directory dialog box, click Browse.

16. In the Browse For Folder dialog box, expand Local Disk (C:), select Inetpub, click Make New Folder, type **Webservice** as the name of the folder, and then click OK.

17. In the Web Site Home Directory dialog box, ensure that the entered path is C:\Inetpub\Webservice, ensure that the Allow Anonymous Access To This Web Site check box is selected, and then click Next.

18. In the Web Site Access Permissions dialog box, review the default settings, click Next, and then click Finish.

19. In the Internet Information Service (IIS) Manager console, right-click the Web Service Web site object, and then select Properties.

20. In the Enable Logging area, click Properties.

> **QUESTION** *Where is the log file for this Web site stored?*

21. In the Logging Properties dialog box, click Cancel.

22. In the Web Service Properties dialog box, click the Home Directory tab.

23. In the Home Directory dialog box, in the Application Settings area, from the Application Pool drop-down list box, select Web Service AppPool, and then click OK.

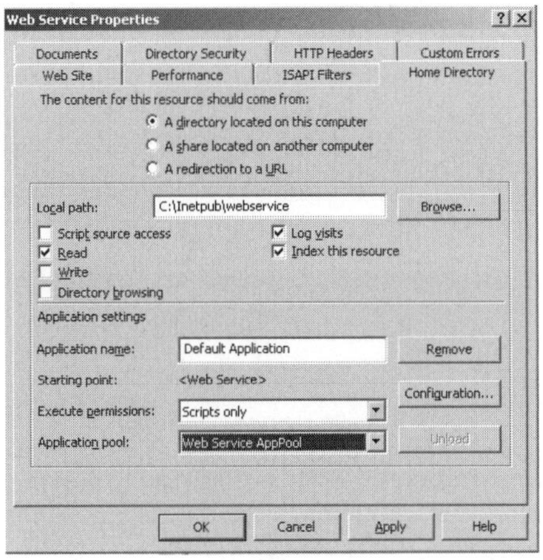

24. Click Start, select Run, type **notepad c:\inetpub\wwwroot\default.htm** and then click OK.

25. In Notepad, replace Home Page with Web Service Home Page.

26. From the File menu, select Save As.

27. In the Save In drop-down list box, navigate to C:\Inetpub\Webservice, and then click Save.

28. Close Notepad.

    Wait until your lab partner has completed the previous steps before proceeding.

29. Open Internet Explorer, type **http://computer*pp*:8000** in the Address box (where *pp* is the two-digit version of your lab partner's student number), and then press Enter. You should see your partner's Default.htm file for the Web Service Web site.

> **QUESTION** If this Web server hosted a .NET Web service application and the application failed, what would happen to other Web sites located on the same computer?

30. Close all open windows.

EXERCISE 12.4: SECURING WEB SERVICES

Estimated completion time: 20 minutes

In this exercise, you will examine the default configuration of IIS 6.0 running on Microsoft Windows Server 2003. You will first examine the services that can potentially be disabled on a computer running Windows Server 2003 that is configured as a dedicated Web server. You will then examine the Web services that are enabled in a default installation of IIS 6.0.

Reducing Attack Surface by Disabling Unnecessary Services

1. Click Start, point to Administrative Tools, and then click Services.
2. In the details pane, double-click Application Management.

   Note the startup type and the description of the service.

   > **QUESTION** *Why would it be a good idea to disable this service on a dedicated Web server?*

3. In the Application Management Properties (Local Computer) dialog box, select the Startup Type drop-down list.

   > **QUESTION** *What are the three possible startup types?*

4. Leave the Startup Type set to Manual, and then, in the Application Management Properties (Local Computer) dialog box, click the Dependencies tab.

   > **QUESTION** *Are there any service dependencies?*

5. In the Application Management Properties (Local Computer) dialog box, click Cancel.
6. In the details pane of the Services console, double-click Distributed File System, note its startup type, and then read the description of the service.

   > **QUESTION** *Why would it be a good idea to disable this service on a dedicated Web server?*

7. In the Distributed File System Properties (Local Computer) dialog box, click Cancel.
8. In the Services console, examine the properties of the following services:
   - ❑ Background Intelligent Transfer Service
   - ❑ Distributed Link Tracking Client
   - ❑ Distributed Link Tracking Server
   - ❑ Error Reporting Service
   - ❑ Netmeeting Remote Desktop Sharing
   - ❑ Print Spooler
   - ❑ Remote Desktop Help Session Manager
   - ❑ Telnet
   - ❑ Terminal Services
   - ❑ Upload Manager

   NOTE *You can disable any of these services on a dedicated Web server, conditional upon a number of factors. For example, you might want to use Terminal Services to perform remote administration, so you would not disable this service. This list is not comprehensive. You might want to disable additional services on a dedicated Web server.*

9. Close the Services console.

Reducing Attack Surface by Prohibiting Unnecessary Web Service Extensions

1. Click Start, point to Administrative Tools, and then select Internet Information Services (IIS) Manager.
2. Expand Computer*zz* (Local Computer), and then select Web Service Extensions.
3. In the details pane, note the Web service extensions and whether they are prohibited or allowed.

   QUESTION *Are any Web service extensions allowed? Why or why not?*

4. In the Web Service Extensions details frame, click the Open Help link, and then read the corresponding article about enabling and disabling dynamic content.

   QUESTION *What is the default configuration of IIS 6.0 for delivering dynamic content?*

5. Close the Microsoft Management Console Help application.

LAB REVIEW QUESTIONS

Estimated completion time: 15 minutes

1. In addition to configuring Web server permissions to authorize access, what other permissions should you configure?
2. Why is NTLM authentication more secure than Basic authentication?
3. What aspect of the CIA (confidentiality, integrity, and availability) triad can Web application pools enhance?
4. One of the default settings for the Internet zone is to prompt for a user name and password. Why is this an appropriate setting for the Internet zone?
5. If you use Basic authentication, what should you do to protect the confidentiality of authentication credentials?

LAB CHALLENGE 12.1: IMPLEMENTING CERTIFICATE-BASED AUTHENTICATION FOR WEB SITES

Estimated completion time: 25 minutes

The administrator in the R and D department has implemented a Web server for the internal use of the R and D departmental employees. Your manager is concerned about the security of some of the virtual directories on this Web server. In particular, she wants specific virtual directories to require the strongest SSL encryption possible. Moreover, she wants to require that user certificates are required for access to these virtual directories. She wants users to be able to acquire their user certificates by using the Web-based certificate enrollment application. You have been asked to implement this solution.

To complete this lab challenge, reconfigure the CertSecure virtual directory you implemented in Exercise 12.2 so that access to it requires user certificates. Then, log on as Jgeist*zz*, and request a certificate by using the Web-based enrollment tools on Computer*xx*. You should note that this exercise is partly a troubleshooting exercise because the account will not be to request the certificate, given the current security settings of Internet Explorer, and you will have to devise a solution to the problems you encounter.

If time permits, disable anonymous authentication on the CertSecure virtual directory and enable and configure certificate mapping for the Jgeist*zz* account.

When you have completed the lab challenge, inform your instructor.

LAB 13

CREATING A DISASTER RECOVERY PLAN

This lab contains the following exercises and activities:

- Exercise 13.1: Backing Up and Restoring Data by Using the Incremental Backup Type
- Exercise 13.2: Backing Up Software Update Services
- Exercise 13.3: Disaster Recovery Planning for a Single Server
- Lab Review Questions
- Lab Challenge 13.1: Backing Up Critical Data

SCENARIO

As network administrator for Contoso Pharmaceuticals, one of your responsibilities is to ensure that an efficient and appropriate backup strategy for data and core network services is in place. In some cases, you must verify that your backup and restoration plan meets requirements that are specified in Service Level Agreements.

After completing this lab, you will be able to:

- **Implement a backup plan by using incremental or differential backups.**
- **Restore a backup based on the backup type.**
- **Back up Software Update Services.**
- **Design a backup and restore strategy as part of a disaster-recovery plan for a single server.**

Estimated lesson time: 90 minutes

BEFORE YOU BEGIN

To complete this lab, you will need to have done the following:

- Installed Software Update Services as specified in Lab 3, "Reducing the Risk of Software Vulnerabilities."

EXERCISE 13.1: BACKING UP AND RESTORING DATA BY USING THE INCREMENTAL BACKUP TYPE

Estimated completion time: 30 minutes

To better understand the different backup types, you will perform a full backup of test data, then modify some of the data, and perform an incremental backup.

Performing Normal and Incremental Backups

1. Log on as Contoso*dd*\Admin*zz*.
2. Open Windows Explorer and browse to C:\Lab Manual\Lab 13\Backup.

   This folder contains text files copied from the Microsoft Windows Server 2003 Enterprise Edition CD.

3. From the View menu, select Details, and then note the file attributes in the Attribute column.

   QUESTION *What attribute type is listed in the Attributes column for each file?*

4. Click Start, point to All Programs, point to Accessories, point to System Tools, and then select Backup.
5. On the Welcome To The Backup Or Restore Wizard page, clear the Always Start In Wizard Mode check box, and then click the Advanced Mode link. The Advanced Mode enables you to work with the Backup interface directly instead of within a wizard. You can revert to the wizard mode at any time by clicking the Wizard Mode link on the Welcome tab of the Backup Utility console.

6. In the Backup Utility console, click the Backup tab.
7. In the folder tree, expand the C drive, browse to C:\Lab Manual\Lab 13\, and then select the Backup folder check box to back up the C:\Lab Manual\Lab 13\Backup folder.
8. In the Backup Media Or File Name box, click Browse, and then click Cancel when prompted to insert a floppy disk into the A drive.
9. On the Save As page, select the Save In drop-down list and browse to C:\Lab Manual\Lab 13, type **Lab13Backup** in the File Name box, and then click Save.

   The screen shot here shows the results of the backup configuration.

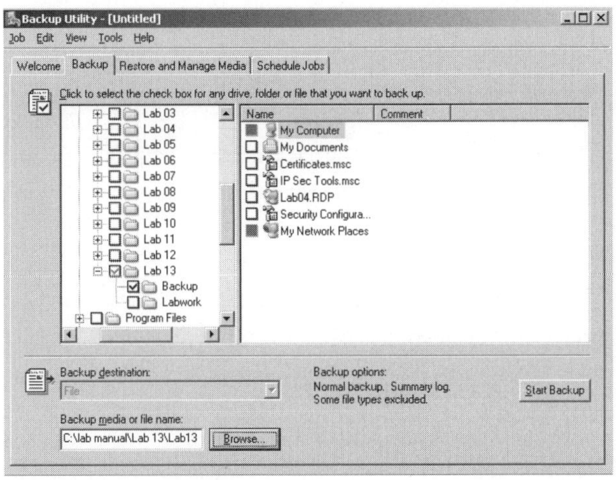

10. In the Backup dialog box, click Start Backup.
11. You now see the Backup Job Information dialog box. You can use this dialog box to perform tasks such as entering a description for the backup or scheduling it to occur at off-peak hours. Click Start Backup to accept the default settings and back up the data.

    The Backup Progress dialog box opens. After a few minutes, the status bar indicates that the backup job is complete.
12. To view the report, click Report.
13. Examine the details of the report, and then close the Notepad window.
14. In the Backup Progress dialog box, click Close.
15. Switch to Windows Explorer, and then view the attributes of the files in the C:\Lab Manual\Lab 13\Backup folder.

    QUESTION *How have the file attributes changed? What does this indicate?*

16. Double-click one of the files to open it in Notepad, press ENTER to make a change to the file, save the file, close Notepad, and then view the file attribute.

    QUESTION *Did the file attribute on the file change?*

17. Switch to the Backup Utility console.
18. On the Backup tab, in the folder tree, expand the C drive, browse to C:\Lab Manual\Lab 13, and then select the Backup folder check box.
19. In the Backup Media Or File Name box, ensure that the C:\Lab Manual\Lab 13\Lab13Backup.bkf file is selected, and then click Start Backup.
20. In the Backup Job Information dialog box, ensure that the Append This Backup To The Media option is selected, and then click Advanced.
21. From the Backup Type drop-down list, select Incremental, and then click OK.

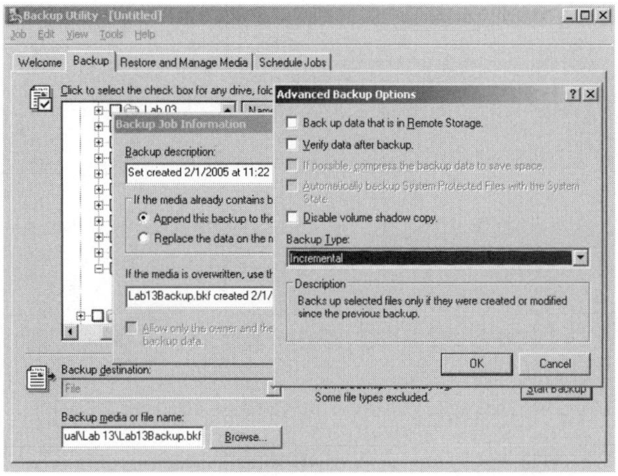

22. In the Backup Job Information dialog box, click Start Backup.

23. When the backup is complete, examine the summary in the Backup Progress dialog box, and then click Close.

24. Switch to Windows Explorer and view the attribute on the file you modified in step 16.

> **QUESTION** *Did the file attribute on the file change?*

> **QUESTION** *If you had performed a differential backup, would the file attribute have changed?*

25. Double-click a different file from the one you modified in step 16, press ENTER to make a change to the file, save the file, close Notepad, and then view the file attribute.

26. Switch to the Backup Utility console.

27. On the Backup tab, in the folder tree, expand the C drive, browse to C:\Lab Manual\Lab 13, and then select the Backup folder check box.

28. In the Backup Media Or File Name box, ensure that the C:\Lab Manual\Lab 13\Lab13Backup.bkf file is selected, and then click Start Backup.

29. In the Backup Job Information dialog box, ensure that the Append This Backup To The Media option is selected, and then click Advanced.

30. From the Backup Type drop-down list, select Incremental, and then click OK.

31. In the Backup Job Information dialog box, click Start Backup.

32. When the backup is complete, examine the summary in the Backup Progress dialog box, and then click Close.

33. Switch to Windows Explorer and view the attribute on the file you modified in step 25.

    You can view the information in the Date Modified column to identify which files you modified.

Restoring Data from a Normal and Incremental Backup

In this section, you will delete the files you backed up and then restore them from the normal and incremental backups. You will first restore the normal backup and then restore the incremental backups in the order that you performed them.

1. In Windows Explorer, browse to C:\Lab Manual\Lab 13\, right-click the Backup folder, and then select Delete.
2. Click Yes to confirm the deletion and send the folder the Recycle Bin.
3. Switch to the Backup Utility console.
4. Click the Restore And Manage Media tab.
5. In the console tree, fully expand the first backup set, and then select the C:\Lab Manual\Lab 13\Backup folder check box.

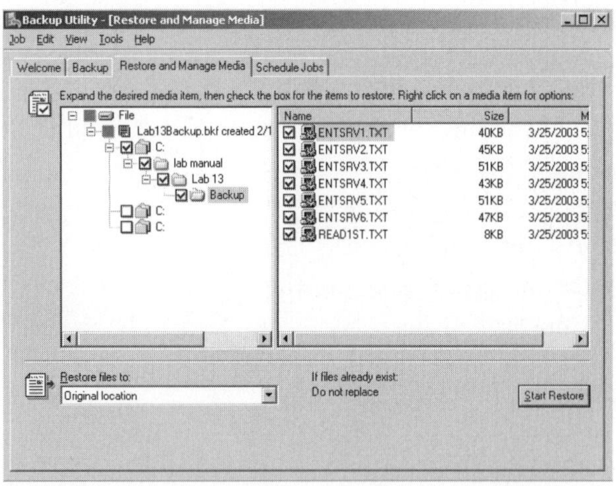

   In the console tree, you may have to double-click on the folder to expand it.

6. Click Start Restore.
7. In the Confirm Restore dialog box, click Advanced, review the settings, and then click OK.

8. Click OK in the Confirm Restore dialog box.

   The Restore Progress dialog box appears.

9. When the restore process is complete, click Report to review the details of the restore process, and then close Notepad.

   You will have to scroll down to see the information about the number of files that are restored.

10. Close Notepad, and then close the Restore Progress dialog box.

11. Switch to Windows Explorer, and then browse to C:\Lab Manual\Lab 13\Backup to confirm the success of the restore process.

    Note that the information in the Date Modified column indicates that all the files were last modified at the same time.

12. Switch to the Backup Utility console, fully expand the second backup set, and then select the C:\Lab Manual\Lab 13\Backup folder check box.

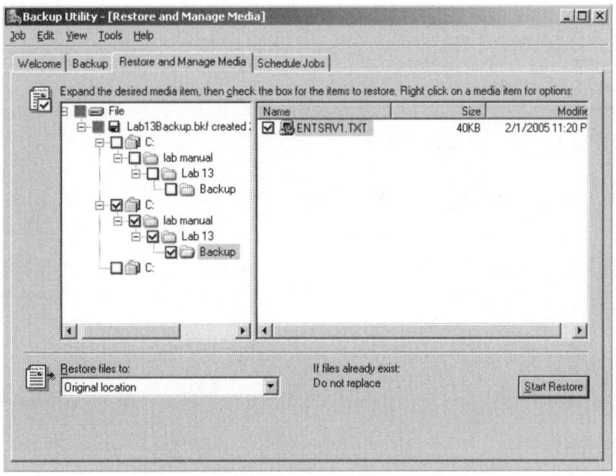

13. From the Tools menu, select Options.

14. In the Options dialog box, click the Restore tab.

15. Select the Replace The File On The Disk Only If The File On Disk Is Older option, and then click OK.

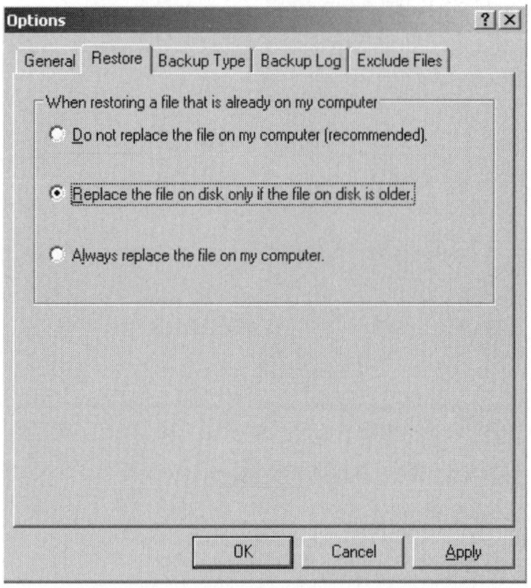

16. In the Backup Utility console, click Start Restore, and in the Confirm Restore dialog box, click OK.

17. When the restore process is complete, close the Restore Progress dialog box.

18. Fully expand the third backup set, and then select the C:\Lab Manual\Lab 13\Backup folder check box.

19. Click Start Restore, and in the Confirm Restore dialog box, click OK.

20. When the restore process is complete, click Report to review the details of the restore jobs, and then close Notepad.

21. Close the Restore Progress dialog box.

22. Switch to Windows Explorer, and then view the files in the C:\Lab Manual\Lab 13\Backup folder.

    You should see that both of the files you modified have been restored. Note that if you had performed a normal backup followed by differential backups, instead of incremental backups, you would have had to perform only two restore operations: first you would restore the normal backup, and then you would restore the last differential backup. When considering backup types, you should always consider the trade-offs implicit in the choice of the backup type. The backup type you choose will determine the amount of time it takes to restore the data.

23. Close all open windows.

EXERCISE 13.2: BACKING UP SOFTWARE UPDATE SERVICES

Estimated completion time: 20 minutes

Some services on the network require special consideration when designing a backup and recovery plan. To restore a service from a failure, you might have to restore more than one set of files, or you might have to restore different types of files, or you might have to take a series of steps in a specific order. In this section, you will execute the steps that are required for you to back up the Software Update Services (SUS) that you installed and configured in Lab 3. To back up SUS, you must back up the Web site directory that contains the SUS administration site, the files containing the SUS content, and the Microsoft Internet Information Services (IIS) metabase. You will begin by backing up the IIS metabase to ensure that you have the most recent copy.

1. Click Start, point to Administrative Tools, and then select Internet Information Services (IIS) Manager.
2. In the console tree, right-click Computer*zz* (local computer), point to All Tasks, and select Backup/Restore Configuration.

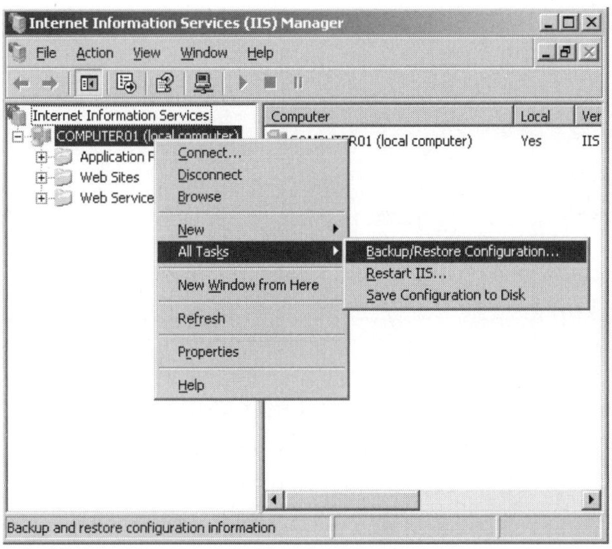

In the Configuration Backup/Restore dialog box, you might see additional instances of backups that were created by means of an automated process.

3. In the Configuration Backup/Restore dialog box, click Create Backup.
4. In the Configuration Backup dialog box, type **SUS Backup** in the Configuration Backup Name box, select the Encrypt Backup Using Password check box, type **P@ssw0rd** in the Password and Confirm Password boxes, and click OK.
5. In the Configuration Backup/Restore dialog box, click Close.
6. Close Internet Information Services (IIS) Manager.
7. Click Start, point to All Programs, point to Accessories, point to System Tools, and then select Backup.

   The Backup Utility dialog box appears if you previously performed the steps in Exercise 13.1. You will have to back up files from three different locations: C:\Inetpub\Wwwroot (the Web site files), C:\Sus (the content storage location), and C:\Windows\System32\Inetsrv\Metaback (the IIS metabase).

8. In the Backup Utility, verify that the Backup tab is selected, and in the folder tree, expand C:\Inetpub, and select the C:\Inetpub\Wwwroot folder check box.

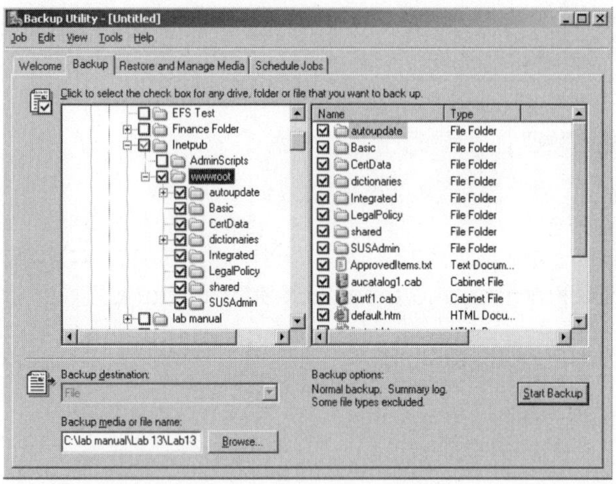

9. In the folder tree, select the C:\Sus check box.

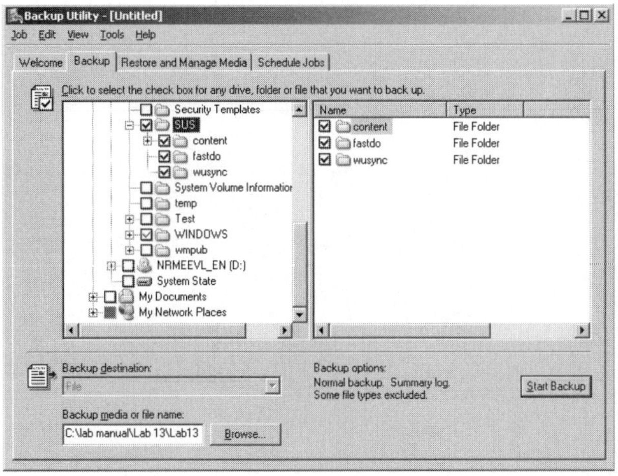

10. In the folder tree, select the C:\Windows\System32\Inetsrv\Metaback check box.

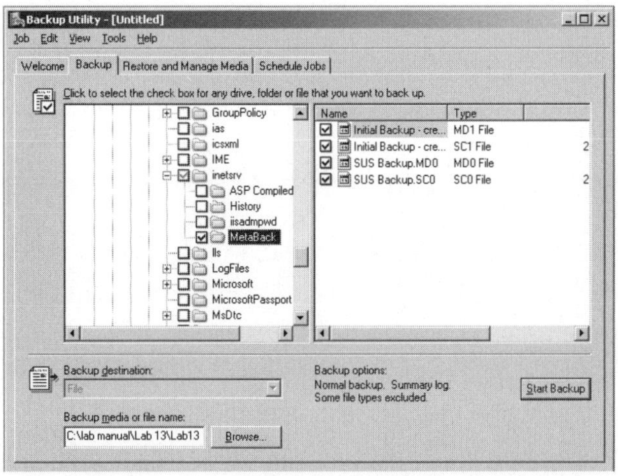

11. On the Backup tab, in the Backup Media Or File Name box, type **c:\lab manual\lab 13\susbackup.bkf**, and then click Start Backup.
12. In the Backup Job Information dialog box, click Start Backup.
13. When the backup is completed, in the Backup Progress box, click Report, and view the information about the backup.

> **QUESTION** It is important to keep a paper log of backups. What might you do at this point?

14. Close Notepad.

15. Close the Backup Progress dialog box, and then close the Backup Utility.

> **QUESTION** Working with your lab partner, take a few moments to list the steps that you would take to recover the SUS service in the event that the server suffered a catastrophic failure. Note that, on Microsoft Windows 2000, IIS 5.0 uses Security Identifiers (SIDs), which makes it impossible for you to restore SUS to new hardware or a new installation of the operation system. However, Windows Server 2003 does not have this limitation.

EXERCISE 13.3: DISASTER RECOVERY PLANNING FOR A SINGLE SERVER

Estimated completion time: 30 minutes

In this exercise, you and your lab partner will work together to create a list of recommendations for ensuring that your backup and recovery times for a critical server meet the minimum requirements as specified by management. Several questions follow the scenario to help you create your list of recommendations. However, you should go beyond the questions to make your recommendations as comprehensive as possible. For example, consider what you might do to improve the fault tolerance and physical security of the server.

You should compile your recommendations in a text file that you create using Notepad or Wordpad. After you have compiled your recommendations, your instructor will lead the class in a discussion of the exercise. Your instructor might require you to submit the text file containing your recommendations for evaluation. If so, the instructor will give you specific instructions for naming and submitting the file.

Scenario

A server used by Contoso Pharmaceuticals contains a large amount of critical data stored in a Microsoft SQL Server 2000 database that is used extensively to support daily operations of the company. The amount of critical data on the server is close to 50 gigabytes (GB), and it is located on a redundant array of independent disks (RAID) 5 volume. The transaction logs for the database are located on a mirrored volume of the same computer. You recently bought a new backup device that is, according to the manufacturer, capable of a native data throughput of about 30 megabits per second (Mbps). The backup device is connected to a dedicated backup computer. This computer is located on the same 100-Mbps Ethernet segment as the server that contains the critical data.

Management has stated that, in the event of a catastrophic failure to the server that contains the critical data, the data must be restored and available to users within an hour. A maximum of two hours' worth of data loss is tolerable.

You test backups and restores of 50 GB of data and the transaction logs and find that backup and restore times are far longer than the required minimums. What should you recommend as a solution to ensure that backups can be restored within the time specified by management?

> **QUESTION** The tape device supports a very high-rate native throughput rate. It should easily be able to restore 50 GB in an hour, even with the Verify option enabled. What are the likely bottlenecks?

> **QUESTION** What kinds of backups should you perform: full, differential, incremental, or a combination of these? How often should you perform them?

> **QUESTION** If you bought backup software that had specific plug-ins for SQL Server 2000 databases, what effect would it have on the rate of backups and restores?

> **QUESTION** Assuming that catastrophic failure means the complete destruction of the computer— for example, if there were a fire in the server room—would you be able to build a computer, load an operating system, install SQL Server 2000, and restore the data within an hour? If not, what solution can you recommend?

LAB REVIEW QUESTIONS

Estimated completion time: 10 minutes

1. You are considering a backup solution for several critical servers on your network. List three or four factors you should consider before deciding on a solution.
2. Describe the difference between a differential backup and an incremental backup.
3. Which backup type, incremental or differential, takes longer to restore?
4. You are designing a backup-and-recovery plan for several core services on your network. Your plan must reflect the possibility that the most experienced administrators might not be available to perform the emergency restoration or that the restoration involves several complex procedures. What must your documentation include?

5. You are the senior administrator of a network that has relatively high security requirements. Several junior administrators have been designated as backup operators and are responsible for backing up the data on servers on the network. Should these administrators have the right to restore data? Why or why not?
6. Where should you store your backup media?

LAB CHALLENGE 13.1: BACKING UP CRITICAL DATA

Estimated completion time: 25 minutes

You have recently been made responsible for maintaining and securing a Windows Server 2003 member server. This server has a particularly important role on your network because it issues computer and user digital certificates, both through autoenrollment and Web enrollment. Upon performing a review of the server, you discover that some of the data on the server is regularly backed up, but the registry, system files, boot files, IIS metabase, and certificate services database are not backed up on a regularly scheduled basis. You decide to create a backup job that will back up these critical files on a weekly basis. You schedule the backup to run at 10:00 P.M. every Saturday evening. You want to create this backup job with the least amount of administrative effort.

After you complete this challenge, take a screen shot of the Backup tab showing the backup selections and a screen shot of the Schedule Job dialog box showing the weekly job. Save these screen shots as Backup and Schedule in the C:\Lab Manual\Lab 13\Labwork folder. If your instructor requires you to submit the screen shots for evaluation, you will be given further instructions.

> **TIP** To take a screen shot, make sure the window element of interest is in the foreground, and then press ALT+PRINTSCREEN to copy the screen shot into the buffer. Open the Paint program, and then press CTRL+V to paste the screen shot into Paint. Finally, save the file in Paint with the appropriate name.